THE DILEMMA AND THE COMPUTER

THE DILEMMA AND THE COMPUTER

Theory, Research, and Applications to
Counseling Psychology

Morton Wagman

PRAEGER SPECIAL STUDIES • PRAEGER SCIENTIFIC

New York • Philadelphia • Eastbourne, UK
Toronto • Hong Kong • Tokyo • Sydney

Library of Congress Cataloging in Publication Data

Wagman, Morton.
  The dilemma and the computer.

  Bibliography: p.
  Includes index.
  1. Counseling — Computer assisted instruction.
2. Problem-solving — Computer assisted instruction.
I. Title.
BF637.C6W27   1984   158'.3   84-3407
ISBN 0-03-069313-6 (alk. paper)

Published in 1984 by Praeger Publishers
CBS Educational and Professional Publishing
a Division of CBS Inc.
521 Fifth Avenue, New York, NY 10175 USA
© 1984 by Praeger Publishers

456789 052 987654321

Printed in the United States of America
on acid-free paper

PREFACE

This book represents a research approach to human dilemmas. While dilemmas as aversive–aversive situations are pervasive and continuous in human existence, a general theory about dilemmas, their nature and resolution, is developed.

In the Introduction, theoretical viewpoints concerning the nature of human reasoning and thinking are discussed. In Part I of the book (Chapters 1 and 2), the dilemma is examined from two perspectives. The dilemma as a purely logical structure is examined in Chapter 1. The dilemma as a psychological experience is examined in Chapter 2.

In Part II (Chapters 3 to 5), various approaches to the dilemma are discussed. Chapter 3 examines the relationship between the dilemma and the cognitive operation of negation, discusses the dilemma in terms of cognitive psychology and psycholinguistics, and places the dilemma in the context of Piaget's INRC group of logical operations. In Chapter 4, the dilemma is approached from the standpoint of several systems of psychotherapy. The dilemma from the perspective of information theory is discussed in Chapter 5.

Part III (Chapters 6 and 7) examines in a laboratory research context the theoretical approaches to the dilemma that were discussed in earlier sections of the book. Thus, in Chapter 6, research is presented that studies the effect of the operation of negation on extrication from psychological dilemmas. In Chapter 7, the logic of implication as a major component of the dilemma is studied in a research context concerned with the comparative effects of a teaching machine or self-contradiction on fallacious scientific and personal reasoning.

In Part IV (Chapters 8 to 11), the theory and research sections presented earlier are developed into an applied research program concerned with the dilemma, the counselor, and the computer. Thus, in Chapter 8, earlier theories of the logical dilemma and the psychological dilemma, concepts of negation and extrication from the dilemma, and the related research are organized into a set of principles constituting the methods of systematic dilemma counseling. Research concerning the effectiveness of dilemma counseling is also discussed in Chapter 8.

Chapter 9 discusses a basic conceptual formulation of the equivalence among the logic of the computer (electronic circuits), the logic of the software (the dilemma counseling method), and the logic of the person (the psychological dilemma). This chapter describes how this basic formulation evolved into the PLATO Computer-Based Dilemma Counseling System (used, internationally, by colleges, universities, business, and government organizations). Chapter 10 discusses research concerned with the effectiveness of and reactions to the PLATO Dilemma Counseling System.

In Chapter 11, a research method for integrating the results of independent studies is presented. This method is applied to the question of the comparative effects of computer counseling and standard counseling as procedures for the resolution of dilemmas.

The book concludes (Chapter 12) with an integrated discussion of the major concepts and research findings.

MORTON WAGMAN
University of Illinois at Urbana-Champaign

CONTENTS

LIST OF TABLES AND FIGURES

TABLES

FIGURES

ACKNOWLEDGMENTS

The author gratefully acknowledges permission to reprint the following material:

Wagman, M. 1978a. "The Comparative Effects of Didactic-Correction and Self-Contradiction on Fallacious Scientific and Personal Reasoning." *Journal of General Psychology,* 99: 67–80. (Chapter 7)

Wagman, M. 1979. "Systematic Dilemma Counseling: Theory, Method, Research." *Psychological Reports,* 44: 55–72. (Chapter 8)

Wagman, M. 1980a. "PLATO DCS, an Interactive Computer System for Personal Counseling." *Journal of Counseling Psychology,* 27: 16–30. Copyright (1980) by the American Psychological Association. Reprinted/adapted by permission of the publisher. (Chapter 9)

Wagman, M., and Kerber, K. W. 1980b. "PLATO DCS, an Interactive Computer System for Personal Counseling: Further Development and Evaluation." *Journal of Counseling Psychology,* 27: 31–9. Copyright (1980) by the American Psychological Association. Reprinted/adapted by permission of the publisher. (Chapter 10)

Wagman, M. 1982. "Solving Dilemmas by Computer or Counselor." *Psychological Reports,* 50: 127–35. (Chapter 11)

The author wishes to express his gratitude to Aileen Smith for her excellent typing of many versions of this manuscript and to William L. Unziker for his assistance in his careful proofreading of versions of this manuscript.

INTRODUCTION

Although human dilemmas may be very diverse and experienced in phenomenologically different ways, there may be a highly general structure that underlies all dilemmas and a highly general theory that permits an approach to solution of all dilemmas. The search for such a general structure and such a theory of generic resolution of dilemmas has guided a research program extending over a period of 15 years. From the beginning, it was clear that the discovery of such a unified general theory would at once have to be more abstract and simple than psychodynamic theories and more closely linked to cognitive and logical processes than to operant and classical conditioning models. The discovery of such an abstract, simple, cognitive, and logical general theory would be extremely valuable, as it might provide a very powerful approach to dilemmas in general and to any psychological dilemma in particular. This book describes the development of such a theory and relevant experimental research conducted by the author with the assistance of graduate students.

Reasoning about dilemmas may be related to reasoning in general. Therefore, most of the rest of this introduction is devoted to an account of general viewpoints regarding the psychology of reasoning.

What is the relationship between logic and reasoning? Are the laws of logic descriptive of thought processes, or are they only normative? There are those who have held that cognitive operations are identical with the laws of logic. For example, this account is briefly reviewed by Cohen and Nagel (1934) as follows: "An old tradition defines logic as the science of the laws of thought." There are those who hold that the laws of logic are not the laws by which we actually do think, exemplified by the statement of Cohen (1944): "That the laws of logic are not the universal laws according to which we do actually think is conclusively shown not only by the most elementary observation or introspection, but by the very existence of fallacies." Nagel similarly remarks:

> Little need be said in refutation of the view that logical principles formulate the "inherent necessities of thought" and are generalized descriptions of the operations of minds. Surely the actual occurrence of beliefs in logically incompatible propositions makes nonsense of the claim that the principle of noncontradiction expresses a universal fact in psychology [1956: 86].

The philosopher Bertrand Russell wrote:

> Throughout logic and mathematics, the existence of the human or any other mind is totally irrelevant; mental processes are studied by means of logic, but the subject-matter of logic does not presuppose mental processes, and would be equally true if there were no mental processes [1904: 351].

Experimental psychological research in the area of reasoning has varied between (1) a de-emphasis on the role of logic in reasoning with a concurrent demonstration of emotional contagion and distortion and (2) an insistence on the logical quality of both everyday and formal reasoning. Thus, Bruner, Goodnow, and Austin (1956), in their *A Study of Thinking*, state, "Much of human reasoning is supported by a kind of thematic process rather than by abstract logic. The principal feature of this thematic process is its pragmatic rather than its logical structure." Similarly, the tendency toward biased conclusions is illustrated by Morgan and Morton:

> A person is likely to accept a conclusion which expresses his convictions with little regard for the correctness or incorrectness of the inferences involved. Our evidence will indicate that the only circumstances under which we can be relatively sure that the inferences of a person will be logical is when they lead to conclusions which he has already accepted [1944: 79].

In the same vein, Lefford (1946) noted that the principles of logical inferences "are techniques which are not the common property of the unsophisticated subject"; he also distinguishes from the logical inference, "Psychological inferences which may be made by the ordinary person. . . . A psychological inference is not valid or invalid except when judged as a logical inference: psychological inference is purely a fact."

These statements would suggest that reasoning and logical reasoning are in separate and nonpermeable compartments. Indeed, a kind of separate compartment called "paleologic" is set up·by Von Domarus (1944) and Arieti (1959) who, on the basis of a case observation, claim that schizophrenics are peculiar in that they state identity on the basis of identical predicates, and that such behavior is also found among infants, primitives, and in dreams of normal individuals.

These writers seem to be making a case for the antilogical quality of human thought. Their case rests upon the high rate of error found in syllogistic reasoning under specified terms of emotional content (Lefford on a bias conclusion agreement, Morgan and Morton) or in psychopathological conditions (Von Domarus and Arieti). The problem of error was handled by the older rational philosophers and the more modern experimental psychologists in a different way. They tended to explain error as the interference with logical laws as laws of thinking by other conditions. These interfering processes could produce error, but they did not thereby destroy the validity of the description of human thought in terms of logical operations. Thus, as Kant (1885) states: "It is easy to see how truth is possible since in it the understanding acts according to its own essential laws." In her article "On the Relation Between Logic and Thought," Henle suggests that:

> Error, however, is difficult to understand since it constitutes "a form of thought inconsistent with the understanding" (Kant 1885). Its source is thus not to be sought in the understanding itself, but rather in the "unobserved influence of the sensibility on the understanding," the sensibility being that faculty which "supplied the material for thought" [1962: 365].

Similarly, Boole comments on the question of error in reasoning:

> The phenomena of incorrect reasoning or error . . . are due to the interference of other laws with those laws of which *right* reasoning is the product. . . . The laws of correct inference may be violated, but they do not the less truly *exist* on this account [1854: 196].

Henle discusses the controversy in the following terms:

> Do errors in deductive reasoning mean that the logical process has been violated? As Mill expresses it, does the occurrence of error mean that the syllogism is a bad one? Or can the error be accounted for otherwise? Is it possible that a process that would follow the rules of logic, if it were spelled out, is discernible even when the reasoning results in error? The distinction being made here is a familiar one in the psychology of learning and thinking. Thus, Koffka (1935) distinguishes between learning as accomplishment and the learning processes responsible for this accomplishment. Kohler's (1927) distinction between "good errors" and stupid ones is likewise relevant. Good errors, he points out, "may, in a certain sense, be absolutely appropriate to the situation" (p. 217), although they solve the problem no more than do stupid ones. Wertheimer (1959), too, distinguishes between solutions obtained by "blind" procedures and "fine, genuine solutions." Again, the difference is one of process, since in both cases the result may be the same.

In the same way, in connection with the present problem, we may ask: given contrasting results — correct solutions and errors in deductive reasoning — what can we say about the thinking processes that account for them? Are the processes necessarily different because their effects are different [1962: 366]?

Evans (1980) criticizes the Henle hypothesis as failing to take account of extralogical response biases in reasoning tasks. An example is a matching response bias, as when subjects invalidly match a negative conclusion to a set of negative premises. Evans is suggesting that subjects may be responding in an arbitrary extralogical way to a reasoning task that is beyond their logical ability. Evans is apparently trying to modify the rationalist position of Henle and others (Revlin and Mayer 1978) that except for misinterpretation of premises, subjects do think logically by demonstrating that logical errors are sometimes not the result of misinterpretation of premises but mechanical response biases. It would appear, however, that such a criticism or restriction of the Henle hypothesis pertains to performance factors, that is, the product of thinking, rather than to process factors.

As many authors have shown, the incidence of error in deductive reasoning depends on the form of the syllogism and its contents, as well as on instructions to the subjects. One such instruction, which may or may not be responded to adequately, is to respond to the material purely in terms of its logical validity aside from personal preferences as to agreement or disagreement with the stated conclusion.

Henle centers in this review article, as well as in her experimental work (Henle and Michael 1956), on the syllogism as though this were coextensive with deductive reasoning. Perhaps more representative of reasoning is logical implication as used both in everyday life and in scientific reasoning (Wason 1964; Inhelder and Piaget 1958; Wagman 1978; Wason and Johnson-Laird 1972; Johnson 1972).

When Kant says that logic is the science of necessary laws of thought, whereas psychology provides only contingent rules of thought, his statement seems somehow clear and yet muddled. I would prefer to consider his "necessary laws of thought" as necessary in the sense of the rules of the game laid down by the particular logician. The first of these logicians may have been Aristotle, who designed syllogisms not to parallel or explain the thought processes of his debating Peripatetics but to provide a simple scheme for testing whether the arguments were valid. It was only much later, during the Age of Scholasticism, that this "testing kit" use of the syllogism became translated into universal laws of thinking and reasoning. If from the relationship $6 - 4 = 2$, it is concluded that $6 - 4 - 2 = 0$, this is the case only because of the laws of the algebra of groups which underlie the particular operations. These algebraic functions are the result of some logician's construction. They have a necessity only because certain agreed-upon characteristics of a mathematical group are given. If some of the underlying group properties are excluded, a semigroup or other type of group is constructed, and certain mathematical operations are not permitted, that is, violate the laws of that particular system, but not the full group from which it was derived. If a man should follow either one of these mathematical groups, he would describe himself and be described as engaged in necessary laws of thought. But only in those respects, that is, only for that particular system, would he be viewed as in error by another man who had assumed that the alternative group was the one to be used.

If we then taught the first man the mathematical subgroup, he would be alternatively right and wrong, as he moved between the group and the semigroup operations. His "thinking" or "reasoning" at these times would rather be referred to as learned or programmed logical operations and would not differ from those performed by a programmed computer. Addressing ourselves to the computer, we would not say that its program was the laws of the computer's thought, for these have no existence outside of the program, and a different program would mean a different "set of computer thoughts." Now, let us look closely at and examine the psychology of the computer. If a voltage irregularity caused a dysfunction in its magnetic relays, we would not complain that there was an error in the program of the mathematical group. If the connecting relays leading to the output printer went haywire and incorrect results were printed, we would not claim that the program of mathematical groups was incorrect. If a resistor in the circuit burned out and the program was progressing at a rate too fast for the limits of the memory bank, we would not claim that the computer program of mathematical groups was incorrect.

Now the question can also be looked at in developmental terms. If a child of six and an adult of 40 are both given a test involving reasoning with logarithms and both fail miserably, this does not prove anything about the invalidity of the *logic* of logarithms. Errors in deductive reasoning can be produced by a variety of factors: testing at a point beyond the stage of the child's or adult's logical development (Inhelder and Piaget 1958), illness (Arieti 1959), emotional bias (Lefford 1946; Morgan and Morton 1944), failure to maintain task practice (Wagman 1978), failure of everyday environment to require formal logical operations (Furth, Youniss, and Ross 1970), and the abstract character of the logical task and associated excessive cognitive load (Wason 1964). The list could be extended. The point is that even where errors do result in terms of the task demand, the product of the subject is not extralogical, but is either a logical response within the same network of the task logic but incorrect because of incorrect assumptions or content (Henle 1962), or the logical response belongs to a different logic, usually one characteristic of a lower level of logical development or instruction, for example, a regression from formal to concrete or even sensorimotor operations (Inhelder and Piaget 1958).

Furthermore, Williams (1965) finds no support for a special "paleological process" in schizophrenics as evidenced by Arieti (1955). Using a group of schizophrenics and a group of college student normals, he found no difference in error rates in the drawing of conclusions for the second figure of the syllogism, which is the one used by Arieti to describe the "paleologic" reasoning in which identity of *A* and *B* is asserted because they have a common trait, all *s* are *m*, all *p* are *m*, therefore all *s* are *p*. Williams's (1965) experimental results suggest that Arieti may have been mistaken in his confusing the reasoning process as the grounds for a drawn inference and the reasoning process as a bolstering or just justification of a personal conclusion. Thus, the schizophrenic woman, quoted by Arieti, who believed that she was the Virgin Mary did not come to this conclusion by way of rational argument, as Arieti suggests, but rather used her ability to reason (and to reason fallaciously, as do college students) to prove or support her cherished belief of her uniqueness. She did not, as Arieti contends, arrive at the fallacious figure 2 conclusion after a careful ratiocination, namely: The Virgin Mary was a virgin. I am a virgin. Therefore, I am the Virgin Mary.

We have already indicated above that the reasoning process may be correct, but the results incorrect because of the use of incorrect assumptions or content. This early argument made by Spinoza (1927), John Stuart Mill (1874), and Henle (1962) is supported by a number of investigations, including especially the work of McGuire (1960). McGuire was able to demonstrate that even in the presence of strong attitudes and opinions, the logical processes and conclusions of his experimental subjects were still predictable on the basis of logical probability assignments made to their premises and biases.

McGuire's logical consistency model of belief change has indicated that there might be illogical effects as well as logical effects of a persuasive communication designed to change a major or minor premise of a controversial syllogistic argument. In particular, McGuire's theory held that the illogical changes would be demonstrated by changes in beliefs and attitudes related to the premises, but not mentioned in a persuasive communication. In view of our above discussion concerning the emphasis in psychological research and theory concerning the difference between man's rational and irrational processes in reasoning and problem solving, it is of special interest to note that in a carefully designed experimental study, McFarland and Thistlethwaite (1970) found support for the logical effects upon conclusion and beliefs, but no support for McGuire's prediction of the illogical effects.

Having considered some issues in the psychology of thinking and reasoning, we will, in the next two chapters, focus more on the nature of the dilemma as a logical (Chapter 1) and as a psychological (Chapter 2) construct.

I

THE DILEMMA

1

THE LOGICAL DILEMMA

In this chapter, we shall examine the logical foundation of the dilemma. Attention will be given to the component logical forms and operations from which the logical dilemma is constructed. These logical forms and operations will be presented in this chapter as a brief course in logic (drawing largely from Copi 1967 and Terrell 1967) for the benefit of those readers not completely familiar with modern symbolic logic. The chapter will also prove useful for clarification of terms in formal logic as they appear in the context of the later theoretical and research section of the book.

PROPOSITIONAL LOGIC

Consider this conditional statement:

If Bill makes his plane connection, then he will arrive on time.

Bill makes his plane connection.

Bill arrives on time.

This proposition can be considered as made up of different components that are related truth-functionally. In order to treat this proposition in symbolic logic terms, we can symbolize the component as follows:

Let p stand for "Bill makes his plane connection."

Let q stand for "Bill arrives on time."

This proposition can then be expressed symbolically as:

If p, then q.

$$\frac{p}{q}.$$

To further symbolize the proposition, we can use a logical operator symbol. The operator is "if . . . then," an implication, and the symbol we will use is the horseshoe ∩, so that the proposition can be expressed:

p∩q

$$\frac{p}{q}.$$

TRUTH TABLES

All logical relations are defined *truth-functionally*, that is to say, any proposition involving a logical operator is assigned a truth value which is dependent solely on the truth or falsity of its *component parts*. For example, consider "and" symbolized by ".". Consider "This plane is small and slow." Its components are p = "This plane is small" and q = "This plane is slow." Symbolically, the proposition is "p.q." Consider what makes this proposition true or false:

In the case where the plane is *both* small and slow, the statement is *true*.

In the case where the plane is small but not slow, the statement is *false*.

In the case where the plane is not small, but is slow, the statement is *false*.

In the case where the plane is *neither* small *nor* slow, the statement is *false*.

Thus, the truth of the compound proposition is given by considering only the truth or falsity of each of the two components of the proposition. The conjunction is *true only* when both conjuncts are true, and false otherwise. This is the case for *any* conjunction and is a truth functional definition of "and." This definition can be presented as a "truth table" that shows the possible combination of truth values of the atomic propositions and the resultant truth value of the compound proposition.

p	.	q
T	T	T
T	F	F
F	F	T
F	F	F

Truth tables for other logical relations will now be presented:
"Or" *disjunction* symbolically ∨

p	∨	q
T	T	T
T	T	F
F	T	T
F	F	F

The above table is for *inclusive* disjunction, or for statements of the sort "p or q or both." There is another form of disjunction, exclusive disjunction, which is used for statements meaning "p or q but *not* both." Its truth table is:

p	∨¹	q
T	F	T
T	T	F
F	T	T
F	F	F

Negation, "not," symbolically "N" (∼):

N	p
F	T
F	T
T	F
T	F

Material implication, if . . . then, symbolically "⊃":

p	⊃	q
T	T	T
T	F	F
F	T	T
F	T	F

and material equivalence, or "if and only if," symbolically " $\equiv$ ":

p	$\equiv$	q
T	T	T
T	F	F
F	F	T
F	T	F

Material equivalence is sometimes called "biconditional," for when material equivalence holds between two statements, it is the case that p⊃q and q⊃p.

Material implication of all the truth functional connectives is always the most troublesome for people to understand. ⊃ is a truth-functional connective, not a causal connective, and since we tend to think of implication as causality, we feel uncomfortable thinking of ⊃ as meaning if . . . then. The best way to understand the logical definition of implication is this—logical analysis always proceeds *minimally*—its goal is to guarantee that one reasons correctly only from truth to truth, it cannot lead to new truth; it provides *only* the minimum conditions for *not* falling into error. Consequently, in defining its connectives, its criterion is to ask what would falsify such a proposition. In the case of the other operators, logical definition coincides with the intuitive. In the case of implication, however, the definition departs from the intuitive. Close scrutiny of implication will justify the logical definition of implication, if falsification is the *only* criterion. Consider, for instance, the implication given earlier:

"If Bill makes his plane connection, then he will arrive on time."

What will make this statement *untrue*? If Bill *misses* his plane connection, and then does not arrive on time, the statement is obviously true. If Bill *misses* his plane connection, *and* then arrives on time, the statement is true, since *something else* could have enabled him to arrive on time. If he makes his plane connection and *arrives on time*, then the statement is true. If, however, he makes his plane connection, and he does not arrive on time, the statement is false, since the purport of the statement was that this could not happen.

RULES OF INFERENCE

Now we proceed to a consideration of the basic *rules of inference*. There are nine argument patterns directly verifiable through the construction of truth tables — that is, it is impossible for the premises to be true while the conclusion is false.

These nine rules of inference are: (∴ = therefore)

1. Addition

p

∴pVq

If p is true, then any disjunctive proposition including it must be true (see truth table for disjunction).

2. Conjunction

p

q

∴p.q

If p and q are both true, then this conjunction must be true (see truth table for conjunction).

3. Simplification

p.q

∴p

If p.q is true, then either conjunct must be true.

4. Disjunctive syllogism

pVq

~p

∴q

If pVq is true, and ~p is true (that is, p is false), then q must be true.

5. Hypothetical syllogism

p⊃q

q⊃r

∴p⊃r

With the above premises, if we were given p, we would reason to r: p⊃q; p; ∴q; q⊃r; ∴r. It is obvious, then, that r is deducible from p, hence p⊃r.

6. *Modus ponens*

p⊃q

p

∴q

Given that p⊃q is true, and p is true, then q cannot be false, from the truth table of ⊃, hence q is true.

7. *Modus tollens*

p⊃q

~q

∴~p

Given that p⊃q, and q is false, then p cannot be true, and must be false, hence ~p.

8. Constructive dilemma

p ⊃ q

r ⊃ s

p∨r

∴ q∨s

Given that p⊃q and r⊃s are true, the given that p∨r is true, at least p is true, or r is true; that being the case, at least q or s must be true (depending on whether r is true), hence, q∨s.

9. Destructive Dilemma

p ⊃ q

r ⊃ s

~q∨~s

∴ ~p∨~r

Given that the premises are true, as before, then at least one of q∨s must be false (i.e., at least one of ~q or ~s must be true), hence at least one of p∨r must be false, hence ~p∨~r.

This concludes our brief course in symbolic logic and the logical basis of the dilemma. In the next chapter we will discuss the relation of logic to psychology and place a psychological interpretation on the logical dilemma.

2

THE PSYCHOLOGICAL DILEMMA

LOGIC AND PSYCHOLOGY

Almost up to the close of the nineteenth century and until the work of Darwin (1871) and Spencer (1896), psychology was undifferentiated from philosophy. Rational man was held to think essentially in terms of the philosophers' logical calculus, especially that based on Aristotle's syllogisms, although later on the propositions of sentential calculus (Whitehead and Russell 1910–1913) man was perceived as obeying inevitably the laws of logical thought.

The work of Darwin, especially his *Descent of Man* (1871), placed the psychology of thought in the general framework of evolution, survival, and environmental adaptation. In fact, in *Descent of Man* Darwin outlined a number of experimental designs intended to test the problem-solving or reasoning ability of animals and this opened a way to a long series of experiments in comparative psychology in which reasoning for a time came to be associated with the behavior of lower animals, including the rat (Heron and Hunter 1922).

But man's rationality was dethroned not only through Darwinian evolutionary perspectives but also through the work of Freud, who in his "Doctrine of Psychosexual Evolutionism" (1935) was forever reducing man's everyday behavior and mishaps to primitive and irrational motives and conflicts, such as in his *Psychopathology of Everyday Life* (Freud 1966). Moreover, the Freudian view seemed to hold that the very rationality of man could sometimes be interpreted as intellectual avoidances and defenses, sometimes with clear obsessional or compulsive symptoms (Fenichel 1945). The early laboratory investigations of human reasoning ability and performance seemed sometimes motivated by the need to separate psychology as a science from its maternal source in philosophy and to extend the Freudian view of man's everyday psychopathology to the lofty realm of erroneous formal syllogistic reasoning (see the Introduction).

Beginning sometime in the 1950s, experimental psychology of reasoning — under a general shift of psychological interest to cognition in the United States by the work of Bruner, Goodnow, and Austin (1956), in England by the work of Bartlett (1958), and beginning even earlier in Geneva, in the immense contributions of Piaget (1949) and his collaborators — dethroned Darwinism and Freudianism and relegated their legacies to secondary importance. The questions of the range and power of man's logical competencies and their underlying information processes were placed in a position of saliency (see Chapter 3), without restoring the earlier philosophical description of man's reasoning, as a priori equivalent to the idealized forms described in various formal, logical systems (see Chapter 3).

During the last 100 years, philosophy and logic have not stood still. Logic as a major branch of philosophy has become a highly specialized science — held by some to be akin to mathematics and by others to be the basis of mathematics or merely a set of transformations from which mathematical operations are derived (Copi 1967; Terrell 1967; Bourbaki 1964). The difference between logic as a science and psychology as a science thus must be observed.

With regard to reasoning, psychology studies how people actually do reason, whereas logic is normative with respect to reasoning, providing a standard of valid reasoning. Valid reasoning and logic, as indicated in the previous chapter, are contentless, very much like mathematical symbols in calculus and algebra are mathematically correct regardless of the reference of the symbols. This gives mathematics and logic both their power and their difficulty — power because of their range of application and difficulty because of their abstract character. Yet, as alluded to in a previous chapter and as will be made clear in the further chapters of this book, logical operations as part of the working tools of all scientists in their inferential behavior in drawing conclusions from their symbolized data may also be an indispensable tool in studying people's everyday competence as they reason themselves into real or fantasized problem situations, grasp the implications of the reasoning problem more or less adequately, and reason themselves more or less clearly out of the perplexing quandary.

PSYCHOLOGICAL INTERPRETATION OF THE DILEMMA

Many times in everyday life people face difficult choice situations only to find themselves baffled again and again. One example is the mother who is perplexed about the placement of her retarded child in either a regular school where he may have to face unfair competition or in a special class for retarded children where he therefore assumes a special school and general societal status and label. The choice is dilemmatic, and her prevailing mood may well be dysphoric with prevailing feelings of anxiety, emotionality, and depression. There is a quality of necessity about the opposed choices. The dilemma seems to run with inevitable logic to the conclusion of bitter unhappiness on either horn.

One of the basic psychological qualities of dilemmas is their requiredness, necessity, or "mustness." Does this derive from the logical dilemma or from the apprehensive helplessness and hopelessness which grip a person in a confronting dilemma?

As expressed in formal logical operations, it is assumed that the relationships between the antecedents and consequents are not open to exceptions. These relationships possess the character of inevitable absolutes. An individual in a psychological dilemma experiences the problem as inescapable and as though bound helpless between the horns of the dilemma. The person, if sophisticated, may go on to assert strenuously that the unpleasant and inescapable outcomes that constitute the dilemma are dictated and constrained by sheer intellectual operations. This is especially likely to happen when the person is in an anxious or depressed mood with associated obsessive thoughts. At these times the requiredness of his plight seems absolutely inescapable. But, in fact, the person at that time is using the logic of conditionals and of the constructive dilemma in an arbitrary fashion. This arbitrariness can easily be demonstrated by negating the consequents which compose the conclusion and reversing them with respect to the antecedents. The result of the operation is a constructive dilemma with equal logical validity and identical arbitrariness, though the conclusion is now benign.

In summary, psychological dilemmas usually have the quality of necessity. The person feels driven, blocked, and helpless between, if not on, the horns of the dilemma. The person feels trapped between what he believes are necessary evils. The person feels desperate, anxious, or depressed in his dilemmatic construction

ROUTES OF EXTRICATION

In order to provide a concrete example of systematic extrication routes from personal dilemmas, we will anticipate the research which will be described in later chapters of this volume and present one of a large number of items given to experimental subjects.

Subjects are handed a card with the following information appearing typed on it:

Can you help this person with this problem or dilemma?
"If I am aggressive, then I am bound to be disliked by a great many peo-

ple; and if I am not aggressive, then I am bound to fail in business. But I must either be aggressive or unaggressive. Therefore, I must certainly either be disliked by a great many people or a failure in business. Either way, I am miserable."

In your opinion, which one of the following alternatives would be most helpful to this person? Please select only one alternative and indicate your choice by placing an x at the left of the following six alternatives. Thank you.

1. Being aggressive does not necessarily lead to people disliking you.

2. Being unaggressive does not necessarily lead to being a failure in business.

3. You do not have to restrict yourself to being either aggressive or unaggressive.

4. Being disliked by a great many people is not necessarily bad.

5. Being a failure in business is not necessarily bad.

6. If you are aggressive, then you will not be a failure in business; and if you are not aggressive, then you will not be disliked by a great many people.

In terms of the logical symbols introduced in Chapter 1 — if p then r, and if q then s, but either p or q, therefore, either r or s — we may note that the formal routes of extrication are in general: that you are not restricted to either p or q; that r will not necessarily follow nor will s necessarily follow; and that if they do, such outcomes are not necessarily bad; and that if one wishes to argue in terms of necessity, then in a similarly arbitrary fashion each of the undesired outcomes carries with it the absence of the other undesired outcome. In this latter case the dysphoric dilemma is translated into a euphoric dilemma and once more it follows that: consequences r and s need not necessarily occur and if they do r and s as occurrences are not necessarily good; and, that one is not sure to come out good in either case since each consequence, carrying with it a positive and negative outcome, brings the subject in this arbitrary style of reasoning back circularly once more to the starting point of the dysphoric dilemma.

GEOMETRIC AND PROBABILISTIC REPRESENTATION OF THE PSYCHOLOGICAL DILEMMA

The following paragraphs will present a geometric representation and measurement of the interrelationships of the dysphoric and euphoric dilemmas together with probabilistic measurement in terms of what will be called the dilemmatic triangles.

THE DILEMMATIC TRIANGLE

The dilemmatic triangle (Figure 2.1) of dysphoria is represented by the person at point H (human being). As the person looks out along either side HP or HQ, the person sees nothing but arrows of dire necessity pinning him

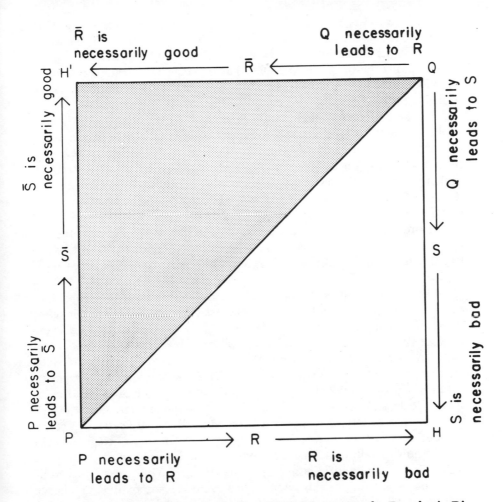

Figure 2.1 The Dilemmatic Triangle. △PHQ Represents the Dysphoric Dilemma. △QH′P Represents the Euphoric Dilemma.

down. The dilemmatic triangle of euphoria is represented by the person at H′ (human being). As the person looks out along either side, H′Q or H′P, the person sees nothing but arrows of delightful necessity, buoying him up.

Points H and H′ are diametrically distant. It is highly unlikely that a human being at either point can consider the possibility of the complementary position. From an objective point of view, it is clear that the two triangles are symmetric and complementary. They are congruent halves of a common square. The square is whole, the triangles of dysphoria and euphoria are equally arbitrary. A human being at point P can proceed to R only by neglecting to proceed to S and vice-versa. A person at point Q can proceed to

S only by neglecting to proceed to R and vice-versa. But all these proceedings are in the constructs of the two triangles. In the construct of the whole square, the person really proceeds along the sides PH and PH' or (starting with Q) along the sides QH and QH'. These perspectives lead to full representation as the square rather than partial arbitrary representation as the two triangles of the dysphoric and euphoric dilemmas.

The area of each triangle can be taken as the measurement of the psychological impact of the dilemma to the person at H or H' seriously involved in it and fully experiencing it. The area of the triangle, that is, the degree of the person's suffering or forced ebullience, is equal to $1/2\,(PR + RH)\,(QS + SH)$ in the case of the dysphoric triangle, and $1/2\,(Q\bar{R} + \bar{R}H')\,(P\bar{S} + SH')$ in the case of the euphoric dilemma. The overbar represents the negation of that letter.

In order to eliminate or reduce to a state of inconsequentiality either dilemma, it is necessary to reduce the area of the triangle. This can be done by reducing or eliminating any of the four line segments involved in each triangle.

Each of these line segments can be considered to have the probability value 1.0 since they have the quality of necessity or certainty. The triangles, therefore, are at maximum area when P (probability) = 1.0. They are also experienced as most dilemmatic by the human being involved when these values hold. To escape from the dilemma of necessity it is only necessary to reduce the probability value below that of 1.0. Thus, for example, the line segment PR has the probability value of 1.0, until the logical route of extrication involved, R does not necessarily follow from P, is applied. How can this be? It can be in a variety of ways. The feared event R usually depends upon a series of intermediate events, the probability of occurrence of each of which may be quite small, and R depends upon the multiplication of these small fractions yielding an infinitesimal quantity. It may be quite easy to demonstrate that R cannot possibly happen, that event R is impossible, and hence that the probability value is reduced to 0. A similar line of reasoning applies to the line segment RH. Application of the logical route of extrication, R is not necessarily bad, denies a probability value of R being bad equal to 1.0. As the probability value of R being bad is reduced, the area of the triangle, the psychological dilemma, is reduced. Under some circumstances, it may be possible to show that R is indeed not bad at all, and that therefore the probability of R being bad is 0. Thus, this line segment plus the line segment PR could both be reduced to 0, and these two operations would produce the area of the triangle being equal to $1/2\,(0 + 0)\,(QS + SH) = 0$.

The length of the line from P to Q can be taken as a measure of the dissimilarity between P and Q. If alternatives P and Q are very highly correlated, then their two geometric point representations are very close to each other. In this case, the size of the square is greatly reduced and the corresponding triangles of the dysphoric and euphoric dilemma are also greatly reduced. Thus, the psychological significance of the dilemma approaches inconsequentiality, as P and Q are more and more correlated. Finally, if it can be demonstrated that P and Q really amount to the same thing, then there is no geometric area of square or triangle and no psychological dilemma. In practice, it may not be difficult to demonstrate that P and Q are indeed highly correlated, as by the method of showing that one operates as a kind of reaction formation to the other.

PROBLEM OF IMPLICIT ASSUMPTION IN DILEMMAS

In terms of extrication routes from dilemmas, the counter-dilemma route: If p then not s, and if q then not r, but either p or q, therefore either not s or not r has a certain appeal in terms of its dramatic upending of the posed dilemma: If p then r, if q then s, and either p or q, therefore either r or s. The appeal is an argumentation *tour de force*, which is a variety of *tu quoque* argument, which appears to be a response in kind to an arbitrary rigid conclusion. But, from a psychological point of view, rather than a logical one, the counter-dilemma has a possibly very significant mood-modifying quality as in our discussion of the euphoric versus the dysphoric dilemma. The particular problem that we wish to discuss, at this point, however, pertains more to the problem of research with dilemmas (as discussed in Chapter 6 of this book, especially in the section on results).

In constructing dilemmas for research, it is necessary to take account of those kinds of dilemmas that assume rather explicitly that r and s as consequents are completely disjunctive and those in which the assumption is more or less implicit. There is also the problem of what inferences the research subject derives from the experimental dilemmatic item.

If the research subject assumes that it is implicit that being a success in business and having friends are not mutually exclusive, or another research subject fails to make this assumption of mutual exclusivity, then the sixth extrication route, the counter-dilemma, will not follow logically and, together with arbitrariness, will probably not be selected as a dilemmatic solution. In fact, a truth table could be set up demonstrating that for these subjects with their assumptions, the counter-dilemma is an invalid argument. However, a truth-table analysis will support the validity of the counter-dilemma argument and its extrication route as sound if the assumption of mutual exclusivity is made: if p then r and not s and if q then s and not r, but either p or q, therefore, (1) either r or s (valid) and (2) not s or not r (valid).

The problem of implicitness versus explicitness of assumptions or premises in this book is discussed in various places but especially in the Introduction. There, the issue of how implicit premises, held by the subject and unknown to the experimenter, lead to incorrect conclusions in reasoning tasks, with an incorrect outcome but a correct process of reasoning. But in the present case the subject's implicit assumption of nonmutual exclusivity would lead to a correct rejection of the proposed dilemmatic solution. To a lesser degree, the problem of implicitness also applies to the premise if p then r, namely, that r (being disliked by many people) is bad (undesirable). It may be indicated, however, that this is a value assumption whereas the nonmutual exclusivity assumption is a logical condition. Further discussion is postponed and presented in a more appropriate research context in Chapter 6.

In the next section of the book we shall discuss various approaches to reasoning with dilemmas: "Negation and the Dilemma" in Chapter 3, "The Dilemma and Systems of Psychotherapy" in Chapter 4, and "Information Theory and the Dilemma" in Chapter 5.

II

APPROACHES TO
THE DILEMMA

3

NEGATION AND THE DILEMMA

INTRODUCTION

The role of negation has been cited by Wertheimer (1959) in his observation that productive thinking often requires the denial of mechanical problem-solving methods. This theme, in variations, is apparent in the work of Maier (1933) on the solution of reasoning problems, in Luchins and Luchins (1950) on set and on consistency or contradiction, and in Guilford's (1967) work on divergent thinking. In the realm of modern philosophy of science, Bakan (1967) understands scientific and artistic creativity as the lifting of repression, which, following Freud, he equates with negation as an intellectual operation, and Bertalanffy (1968) in his endorsement of formal general-systems theory and in his more psychological critique on modern radical behaviorism as constituting a robot man model follows a general intellectual and scientific model of challenge through negation of current paradigms or procedures. An interesting twist is taken by Rychlack (1968), who, intent on developing a special philosophy of science for the area of personality psychology, differentiates between dialectic reasoning as derived from Hegel and demonstrative reasoning as derived from Bakan. According to Rychlack, whereas the tradition of Bakanian demonstrative reasoning is appropriate for a science such as physics, Hegelian dialectic reasoning by cyclical negations of thesis and antithesis is appropriate for the science of personality characterized by ever-changing patterns of conflictful and oppositional tendencies.

As an approach to the theoretical understanding of the cognition of the dilemma and of its resolution, the concept of negation is examined, in the first part of this chapter, from the standpoint of several foci of cognitive research, such as psycholinguistics, concept formation, and reasoning with conditionals and, in the second part of this chapter, from the standpoint of the formal level of thought and particularly the INRC group of logical operations.

PSYCHOLINGUISTIC STUDIES OF NEGATION

The work of Chomsky (1957) has inspired a series of research investigations concerned with the linguistic approach to negation. Chomsky's (1957) transformational grammar is clear in the work of Gough (1965), who confirmed the hypothesis that it takes longer to understand a sentence that has more transformations away from the kernel. Thus, the sentence "John is running" constitutes the kernel of the sentence "John is not running," which involves the kernel plus a negative transformation. The hypothesis of Gough and others, which now has been fairly well rejected, was that it should take longer to comprehend or verify a sentence or picture that has a transformation in it than it does for a sentence or picture that only has the kernel. It was supposed or theorized that the steps involved storing the kernel in memory and storing the footnote or tags (transformational tags) of the negation, for example, "not." In this account the person stores "John is running" and stores "not." The person then combines the stored content producing "John is not running," and therefore the time involved is longer.

In the summary that Gough gives for the second article, he says:

> Active sentences will verify faster than passive and affirmative faster than negative contrary to a hypothesis that the hearer immediately decodes a complex sentence by transforming it into its underlying structures [Gough 1966: 492].

Thus, Gough rejects the hypothesis concerning the storing of transformational tags.

In "Grammatical Transformations in Sentence Comprehension in Childhood and Adulthood," Slobin states, "This study is one of several recent attempts . . . to use the grammatical theory laid forth in Chomsky's *Syntactic Structures* (1957) and can be characterized as generative and transformational" (1966: 219). Referring to articles by McMahon (1963) and Gough (1965), Slobin states, "But the passive, which is grammatically more complex than the negative, consistently requires less time (less verification time) to evaluate than the negative" (1966: 220). The hypothesis they have been using is that the kernel or the active form without any transformation should be the easiest to verify and the fastest. The negative should be next, so the passive should be the next hardest, and the passive negative the most difficult. But it turned out in all these experiments that the negative took more time to evaluate than the passive. Therefore, Slobin states, "Thus the semantic variable of affirmation–negation seemed to be more important than the grammatical variables of transformational complexity in this case" (1966: 220).

On a more theoretical note, Slobin concludes, "Semantic factors, such as negation and reversibility, play an important role in the theoretical gap between competence and performance, and considerably alter behavioral prediction made solely on the basis of a syntactic psycholinguistic theory" (1966: 226). The tenor of this research was apparently to demonstrate that Chomsky's (1957) syntactic conceptualization could not stand alone, and it is now known that it is not possible to eliminate either syntactic or semantic components from theories of sentence comprehension.

Lexical Marking and Processing Time

In more recent investigations, some researchers adhere to their theory of lexical marking, but they acknowledge that the transformations necessary to interpret negative information are not completely accounted for by a mechanical model of additional time for processing more components. Instead, there are qualitative variations in the meanings of affirmative and negative components in how they are interpreted. Researchers have not attained a consensus concerning the nature of those variations, and the research findings such a theory must explain are complex.

Catlin and Jones (1976) studied the verification or falsification of the correspondence between a sentence and a picture. Falsification time was longer when the picture was presented first than when the sentence was presented first. However, there was no dependable difference across the conditions for negation time, the additional time needed to evaluate a sentence containing a negative.

The findings of several recent experiments demonstrate that lexical marking of negatives does not always result in longer processing time than for unmarked affirmatives. In a sentence verification task, Thomas and Hemenway (1981) found that subjects took less time to evaluate the sentence "The treaty failed" when instructions had defined the rule for passage, regardless of whether the sentence was true or false. This result was explained by congruity between the predicate of the sentence (failed) and the critical status ("pass" or "fail") that determined decision rule. This result was found regardless of whether the subjects were evaluating the number of votes for or against the treaty. Clearly, these effects cannot be attributed to the simple model that unmarked components are processed faster than marked components. Complex differences are evident in semantic processing of affirmative and negative stimuli.

Research on the solution of two-term and three-term series problems (linear syllogisms) has moved from the spatial paralogic theory of DeSoto, London, and Handel (1965) to the grammatical–spatial theory of Huttenlocher (1968) to the linguistic approach of Clark (1969). Clark (1969) offers principles to explain differences in various types of three-term series problems including negative versus positive terms and order of comparisons.

Clark's principle of lexical marking would describe affirmatives as unmarked, more easily stored, and more quickly retrieved than negatives. Thus, three-term series problems that include a negative require an additional step and thus more time than an equivalent logical form, for example, "If John isn't as good as Pete and John isn't as bad as Dick, then who is best, Dick, Pete, or John?"

Linguistic versus Spatial Representations

Ormrod (1979) compared the conflicting theories of Clark and Huttenlocher. Ormrod's experimental data indicated that different strategies—either spatial or linguistic—are used, depending on differences in demands on memory and input-processing interference. These different cognitive demands are instigated by the method of problem presentation (Presson, 1982). Regarding the Huttenlocher–Clark controversy, Ormrod concluded that when problem solving requires deducing information not specifically given in the problem, Huttenlocher's spatial/imagal theory is a better explanation than Clark's linguistic processing theory, in which the solution is achieved by an integration of the original input sentences.

Beech (1980) and Williams (1979) also have proposed resolutions of the spatial linguistic theories. Beech reported experimental evidence in favor of a parsimonious model of interaction between the two theories of representation, in which a negative sentence is combinatorily stored as an image and a proposition stating that the image is false. Williams, in a study of linear syllogisms, concluded that linguistic and imagery theories are complementary and that linguistic theory predictions about sentence processing are supported by latency times, but error rates support an imagery theory of problem solving.

A general conclusion can be drawn from these psycholinguistic studies of negation. Different cognitive processes are involved in the interpretation of negatives and affirmatives, and there are corresponding differences in modes of processing linguistic information (Ratcliff and McKoon 1982) containing negatives and affirmatives.

NEGATION IN CONCEPT FORMATION STUDIES

The research on the relative difficulty of concept formation based on negative versus positive instances is rather complex. In binary situations, for example, odd–even, it has been demonstrated that concepts are more readily formed from positive than negative instances (Dominowski 1968). Brinley and Sardello (1970) indicated memory load as a possible factor since in positive instances the set of possible solutions is displayed, but in negative instances the set of possible solutions has to be remembered and generated by the subject. When a list of possible solutions was provided to the subject, the differential effect of negative versus positive instances disappeared.

In terms of the present research with dilemmas, a similar explanation might hold for the difficulty of extricating from dilemmas that are positive situations to the generation of negative instances by which the validity of an extrication route and its content could be supported.

A further aspect of this problem may be relative cognition of associational and dissociational information and, similarly, relative cognition of information that is consistent or inconsistent with a hypothesized implicational principle.

Bear and Hodun (1975) taught subjects an implicational rule, then presented items of information that were either clearly consistent or inconsistent with the rule or else ambiguous because of incomplete information. Consistent items were more frequently recalled as being consistent than vice versa, and incomplete information was more frequently fabricated to be consistent than inconsistent.

Phillips and Epstein (1979) found higher performance on a cued recall task when word pairs were learned by encoding similarities between them than when word pairs were learned by encoding differences between them. They concluded from these findings that forming a meaningful associative relationship between pair members was more effective than forming a dissociational relationship for recalling pair membership. This result implies that information derived from negative instances of a concept might be forgotten, and the cumulative knowledge concerning what is not contained in the concept, potentially available from successive negative instances, would be irretrievable.

Brichacek, Katetov, and Pultr (1978) expressed doubt as to whether subjects assimilated information available from negative instances. Reviewing the research literature, they observed that subjects frequently offered solutions they should have been able to rule out on the basis of negative instances they had apparently disregarded. They also noted consistent performance differences favoring a series of positive instances over a series of negative instances, whereas an intermediated performance level was typically reported for a heterogeneous series of positive and negative instances. Complementary to these performance results, they reported that subjects also preferred to be presented with positive rather than negative instances.

The relative effects of negative versus positive instances seem to interact with the particular logical form (conjunction, disjunction, conditional) and with the inferential strategies that these forms may permit. Bourne and Guy

(1968) and Kendler (1964) indicate that positive instances raise performance in conjunctive concept tasks. Negative instances lead to more efficient operation with conditional forms (Bourne and Guy 1968). In disjunctive concepts, negative instances are more efficient than positive instances (Carroll 1964; Davidson 1969). Inferential strategy is facilitated by positive instances in the case of conjunctive concepts, but is facilitated by negative instances in the case of disjunctive concepts and implication concepts. Labeling the instances positive or negative appears secondary to the nature of the inferential process, and this emphasis on inference drawing or reasoning seems in strong opposition to Clark's (1969) reduction of deductive reasoning to linguistic processes, such as linguistic marking.

REASONING STRATEGIES AND NEGATION

Suppose we know that event X is determined by either condition a or by condition b, but not by both and not by any other condition. Our hypothesis may favor condition a and we can proceed to test it directly to search for verification or we can test condition b and by the negative information produced by the disconfirmation of b infer support for condition a. The mode of reasoning with negative information is different than with positive information, even though logically the two are equivalent. Logically, aversive training and reward training are merely binary, but their psychological effects are not simply opposite and equal (Wason 1960). Dysphoric dilemmas and euphoric dilemmas are not merely opposite *scalar* qualities but have differential effects on reasoning as will be discussed in Chapter 6.

In deductive reasoning, the effects of negatives seem at least dependent on the nature of the logical construction, the construction language, and assumptions regarding the logical system or logical universe involved.

Effects of Negatives on Deductive Inferences

Roberge (1974, 1976a, 1976b) has conducted a series of experiments that demonstrate that reasoning with negation is complex and highly dependent upon specific conditions. As an example, disjunctive major premises with a negative in one component resulted in more errors than disjunctive major premises with both components either positive or negative. However, disjunctive arguments with affirmative minor premises were more troublesome than those with negative minor premises (Roberge 1976a). As another example of the effect of specific conditions on reasoning performance, Roberge (1976b) reported that arguments involving confirmation of the first component of a disjunction and negation of the second component were easier to evaluate than those in which the confirmation and denial were reversed. Evidently, a full account of reasoning with negation will have to take into account not only the presence or absence of negation but also the ordering of affirmative or negative components in disjunctive arguments.

Roberge (1974) also reported that the effect of negation in the major premises varied with the form of reasoning, either disjunctive or the logically equivalent conditional. In this experiment, Roberge also reported that subjects were more likely to erroneously verify negative statements than affirmative statements and less likely to correctly falsify negative statements than affirmative statements.

Wason (1960) studied the ability of subjects to utilize negative information so as to eliminate hypotheses and discover a rule. Experimenter directions were: "You will be given three numbers which conform to a simple rule that I have in mind. Your aim is to discover this rule by writing down sets of three numbers together with reasons for your choice" (Wason 1960: 131). Subjects began their rule search with the number sequence: 2, 4, 6. The problem solution was simple, perhaps too simple: three numbers in increasing order of magnitude. In a way, these British university students may have been diverted as they tried rather complicated multiplicative ratios, logarithms, and so on as positive instances of a complicated mathematical rule. This confirmatory procedure did not, however, lead to a rapid shortening of the myriad possibilities. With few exceptions, subjects seemed to avoid a strategy of negative examples that would eliminate a hypothesis. When this strategy was used by the occasional subject, it was very efficient in rapid elimination of large classes of possibilities and the discovery of the experimenter's rule. Wason (1960) discussed this finding in terms of a bias toward verification, and this explanation is discussed by Wagman (1969) and extended to other areas of psychology, especially including abnormal psychology.

Effects of Bias toward Verification on Deductive Inferences

Research examining the bias toward verification suggests that there are two complementary facets of this problem. The first facet is the disregard of the value of falsification in testing a hypothesis. The second facet is the disregard of the relative values of alternative hypotheses. Therefore, surmounting the first deficit does not always produce successful inferences if the subject's approach is too rigid.

With respect to the first facet, two studies by Mynatt, Doherty, and Tweney (1977, 1978) permitted subjects to design experiments to help them induce the laws of particle motion in an experimental environment. In both studies, subjects showed a strong bias for choosing a test that would probably confirm their hypothesis rather than seeking to disconfirm it, and this bias was resistant to instructions to use a falsification strategy. When falsifying information was encountered in the first study, subjects employed it appropriately to reject incorrect hypotheses. However, in the second study, the environment was made significantly more complex, and in this circumstance subjects failed to employ disconfirming evidence that was discovered. Additionally, when subjects were induced to employ a falsification strategy in this complex environment, it seemed to surpass their cognitive load and was generally counterproductive. Thus, it appears, consonant with the findings in concept learning studies, subjects are deficient both in searching for negative evidence and in employing it productively.

Interesting and significant advances were achieved by Tweney et al. (1980) in a series of experiments designed to surmount the confirmation bias in Wason's (1960) 2-4-6 rule discovery task. Unless subjects were specifically instructed in the advantages of a disconfirmation strategy, they failed to employ that strategy. However, the use of disconfirmation strategies did not improve performance in discovering the relational rule. Even when negative instances were generated and tested, the knowledge gained was not used effectively. Following a recommendation by Wason, the researchers modified the nature of the task in one experiment. In place of subject's instances being labeled positive or negative instances of the rule, they were labeled DAX and MED, respectively. Subjects were instructed to discover two interrelated rules which defined the DAX and MED categories. The surprising result was that subjects in this condition were much more effective discovering the rule for DAX than were subjects in other conditions.

Theorizing about possible reasons for the dramatic increase in performance, the researchers proposed that the innovation permitted subjects to avoid rigid testing of a single hypothesis, while they had been unable to overcome that tendency in other conditions. Tweney et al. concluded that negative information became relevant because it related to the MED rule, and they wondered whether negative feedback in Wason's original 2-4-6 task blocked the subjects' ability to integrate knowledge. Possibly this implies an emotional response to negative information.

Concerning the failure to entertain alternative hypotheses, Peterson (1980) has observed that if the correct solution to a problem is not present in a set of hypotheses the subject regards as potentially relevant at the beginning of a task, the problem will not be solved. Subjects in Peterson's research were to infer a contingency rule for a sequence of binary events that in some cases was random. Inference of randomness (noncontingency) was never drawn unless it was prompted by instructions prior to the task.

These experimental studies on the verification bias suggest a general principle that performance can be greatly constricted when prior assumptions about potential solutions to a task limit the inferences drawn from observed events.

NEGATION AND IMPLICATION

The article "Reasoning About a Rule" (Wason 1968) is concerned with the difficulty of *modus tollens,* or the assertion of the contrapositive inference: if p then q, and not q . . . not p. To accomplish the contrapositive, it is necessary to transform (falsify or negate) the information contained in the q component of the conditional statement. The difficulty in making the contrapositive inference lies in the well-established bias, based on lifelong history of learning, that produces a mental set toward expecting that a relationship of truth, correspondence, or a match should hold between sentences and states of affairs. We encounter truth more often than falsity in such statements. We seldom falsify a statement in order to make an inference. Wason attempted two therapeutic exercises to dissolve the mental set toward the expectancy of correspondence or truth or match of sentence with a state of affairs, but both of these failed to eliminate this set, which is therefore highly resistant. Wason also concluded his article by raising the question as to whether his subjects, undergraduate students, had indeed reached the Piagetian stage of formal operational thought.

In Wason's experiment, subjects were asked which cards they would have to turn over if they were to prove that the experimenter was making a false statement in stating that "If there is a vowel on one side of the card, then there is an even number on the other side." Four cards were used: p (vowel), not p (consonant), q (even number), and not q (odd number). Almost all subjects chose p, 60% to 70% chose q, a small minority chose not q, and hardly anyone chose not p. These results are explained according to Wason by the following theory: Subjects believe that there are three outcomes to any conditional statement — if p, then q. P and q prove the statement true, p and not q prove the statement false, and not p combined with either q or not q is irrelevant. Thus, subjects turn over the card p and then they turn over the card q (the even number) to see if indeed p does show up (the vowel). In doing so they are committing the fallacy of affirmation of the consequent. They seldom turn over not p, therefore, the fallacy of negating the antecedent is rare, because they regard this possibility as irrelevant. That a card is not a vowel card, in their thinking, is irrelevant as to whether or not there is an even or odd number on the other side. All of this explains the "reasonableness" of the subjects' making the inference, though fallacious, that if q then p. But the failure to test the contrapositive, *modus tollens,* that if not q then not p, to prove the experimenter was lying, involves the explanation in which one has to see the state of affairs as involving a not q — that is, an odd number and realizing that this perceived odd number is an example of not q in the conditional statement itself. This requires transforming statements by negation — or falsity — and the construction or evaluation of such sentences as in Wason's previous research is really rather difficult. Thus, this difficulty could account for the low frequency with which the contrapositive inference or test is made. Wason then attempts to encourage the contrapositive by projecting falsity onto the statements, but both of these fail. He then makes his conclusion, as stated above, about the expected correspondence between the state of affairs (vowels, consonants, even numbers, odd numbers on the cards) and the sentence: "If there is a vowel on one side of the card, then there is an even number on the other side." The other possible explanation of not arriving at Piaget's logical operational thought stage is also considered.

VanDuyne (1976) explored the connection between performance on Wason's selection task and the verification bias by manipulating the belief that the conditional statement was true. VanDuyne theorized that subjects seek disconfirmation only for rules they believe have exceptions. In support of this theory, he reviewed studies of the selection task in which insight was much more frequent for the conditional "If a letter is sealed it has a 50 lire stamp on it" than for the conditional "If it is raining the street is wet." In VanDuyne's test of this theory, performance was stronger when the conditional was a sentence the subject believed was sometimes true than when the subject believed the sentence was always true. In the latter condition, subjects were less likely to think of disconfirming the consequence. However, complete insight was infrequent in both conditions.

Experimental data demonstrate that the expectation of correspondence between sentences and states of affairs disrupts the learning of conceptual rules. Salatas and Bourne (1974) compared learning of eight bidimensional conceptual rules (e.g., conjunctive, disjunctive, biconditional, conditional, etc.). Subjects had the most difficulty learning rules in which stimuli possessing both defining attributes (true–true) belonging to the negative category (not belonging to the class), stimuli possessing neither attribute (false–false) belonging to the positive category, or true–true and false–false stimuli belonging in the same category. Subjects found it difficult to make sense out of these instances in order to discover the general rule.

Newman (1974) ascribed this difficulty to the directional quality of the sorting category labels "positive" and "negative," which is congruent with the attribute labels "true" and "false" for primary rules and reversed (incongruent) for complementary rules. Counter-intuitive classification is necessary for a complementary rule, which makes it more difficult to learn than the corresponding primary rule. As an experimental manipulation, Newman substituted neutral labels for the categories in place of "positive" and "negative." This semantic manipulation eliminated the typical difference in difficulty between primary and complementary rules. Mean performance on both types was then between the performance levels on the two types under the condition when they have directional labels.

In attempting to teach subjects to reason correctly, Brown et al. (1980) proposed using an additional concept for subjects to consider: the distinction between competence and performance. From the results of their experiment, Brown et al. suggested that it is more difficult to produce arguments involving negation than simply to evaluate them. Subjects participated in the Wason selection task and, in a second task, evaluated the truth or falsity of propositions such as "all p are q," "all p are q̄," "all q are p̄," "some q̄ are p," and so on. Performance on the two tasks was uncorrelated. The importance of this finding was that correct interpretation of implications does not ensure a correct response on the selection task; therefore, Brown et al. (contra Wason) conclude that incorrect responses on the selection task do not imply inability to reason with implication.

Leahey (1977) demonstrated that subjects could be trained to gain insight into implication and validly use inferences that previously had been used fallaciously. Wagman (1978) found that, as compared with Wason's (1964) method of self-contradiction which depended on the emergence of self-insight during the experiment, a method of information feedback (didactic correction) was much more effective in reducing fallacious reasoning. Roth (1979) demonstrated a different strategy of improving performance on the selection task. This strategy stressed performance in reasoning, rather than the comprehension of logical rules. Subjects were given the Wason selection task, but omitting "p" (the antecedent) as an available choice among the cards they could turn over. This prompted subjects to examine "q̄" in order to discover the occurrence of "p and q̄." Having learned this inferential reasoning process on the reduced array of choices, subjects then performed with insight into the selection task with the standard array.

Wason also offered the possible explanation that subjects had not attained Piaget's formal operational stage of cognition. Some evidence (Roberge and Flexer 1982; Griggs and Newstead 1982) can be found that performance on reasoning tasks (except for subjects misconstruing the conditional as a biconditional, perhaps a linguistic error rather than a logical error) improves with age (Taplin, Staudenmayer, and Taddonio 1974); however, that explanation does not seem entirely satisfactory in view of the research evidence presented above for deficits in performance rather than competence. In addition, Demetriou and Efklides (1979) found differences in performance on a test of the integration of formal operations in a latticed INRC group structure (Piaget's formal level of thought is discussed later in this chapter) among same-age subjects (college students) that were accounted for by factors of education and sex.

APPLICATION TO THE DILEMMA

Cast in logical symbols, the personal dilemma is: if p then r, and if q then s, but either p or q (and, implicitly, both r and s are bad), therefore either r or s (unhappiness is inescapable). A logical resolution is to negate r and s and reverse them with respect to the antecedents (if p then not s and if q then not r), thus yielding a not s or not r situation, which produces positive and happy outcomes.

This negating of the implicates is sometimes called "destructive dilemma." Its similarity to *modus tollens* or the contrapositive inference seems clear. Accepting Wason's (1960, 1964) findings that the contrapositive is exceedingly difficult to elicit and that this difficulty depends upon certain deep-seated sets, the reason for the perpetuation of personal dilemmas, in which anxious, obsessive, and depressed persons are inextricably involved, can be partially explained. In this explanation, a distinction needs to be drawn between (1) the purely inferential difficulty involved in making the contrapositive inference, with the long-standing set toward expecting correspondence, match, or truth between a sentence and a state of affairs and (2) the role of emotional or dynamic factors in the dilemma.

Dobson and Dobson (1981) found differences in conceptual problem-solving styles and efficiency between depressed and nondepressed college students. Depressives used a more conservative style which was less efficient, as it required more steps to reach a problem solution. Although both groups were able to improve their performance scores in the second phase of the study, nondepressives perceived an increase in their own performance when it improved in the second phase of the study, while the depressives did not. Thus, expectations for and ratings of performance reflected a fixed perception of improvement for the depressives, but reflected a changing perception of improvement, in keeping with objective measures of improvement, for the nondepressives.

In the preceding section, a variety of experimental studies that center on the comparative effectiveness of different methods of teaching the strategy of *modus tollens* has been discussed. These methods might be applied in a teaching program aimed at effective extrication from psychological dilemmas.

A new and interesting finding concerning *modus tollens* inferences was made by Cope (1979). Given nonbinary conditional statements, *modus tollens* inferences are made less often than when binary conditional statements are given. Cope offers the intriguing explanation that given the usual difficulty subjects have with negatives, subjects will have special difficulty with negatives in nonbinary conditionals because logically these cannot refer to single items. In attempting to process such inferences, subjects will experience an overloading of the cognitive system and thereby result in reasoning errors. A possible application of Cope's finding an explanation regarding *modus tollens* inferences in nonbinary statements could teach an effective method of reformulating psychological dilemmas so that the new formulation would involve binary rather than nonbinary conditional statements, thereby facilitating the use of *modus tollens* as an effective procedure for extrication from the dilemma. Experimental research with such methods, as well as others, is extensively discussed in later chapters of this book.

The role of logical factors in making the contrapositive inference, or destructive dilemma inference, is that negation and falsity are more difficult to deal with than assertion and truth; we meet truth more often than falsity, and we rarely assert something to be false in order to make a deduction from it.

What are the sentences and what are the states of affairs between which there is a set toward experiencing truth, correspondence, or match in the case of personal dilemmas? These sentences are the anxious and depressed person's thoughts rather than an experimenter's overt statement. But in an experiment, the experimenter's statements become the subject matter of the subject's self-sentences or thoughts. Not all anxious or depressed persons, unless they also happen to be logicians, experience their personal dilemmas in the form of sharp dilemmas. Some, however, after much cognitive turmoil, do come out with a whether or not self-statement regarding their condition. Some clinicians can and do reduce the client's crisis to a . . . well, it comes down to this then . . . you feel that either . . . or. . . . Thus, either by the clinician's presenting the conditional alternatives to the client or by the client having arrived at them himself, a resemblance occurs between the clinical situation and the experimental situation discussed above.

But what are the relations between the sentences involved in the personal dilemma and the state of affairs? In the personal dilemma, the "truth, matching, or correspondence" set can involve (1) a difficult state of affairs producing appropriate dysphoric self-statements or (2) dysphoric self-statements producing perception of a difficult state of affairs. In either case, mutual interaction and mutual reinforcement between conditional self-statements and states of affairs are likely to occur. The expectation of correspondence between conditional self-statements, if p then q, and a state of affairs leads to the search for representatives of q in the state of affairs and to representatives of p in the state of affairs, but to the overlooking or nonselection of representatives of not q in the state of affairs.

To make this concrete and relate it to dilemmas, consider once again the aggression dilemma. A person holding these self-statements will seek for confirmation, that is, he will look for instances where he is aggressive and disliked and instances where he is nonaggressive and a failure. He will overlook the contrapositive instances, instances where he is aggressive yet liked and where he is nonaggressive but successful. Is this choice distribution a function of deficit in formal logical operations, as suggested by Wason (even in nonemotional situations), or is it also a function of emotional and psychodynamic factors such as mood state? If the mood state is happy and ebullient, conditional self-statements with a different content and different dilemmatic outcome occur. But the relation still holds between the conditional statements and states of affairs. Therefore, correspondence, interaction, and mutual reinforcement among conditional self-statements, personal dilemmas (happy or unhappy), and states of affairs prevail. The tendency, therefore, would be toward selecting from the states of affairs p and q exemplars rather than not q. This biased selection is illogical, since it inhibits the demonstration of the contrapositive inference and is deceptive with regard to mood-lowering or mood-raising consequences.

But why do people persist in such self-deception? The traditional motivational explanation in terms of mood determination may be replaced by a cognitive explanation involving people's limited command of formal logical operations.

NEGATION AS AN OPERATION

The concept of negation itself is indeed a rather difficult one for most persons, especially young children. In a recent investigation (Slobin 1966), it was found that children refuse to believe that a statement that included the word "not" could be true. In their experience, truth is associated with affirmative forms and falsity with negative forms of statements. But the extrication from the dilemmatic statement requires the establishment of truth by the employment of "not" in each of the six routes of extrication. P does not necessarily lead to r, and q does not necessarily lead to s, and r is not necessarily bad, and s is not necessarily bad, and you are not necessarily restricted to either p or q, and it may be just as arbitrary or specious to construct the counter-dilemma (if p then not s and if q then not r, but either p or q, therefore either not s or not r). Many children find it difficult to accept such statements because of the presence of the negative as true. Even adults feel a little uncertain about dealing with statements in negative form, and research indicates that, indeed, true negative statements are more difficult to verify than false positive statements. Just as in the long course of human development positive instances are more frequent and are more frequently reinforced than negative instances, so associative responses are more frequent than responses in the form of the logic of conditionals. Responses to stressful situations are more likely to be of an associative than of a conditional character. When individuals do translate their associative responses to threat into conditional statements, they are likely to leave it at that without attempting to solve the conditionals. This is because of their lack of experience and lack of specific training with the logic of conditionals. We would get along as badly with the handling of mathematical and arithmetical concepts or even with the working out of comparative interest rates and other aspects of personal finance and budgeting without the long years of training and other instruction begun from the earliest primary grades. Piaget and Inhelder (1959) indicate that it isn't until well after the tenth grade that most children even begin to enter into the stage of logical operations, and the work of Wason and others (discussed earlier in this chapter) indicates that students do rather poorly in solving problems that involve conceptual rules in the form of conditionals. They do even worse when the task requires demonstrating mastery of rules and projecting falsity (negate) on a conditional statement or on its antecedent or consequent part. But this projection of falsity is exactly what is involved in finding routes of extrication from unrealistic personal dilemmas.

At the level of formal logical operations, as described by Piaget and Inhelder (1959), a person is capable of the mature flexible use of the operation of negation in combinatory analysis and in the INRC group of logical operations.

THE INRC GROUP AND THE DILEMMA

In Piaget's theory, after the development of the concrete level of operations, two new structures, the INRC group and combinatory operations, make possible constructive operations on implication (if p then r) and on disjunction (r or s). The INRC group is formed by connecting into a Kleinian structure the operations of inversions (N) and reciprocate (R), together with the inverse of the reciprocal the correlative, (C) (NR = C, the operations of inversion operating on the reciprocates produces the correlative C) and the identity operation, I, which equals NRC (I = NRC = N (N) = N^2). Thus the INRC group is a set of operations that act on the operations or elements of some other logical, mathematical, or physical structure that itself has an involuted operation, that is, an operation that is its own inverse ($N^2 = I$). The dilemma as such an involuted structure makes possible the bearing of formal level of operations, in particular the INRC group of operations, N (if p then r, if q then s) = (if p then not s, if q then not r).

If we define C as the operation which interchanges the order of the consequents r and s: C(r, s) = (s, r) and R as the operation that changes the signs of r and s, R(r, s) = (not r, not s), then N should equal CR and since the operations of the structure are commutative N = CR = RC (euphoric dilemma ↔ dysphoric dilemma).

The presence of double arrows along the sides and diagonal of the square (Figure 3.1) demonstrates a principle of reversibility with respect to direction of application of the particular operation — negation, reciprocity, correlative. There are, then, states of equilibria, a given equilibrium at any one moment but (as in the concept of potential energy in physics) changes in their equilibrating actions achievable by operations on operations. The content of these operations and of course that of the dilemma may be taken to indicate from the psychological point of view that the dilemma is at the level of formal op-

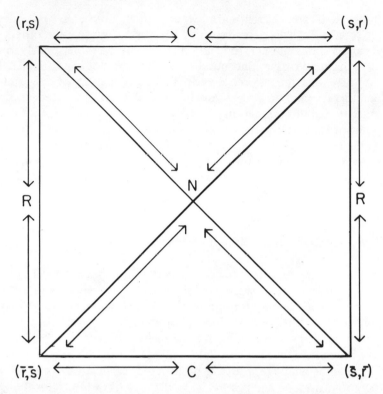

Figure 3.1 State Diagram for Applying the INRC Group of Operations to the Dilemma.

erations, and also potentially in various states of equilibria and not fixed or rigid.

From Figure 3.1 it may be seen that the two vertical sides involve the operation R, which is a kind of inversion or negation of sign, and that either following or preceding these by the operation C yields the diagonal N (RC = N, CR = N). More directly, the diagonal from upper left to lower right (r, s to s̄, r̄) is a representation of the involuted structure of the dysphoric dilemma ↔ euphoric dilemma. One can move in any direction around the square or along diagonals to accomplish various dilemmatic solutions, this provided, though, that the individual has reached this formal level of development of logical operations. This would permit the person to understand that going around the square, starting at the upper left corner (r, s), produces the movement from (r, s) through the order inversion (C) yields (s, r) and through the reciprocity of sign change (R) yields (s̄, r̄), which is equal to N (the negation of the dysphoric dilemma and production of the euphoric dilemma). But the principle of reversibility would permit the operation of negation on negation

$[N(CR) = N(N) = I$, (identity)], that is, the dysphoric dilemma is restored, the person is back at the upper left hand corner (r, s). It is also clear from Figure 3.1 that $R^2 = I$, a reciprocity of a reciprocity is an identity, reversal of reversal of sign is the original sign. $C^2 = I$, the correlative of the correlative is I, the original order results from an even number of operations of C on itself as an operator. It may be noted that, as described in Chapter 6, many subjects incorrectly solved the euphoric dilemmas by transforming them into dysphoric dilemmas and then proceeding to solve these. That they failed to make the complementary error of transforming dysphoric dilemmas into euphoric dilemmas may be taken as evidence for the intrusion of emotional bias or, in the present context, their failure to have mastered firmly enough the INRC group of operations.

4

THE DILEMMA AND SYSTEMS
OF PSYCHOTHERAPY

INTRODUCTION

Just as elsewhere in this book, the dilemma is approached from the vantage point of reasoning and negation in Chapter 3, or from the vantage point of information theory in Chapter 5; so in this chapter it is intended to present an approach to the dilemma from the vantage point of psychotherapy theory and method. The dilemma therapy structure in its various modes is compared with the various psychotherapy procedures discussed under the general headings of: psychoanalytic therapy, existential therapy, behavior therapy, and cognitive therapy. The dilemma is taken either in the whole, in its euphoric or dysphoric modes, or in its structural elements. The material dealing with the four major classes of psychotherapy is examined to determine how these therapeutic systems have approached the dilemma or its various elements.

This chapter is organized into five major sections. Each of the first four major sections presents a commentary on a particular psychotherapeutic system with regard to its approach to the psychological dilemma. In section one, the psychoanalytic therapy systems of Freud, Adler, Jung, Rank, Horney, and Sullivan are presented. Section two presents existential systems including the work of Rogers, Frankl, and Perls. In section three, the behavior therapies of Dollard and Miller, Wolpe, and Phillips and Weiner are presented. In section four, commentary is presented regarding cognitive therapies of Ellis, Kelly, and Tyler. Section five concludes the chapter with a summary of those systems that appear to make some useful contribution to the construal and resolution of the psychological dilemma.

In order to discuss more clearly the relationship between dilemmas and psychotherapy, it will be helpful to identify generic considerations, concepts,

36

and factors common to most psychotherapeutic approaches (Appelbaum 1982; Smith 1982) and to the dilemmatic therapy. Among these issues are:

(1) rational-emotional balance or emphasis (Lazarus 1982)
(2) emphasis on past–present–future
(3) emphasis on understanding versus action
(4) emphasis on change versus choice
(5) placebo effects (encouragement, interest, sympathy, objectivity, hope, and expectations)
(6) neurosis as a failure of higher processes (interference with reasoning as a consequence of emotional problem or emotional problem as a consequence of inadequate or botched reasoning).

Specific considerations relating dilemmatic therapy to general psychotherapy have to do with those systems whose elements, in part or whole, can be represented in the theory of dilemmatic formulation, dilemmatic extrication routes, and the euphoric versus (or complementary to) the dysphoric dilemma.

It is intended to take up in turn many of the standard psychotherapies and to compare dilemmatic analysis with each of these in terms of the relevant specific considerations and commenting on generic considerations as seem appropriate. That the dilemmatic method will turn out to be related only to parts of a very complex system such as Freudian analysis and related more congruently with an existential choice system may be anticipated, but it may also be anticipated that the dilemmatic therapeutic system will relate to each of the major psychotherapies and counseling systems in a significant way and that close comparison should yield both interesting, clear generalities and challenging, divergent differences and complexities.

PSYCHOANALYTIC THERAPIES

Freudian Psychoanalysis

Symptoms, though produced through unconscious processes and having an unconscious meaning, can be made to disappear when brought into contact with conscious processes. Presumably the conscious processes include discernment, judgment, and, not the least of all, reasoning. In this conscious working through, choices between continued fixation on a maternal love object or on a more fitting love object, carry consequences. It should be clear that these alternative choices, consequences, and evaluations, necessary or otherwise, can easily be fitted into the dilemmatic paradigm. Thus, the patient's ability to use dilemmatic formulation and dilemmatic extrication routes relate significantly to escaping from the Oedipal dilemma and its associated neurotic symptoms and to the general strengthening of his "ego" operations.

> The symptom is formed as a substitute for something else which remains submerged. Certain mental processes would, under normal conditions, develop until the person became aware of them consciously. This has not happened; and, instead, the symptom has arisen out of these processes which have been interrupted and interfered with in some way and have had to remain unconscious. Thus something in the nature of exchange has occurred; if we can succeed in reversing this process by our therapy we shall have performed our task of dispersing the symptom [Freud 1935: 247].

The concepts of abreaction and catharsis, especially as they were employed in the treatment of classical (now rare) cases of hysteria with their motor paralyses, sensory anesthesias, and disturbances of personal identity and personal memories (amnesia, fugue, somnambulism, multiple personality), are, in terms of generic considerations, toward the emotional pole of the emotional–rational continuum dimension and toward the change pole of the change–choice dimension. However, since it was an irrational interpretation by a child of his childhood emotional trauma that was involved in keeping memory separate from the rest of the patient's associations and self, the deductive reasoning involved in the negation of these necessary interpretations or consequences of the event, especially with regard to their "badness" or inevitability, became significant in the final stages of treatment and permitted a mature reorganization of memory interpretations and associated effects that provided a posttherapy bulwark against the temptation of regression to childish forms of dilemmatic reasoning with its rigid formulations and inevitable meanings and outcomes. In passing, it is of interest to note similarities between Freud's methods and explanations and those of Joseph Wolpe in his reciprocal inhibition therapy with respect to the use of light hypnosis to make memories or images more vivid, the use of suggestion, and the abreaction of humiliating memories when brought into contact (reciprocally inhibited) by the presence of the therapist, reminder of safety, and reminder of various compensations such as distinctions and accomplishments.

> Again, a person's memory of a humiliation is corrected by his putting the facts right, by considering his own worth, etc. In this way a normal person is able to bring about the disappearance of the accompanying affect through the process of association.
>
> * * *
>
> Our observations have shown, on the other hand, that the memories which have become the determinants of hysterical phenomena persist for a long time with astonishing freshness and with the whole of their affective colouring.

* * *

It will now be understood how it is that the psychotherapeutic procedure which we have described in these pages has a curative effect. *It brings to an end the operative force of the idea which was not abreacted in the first instance, by allowing its strangulated affect to find a way out through speech; and it subjects it to associative correction by introducing it into normal consciousness (under light hypnosis) or by removing it through the physician's suggestion, as is done in somnambulism accompanied by amnesia* [Freud 1935: 8, 17].

Strong resistance places intellectual criticism and decision making in the service of vigorous and desperate emotions, when resistance is milder, when the interference is less, and when critical, intellectual judgment is freer and more accurately dependable. The dependence of such intellectual operations upon positive or negative emotions should be less when resistance is less, and under these circumstances the demonstration of the transmutations between euphoric and dysphoric dilemmas as well as the negation of the necessary consequence of a particular choice or its necessary value quality should permit a reduction in inappropriate despairing or euphoric emotions, returning these effects to direct influence by the dilemmatic intellectual operations.

Even though he may have previously understood and accepted a great deal, yet now all these gains seem to be obliterated; in his struggles to oppose at all costs he can behave just as though he were mentally deficient, a form of "emotional stupidity." If he can be successfully helped to overcome this new resistance he regains his insight and comprehension [Freud 1935: 257].

Freud corrects the common fallacy of affirmation of the consequent: All neuroses involve frustration, but the reverse does not hold. He also takes an interactionist viewpoint on the issue of biological versus exogenous factors in etiology and, in passing, takes a rather arbitrary reasoning gambit to the effect that when a part of a scientific theory is split off from the whole, it necessarily is somehow less adequate or true, namely, Jungian analytic psychology and Adlerian individual psychology. This dilemmatic extrication route is one that will be met, no doubt, in the consideration of other contending therapy theories, including dilemmatic extrication theory.

Freud states that these etiological theories bear only on transference neuroses: anxiety, hysteria, and obsession neurosis. Psychoanalysis is not concerned with conscious conflict, but with conflict between two parts, one of which is unconscious. When that part is made conscious, psychoanalysis resolves itself into any kind of choice or dilemma situation. Freud says that analysis does not give advice or guidance on important matters of career, marriage, and so on, but leaves these to the individual after resolving the unconscious conflicts and also takes the viewpoint that it is the individual's responsibility to work through all possibilities in his dilemma and finally to make his choice and take his stand, including one of remaining in his present maladjusted state of conflict or dilemma.

On the criteria of difference between the healthy person and the neurotic person, Freud sees only a quantitative difference in terms of the practical limitations, small or great, placed on the individual's enjoyment and achievement. Comparison with the dilemmatic approach yields essentially the same impression. Dilemmas are present in varying degree in individuals impaired personally, socially, vocationally, and in themselves have to be judged in terms of the practical limitations placed on the individual's life.

Individual Psychology (Alfred Adler)

Adler does not consider the person or personality to be composed of numerous conflicting elements and particles of id, ego, and superego functions in various topographic and economic relationships to each other, but rather to be a whole, that is teleologically directed toward a particular goal or style of life. Dilemmatic therapy also dispenses with theories of personality be they psychoanalytic or of any other persuasion and focuses on the individual as involved in a series of choice or decisional actions. Dilemmatic therapy does not, however, as Adlerian therapy, insist on, so directly at least, the choice of social goals over narcissistic, neurotic possibilities. The extrication routes and the transmutations between the euphoric form and dysphoric form and the creative catalyst provided by questions as to why and how such extrication consequences are possible or feasible all help to ensure a patient, judicious, and wise final choice rather than a narrow arbitrary choice dictated by desperation. When all of this has been done by the client in writing and in thought and feeling, with or without involvement with a dilemmatic counselor or therapist, and possibilities have been tested through action, the person will have moved to a healthier level of development in the domain covered by that particular dilemma, broad or narrow. Positive achievement should follow this wise choice and action, and self-esteem should be raised. As development proceeds, new problems and new dilemmas will occur. This is an inevitable part of personal and social growth. Working through these will require the application of the previously successful dilemmatic principles and the person will thus continually learn how to pose and how to solve dilemmas and thus how to make less arbitrary neurotic and disastrous choices and decisions.

As in dilemmatic therapy, Adlerian individual psychology therapy views man as basically free to make choices and decisions. Adler views the neurotic as fearful of conflicts and responsive to them by delaying tactics and avoidance of responsibility. Furthermore, neurotics choose magnificently unattainable goals. Proper life goals, according to Adler, are those involving social interests, fellowship, want, and participation in the world of other people within a given social structure. The neurotic is not so much sick as erroneously educated. Reeducation should involve choice of more appropriately achievable goals: goals of social betterment, goals of escape from self-centeredness and vanity, and goals of success in the form of helping and participating with others. Fellowship and equal participation with the therapist and not childlike transference reactions are to be fostered and, even more significantly, reeducation takes the form of environmental therapy as the person is actively encouraged to live his newfound choices through maximizing social interest rather than narcissistic interest.

I. Every neurosis can be understood as an attempt to free oneself from a feeling of inferiority in order to gain a feeling of superiority.

II. The path of the neurosis does not lead to the direction of social functioning, nor does it aim at solving given life-problems but finds an outlet for itself in the small family circle, thus achieving the isolation of the patient.

III. The larger unit of the social group is either completely or very extensively pushed aside by a mechanism consisting of hyper-sensitiveness and intolerance. Only a small group is left over for maneuvers aiming at the various types of superiority to expend themselves upon. At the same time protection and the withdrawal from the demands of the community and the decisions of life are made possible. . . .

IX. Logic, the will to live, love, human sympathy, cooperation and language, all arise out of the needs of human communal life. Against the latter are directed automatically all the plans of the neurotic individual striving for isolation and lusting for power.

* * *

We insist that, without worrying about the *tendencies, milieu and experiences*, all psychical powers are under the control of a directive idea and all expressions of emotion, feeling, thinking, willing, acting, dreaming as well as psycho-pathological phenomena, are permeated by one unified life-plan [Adler 1929: 23–24, 25].

According to Adler, the nervous person is distinguished from the healthy person by way of the greater rigidity and desperate character of his life plan and goal. As indicated previously, dilemmatic therapy through its encouragement of consideration to be given to alternative pathways and objectives and through its examination of creative solutions posed to the extrication routes is intended to reduce the rigidity of fixed dilemmatic life orientations. The cognitive character of Adler's basic notions of lifestyle, goal, and the importance of subjective evaluation, is consonant with dilemmatic therapy as is the occasional and appropriate use of humor, the emphasis on man's freedom to construct different and possibly more healthy and flexible lifestyles, and the important attitudes of encouragement and freedom from coercion on the part of the counselor that permit such cognitive operations and reorganizations.

> The same tendency of the life-line is disclosed in the world-view and the life-view of the patient, as well as in his outlook upon and his grouping of experiences. Falsifications and conscious additions, purposive special applications markedly one-sided, unbounded fears and expectations clearly impossible for fulfillment, are encountered at every step and they always serve the patient's life-plan with its glorious last act [Adler 1929: 46].

Adler notes the function of selective memory recall as a strengthening for current optimistic or pessimistic mood states. The theory of dilemmas, especially of the dilemmatic triangle (see Chapter 2), asserts a similar parallel, but this time between contemporary or future events and their associated euphoric and dysphoric moods.

> The use of memories to stabilize a mood can be plainly seen in everyday behavior. If a man suffers a defeat and is discouraged by it, he recalls a previous instance of defeat. If he is melancholy, all his memories are melancholy. When he is cheerful and courageous he selects quite other memories; the incidents he recalls are pleasant, they confirm his optimism [Adler 1931, 72].

Analytical Psychology (Carl Jung)

The following material from the work of Carl Jung is remarkable for its flexible view of methods for diversities of individuals and problems, even to the point of permitting the patient to keep his neurosis so as not to sacrifice his constructive personality, and for the application of methods of suggestion, hypnosis, and the like (behavior modification methods) for the collective person designed to produce change and cure, and the method of dialectic individuation with the complex intelligent and cultivated person for the problem of assisting, if possible, his self-development (Alexander 1982). Also to be noted are his remarks concerning placebo effects. On the dimension of placebo effects via hypnosis, prestige suggestion, and so on, versus dialectic method of individuation, it may be noted that dilemmatic therapy with transmutation between the dysphoric and euphoric forms and their detailed characteristics, including the one of retaining some neurotic styles, provides an achievable perspective on man's problems that could produce a vivid balancing of life and its choices and its individual meaning.

> The old hypnotism or the still older animal magnetism achieved, in principle, just as much as technically irreproachable modern analysis, or for that matter the amulets of the primitive medicineman. It all depends on the method the therapist happens to believe in. His belief is what does the trick. If he really believes, then

he will do his utmost for the sufferer with seriousness and perseverance, and this freely given effort and devotion will have a curative effect. . . . Thus, from the psychological (not the clinical) point of view, we can divide the psychoneuroses into two main groups: the one comprising collective people with underdeveloped individuality, the other individualists with atrophied collective adaptation. The therapeutic attitude differs accordingly, for it is abundantly clear that a neurotic individualist can only be cured by recognizing the collective man in himself — hence the need for collective adaptation. It is therefore right to bring him down to the level of collective truth. On the other hand, psychotherapists are familiar with the collectively adapted person who has everything and does everything that could possibly be required as a guarantee of health, but yet is ill. It would be a bad mistake, which is nevertheless often committed, to normalize such a person and try to bring him down to the collective level. In certain cases all possibility of individual development is thereby destroyed.

* * *

The more deeply we penetrate the nature of the psyche, the more the conviction grows upon us that the diversity, the multi-dimensionality of human nature requires the greatest variety of standpoints and methods in order to satisfy the variety of psychic dispositions. . . . Inasmuch as a man is merely collective, he can be changed by suggestion to the point of becoming — or seeming to become — different from what he was before. But inasmuch as he is an individual he can only become what he is and always was. To the extent that "cure" means turning a sick man into a healthy one, cure is change. Wherever this is possible, where it does not demand too great a sacrifice of personality, we should change the sick man therapeutically. . . . The doctor must leave the individual way to healing open, and then the cure will bring about no alteration of personality, but will be the process we call "individuation," in which the patient becomes what he really is. If the worst comes to the worst, he will even put up with his neurosis, once he has understood the meanings of his illness [Jung 1910: 6, 7, 10].

Will Therapy (Otto Rank)

Perhaps the major similarity of the Rankian therapy to dilemmatic therapy is the emphasis on the activity, self-guidance, self-responsibility, current new and creative problems and situations, the avoidance of forcing the maladjusted or neurotic individual to fit a specified personality theory schema, the emphasis on the growing psychological freedom of the individual, and the need for continual renewal as new problems and dilemmas arise.

Transference not only contains something passive, temporary, derived, but actually represents that aspect of the relationship to the analyst. But passivity, dependence, or weakness of will in any form is just the difficulty on account of which the neurotic comes for treatment, therefore transference cannot be the therapy to which we attach the idea of something positive.

What is naturally and spontaneously effective in the transference situation and, rightly understood and handled, is also effective therapeutically is the same thing that is potent in every relationship between two human beings, namely the will. Two wills clash, either the one overthrows the other or both struggle with and against the other for supremacy.

* * *

For the first thing the patient does when he begins treatment, is to project his will-to-health onto the analyst who represents it as it were, just by virtue of his profession. That is, the patient himself no longer needs to will to become well, as the analyst must and will make him sound. This is an example of the tendency of the patient just described to make the therapist represent positive will, and to keep for himself the negative role, a tendency on whose correct understanding the whole psychotherapeutic process stands or falls. Its success depends on just this, the ability to allow this will-to-health to be preserved and strengthened in the patient himself, instead of permitting it to be projected upon the analyst. This is possible only when the whole therapeutic situation in all its manifestations is evaluated constructively in terms of the will problem. The positive strengthening of the will-to-health to the level of an actual becoming well and remaining well depends completely and entirely upon the will of the patient which even for the period of this treatment must take over the capacity for becoming well and later for remaining well.

* * *

The therapeutic factor lies in the verbalizing of the conscious emotions, while the so-called "making conscious of the unconscious," always remaining an interpretation of very doubtful value, a substitution of one rationalization for another if it does not actually deteriorate into a duel of wills with the analyst. The verbalizing is important because it represents first of all a self guidance of the individual, an act of will, in which will and consciousness, these two fundamental factors of our psychic life, come together [Rank 1945: 7, 20–22].

Interpersonal Relations Therapy (Harry Stack Sullivan)

The anticipation of necessary undesirable consequences of action in the near future is one of the factors dealt with through extrication routes and dilemmatic therapy. A parallel formulation can be seen in Sullivan's concern with foresight of anticipated anxiety concerning expected quality of interpersonal relations.

I touch here on what I believe is the most remarkable of human characteristics, the importance exercised by often but vaguely formulated aspirations, anticipations, and expectations which can be summed up in the term, foresight, the manifest influence of which makes the near future a thoroughly real factor in explaining human events. I hope that you will resist the idea that something clearly teleological is being introduced here: I am saying that, *circumstances not interfering*, man the person lives with his past, the present, and the neighboring future all clearly relevant in explaining his thought and action; and the near future is influential to a degree nowhere else remotely approached among the species of the living.

Note that I have said "circumstances not interfering." It is from study of the interferences which reduce, or otherwise modify, the functional activity of foresight that a great deal of light has been thrown on the nature of man in his doings with others. The felt component of any of this congeries of tensions includes the experience of *anxiety*; action which *avoids* or *relieves* any of these tensions is experienced as continued or enhanced *self-esteem* or *self-respect*, significantly different from what is ordinarily meant by self-satisfaction. All the factors entering into the vicissitudes of self-esteem, are wholly a matter of past experience with people, the given interpersonal situation, and foresight of what will happen.

There is nothing I can conceive in the way of interpersonal action about which one could not be trained to be anxious, so that if such an action is foreseen one feels anxious, and if it occurs one's self-esteem is reduced [Sullivan 1964: 3–5].

Dilemmatic counseling hopes to achieve for each person some measured increase in judicious and appropriate problem solving through its various methods. In the following, Sullivan emphasizes the importance of the client clarifying through the psychiatric interview his interpersonal operations and presumably thereby improving interpersonal performance. As in dilemmatic counseling, Sullivanian psychotherapy tries to teach the individual some useful practical orientation or skill.

The *quid pro quo* which leads to the best psychiatric interview—as well as the best interview for employment or for other purposes—is that the person being interviewed realizes, quite early, that he is going to learn something useful about the way he lives. In such circumstances, he may very well become communicative; otherwise, he will show as much caution as his intellect and background permit, giving no information that he conceives might in any way do him harm. To repeat, that the person will leave with some measure of increased clarity about himself and his living with other people is an essential goal of the psychiatric interview [Sullivan 1954: 19].

Character Analysis (Karen Horney)

Horney's emphasis on conflicting insatiable strivings and on moral imperatives of shoulds as part of the idealized self or pride system can easily be placed into the dilemmatic approach as formulated disjunctive alternatives, necessary consequences, necessary virtues, and necessary defects. Her basic concepts are very similar to Adler's notions. Compare, for example, will to power and superiority complex with compulsive striving for glory and success, neurotic submission, and illness with compulsive submissive and complaint strivings, inferiority complex with negative evaluation and self-hatred, and so on. Therefore, some, at least, of the comparisons between the dilemmatic approach and Adler system presented above may also hold for Horney's conceptual and therapeutic approach. It may turn out that only her language has a more modern ring and this difference, based on contemporary literary style, may be a thread running through therapy systems with which dilemmatic therapy is congruent. The transformations of dilemmatic symbolic logic may have an advantageous clarifying or unifying value and function regarding such differences in literary style.

> To begin with, for Freud the superego is a normal phenomenon representing conscience and morality; it is neurotic if particularly cruel and sadistic. For me the equivalent shoulds and taboos of whatever kind and degree are altogether a neurotic force counterfeiting morality and conscience. . . . According to my views, the inner dictates are an expression of the individual's unconscious drive to make himself over into something he is not (godlike, a perfect being), and he hates himself for not being able to do so. . . . It follows from these differences that the therapeutic aim on this score is different. Freud can aim merely at reducing the severity of the superego while I aim at the individual's being able to dispense with his inner dictates altogether and to assume the direction of his life in accordance with his true wishes and beliefs.
>
> * * *
>
> Freud was pessimistic but he did not see the human tragedy in neurosis. We see tragic waste in human experience only if there are constructive creative strivings and these are wrecked by obstructive or destructive forces. And not only did Freud not have any clear vision of constructive forces in man; he had to deny their authentic and libidinal forces, their derivatives and their combinations. Creativity and love *(eros)* for him were sublimated forms of libidinal drives. In most general terms, what we regard as a healthy striving toward self-realization for Freud was — and could be — only an expression of narcissistic libido [Horney 1939: Chapter 2].

With regard to the goals of character analysis therapy, Horney is clear that the goal is not the cure of the specific phobia, insomnia, or other such circumscribed condition, but rather involves the integration of the self, self-realization, acceptance of responsibility, control of creative powers, and, in short, self-development. It is thus a function of character analytic therapy to remove the obstacles to true self-realization and development. These goals are at once more ambitious, more time consuming, and more fraught with problems than the one of removing and curing a specific focalized symptom. Success rates of cure, therefore, measured for self-development goals versus circumscribed goals, as appear in behavior therapy procedures, are especially incommensurate. How commensurate are the goals of the dilemmatic approach?

> In order to arrive at a rough estimate of the difficulties of the therapeutic process we must consider what it involves for the patient. Briefly, he must overcome all those needs, drives, or attitudes which obstruct his growth: only when he

begins to relinquish his illusions about himself and his illusory goals has he a chance to find his real potentialities and to develop them. Only to the extent to which he gives up his false pride can he become less hostile to himself and evolve a solid self-confidence. Only as his shoulds lose their coercive power can he discover his real feelings, wishes, beliefs and ideals. Only when he faces his existing conflicts has he the chance for a real integration — and so forth [Horney 1939: 335].

EXISTENTIAL THERAPIES

Client-Centered Therapy (Carl Rogers)

Rogerian therapy lays great emphasis on the therapeutic relationship as the main tool of change, change occurring within the interview, focus on the activity of the client rather than of the therapist, concern with the client's motives and perceptions rather than that of the therapist, a concern with growth and development, client's insight, choices, and decision making. In these respects, client-centered therapy is quite similar to Rankian therapy or relationship therapy as discussed above and comparisons with the dilemmatic approach may also be similar. The client-centered counselor reflects the emotional quality of statements of problems and conflicts presented by the client. The acceptance of negative feelings and the acceptance of positive feelings by the client-centered counselor may be seen as analogous to the construction of the dysphoric dilemma and of the euphoric dilemma and of their interrelationships. The attempt to work out more balanced and freer flowing solutions directed toward more mature development is characteristic of both approaches.

> One further general characteristic of this newer viewpoint should be mentioned. For the first time this approach lays stress upon the therapeutic relationship itself as a growth experience. In all the other approaches mentioned, the individual is expected to grow and change and make better decisions after he leaves the interview hour. In the newer practice, the therapeutic contact is itself a growth experience. Here the individual learns to understand himself, to make a significant independent choice, to relate himself successfully to another person in a more adult fashion.
>
> * * *
>
> Thus, through words, actions, or both, the client is helped to feel that the counseling hour is his — to use, to take responsibility for, an opportunity freely to be himself. With children words are of less use, and the situation must be defined almost entirely in terms of freedoms and responsibilities, but the underlying dynamics seem much the same.
>
> III. The counselor encourages free expression of feelings in regard to the problem. To some extent this is brought about by the counselor's friendly, in-

terested, receptive attitude. To some extent it is due to improved skill in treatment interviewing. Little by little we have learned to keep from blocking the flow of hostility and anxiety, the feelings of concern and the feelings of guilt, the ambivalences and the indecisions which come out freely if we have succeeded in making the client feel that the hour is truly his, to use as he wishes. I suppose that it is here that counselors have exercised the most imagination and have most rapidly improved their techniques of catharsis.

* * *

VI. The counselor accepts and recognizes the positive feelings which are expressed, in the same manner in which he has accepted and recognized the negative feeling. These positive feelings are not accepted with approbation or praise. Moralistic values do not enter into this type of therapy. The positive feelings are accepted as no more and no less a part of the personality than the negative feelings. It is this acceptance of both the mature and the immature impulses, of the aggressive and the social attitudes, of the guilt feelings and the positive expressions, which gives the individual an opportunity for the first time in his life to understand himself as he is. He has no need to be defensive about his negative feelings. He is given no opportunity to overvalue his positive feelings. And in this type of situation, insight and self-understanding come bubbling through spontaneously [Rogers 1942: 29, 35, 42].

Logotherapy (Victor Frankl)

The method of paradoxical intention has been introduced by Victor Frankl as a psychotherapeutic technique especially tailored for anticipatory fears of some person or event. Instead of worrying and backing off from a particular event or object, a patient is encouraged to wish very strenuously for contact with the object or occurrence of the event. This produces a certain distance and perspective about the situation giving rise frequently to humor. Presumably with repetition of this technique, the fear is gradually overcome.

Several things should be noted about this technique. In the first place, humor, like self-assertion, affection, pride, and so on, is known to be counteractive to feelings of anxiety. In the second place, the patient might be said to face the bugaboo and to find it less terrifying. Presumably, the technique would permit a patient to imagine it to be even more terrifying and wishing for it to produce a greater feeling of humor or surprise. Interpretive psychotherapy constantly produces the feeling of surprise mixed with humor when a particular fear is uncovered as an unsuitable and unnecessary defense. In behavior modification terms, paradoxical intention permits extinction of the fear by supplying a humorous or distancing response to the wish for object or event. The procedure accomplishes what would be accomplished if the patient could directly contact the object in real life or participate in the event in real life. In doing so, he would find out that his fears were unnecessary and might well laugh at himself. The procedure of paradoxical intention is one of many techniques which in combination with others should prove useful and when selectively used for certain kinds of patients should be especially helpful.

Can we write the procedure of paradoxical intention in logical symbolic terms? It has the form: I am afraid that if contact is made with p or event p occurs, that a terrible, awful, hideous consequence r will necessarily follow. Now wish intently for r. This constitutes a denial of r and permits together with p the falsification of the original conditional statement. Thus, if p then r (r is bad); not r . . . therefore, p and not r . . . therefore, p and r is false.

In dilemmas, of course, two sets of conditionals are involved, but the denial of r and s is in principle the same as when in paradoxical intention there is only one conditional statement. An example might be useful. I am afraid to ask because if I ask, then I am sure to be refused; and if I do not ask, then I am sure to be in a state of unpleasant tension. But I must either ask or not ask . . . therefore, either be refused or be in a state of unpleasant tension. By negating the consequents and reversing them, with respect to the antecedents, we have: If I ask, then I am sure not to be in a state of unpleasant tension; and if I do not ask, then I am sure not to be refused. But I must either ask or not ask . . . therefore either I am sure not to be in a state of unpleasant tension or I am sure not to be refused. This upending of the dilemma also has a certain quality of surprise or possible humor and certainly lends some distance or perspective as is true for the paradoxical intention procedure.

In the context of logotherapy, Frankl uses the specific tools of paradoxical intention and de-reflection as described below. It is to be noted that the method of "extrication from dilemmas" includes the following elements:

1. Humor and perspective may be stimulated by various procedures such as the juxtaposition of the dilemma and counter-dilemma or the constructive presence of both euphoric and dysphoric alternatives within the same extrication route.
2. Alterations in attention as the individual is distracted from the condition of excessive self-preoccupation and bogged down in an inescapable trap to the condition of possibilities of new alternatives or action.
3. The creative possibilities of taking different attitudes or different value perspectives toward an existing problem.
4. Enhancement of the possibility not only of changing attitude or value constructions but also of finding real, concrete, and specific problem solutions.
5. The exhaustive analysis and complete examination of possible alternatives provided by the dilemmatic analytic method may increase the scope, quantity, and general excellence of problem solutions.
6. The treatment of cases of depression and anxiety may be facilitated by the dilemmatic analytic method in a number of ways including the denial of the necessity of certain consequences and the assertion of their opposite.

7. The treatment of obsessional cases in which rationalization and intellectualization are frequently employed to construct rigid dysphoric dilemmas may be expedited through a judicious selection of extrication routes and ensuing changes in inflexible attitudes that support obsessional thought.
8. The correcting of unrealistic, naively optimistic attitudes and expectations may be brought about by the construction of the euphoric dilemma and its solution through an appropriate extrication route.
9. Everyday problems of choice and of interpersonal relations (not of neurotic proportion) may be usefully approached by the dilemmatic procedures.
10. The dilemmatic method may be useful in significant life-choice and decisions such as those in marriage and career.
11. The dilemmatic method holds that, within limits, people can command their lives in great measure by the specific attitudes they take toward it. Different dilemmatic alternatives produce different automatic and emotional reactive experiences and in turn the possibility of creative solutions and more adaptive behavior. A person's thoughts, emotions, and behavior respond automatically to the particular dilemmatic formulation, counter-dilemma, or extrication route which he selects and imposes.

A phobic person usually tries to avoid the situation in which his anxiety arises, while the obsessive–compulsive tries to suppress, and thus to fight, his threatening ideas. In either case the result is a strengthening of the symptom. Conversely, if we succeed in bringing the patient to the point where he ceases to flee from or fight his symptoms, but on the contrary, even exaggerates them, then we may observe that the symptom diminishes and that the patient is no longer haunted by it. . . . In reference to this phenomenon, Logotherapy includes a therapeutic device known as "de-reflection," designed to counteract the compulsive inclination to self-observation. In other words, what has to be achieved in such cases is more than trying to "ironize" the trouble by using paradoxical intention and its humorous formulation: one should also be able to *ignore* the trouble to some degree. Such ignoring, or de-reflection, however, can only be attained to the degree in which the patient's awareness is directed toward positive aspects. De-reflection, in itself, contains both a negative and a positive aspect. The patient must be de-reflected *from* his anticipatory anxiety *to* something else.

* * *

In addition to this personal aspect, a social factor is involved as well. More and more we meet individuals who are suffering from what logotherapy calls man's "existential vacuum" (2, 22, 23). Such patients complain of a feeling of a *total and ultimate meaninglessness* in their lives. They display an inner void or emptiness in which neurotic symptoms may abound. Filling this vacuum may thus assist the patient in overcoming his neurosis by helping him become aware of the full spectrum of his concrete and personal meaning and value possibilities, or, in other words, by confronting him with the *"logos" of his existence.*

* * *

Being human fades away unless it commits itself to some freely chosen meaning. The emphasis lies on free choice. . . . The psychotherapy that confronts man with meaning and purpose is likely to be criticized as demanding too much of the patient. Actually, however, man of today is less endangered and threatened by being overdemanded than by being underdemanded. There is not only a pathology of stress, but also a pathology of the *absence* of tension. And what we have to fear in an age of existential frustration is not so much tension per se as it is the lack of tension that is created by the loss of meaning. I deem it a dangerous misconception of mental health that what man needs in the first place is homeostasis *a tout prix*. What man really needs is a sound amount of tension aroused by the challenge of a meaning he has to fulfill. This tension is inherent in being human and hence indispensable for mental well-being. What I call noodynamics is the dynamics in a field of tension whose poles are represented by man and the meaning that beckons him. By noodynamics man's life is put in order and structure like iron filings in a magnetic field of force. In contrast to psychodynamics, noodynamics leaves to man the freedom to choose between fulfilling or declining the meaning that awaits him [Frankl 1962: 101–3].

Man's primary concern is not self-actualization, but fulfillment of meaning. In logotherapy we speak of a will-to-meaning; with this we designate man's striving to fulfill as much meaning in his existence as possible, and to realize as much value in his life as possible [Frankl 1959: 159].

Gestalt Psychotherapy (Frederick S. Perls, Ralph F. Hefferline, Paul Goodman)

There are emphases in Gestalt therapy on an active, continuous, exciting, problem-solving, contact-maintaining experience in which individuals both recognize how they are blocking themselves by their tensions, retrogressions, anxieties, and so on and how they can apply already learned techniques or techniques in the process of acquisition to stay in contact with the ongoing problem-solving activity of life and its excitements. Where the neurotic falters and becomes confused, regresses, or abandons himself to anxiety, the normal individual strives to stay with it, to remove inner obstacles, to apply new techniques and powers, and to continue to develop himself with his points of interest and concern. Normal individuals are thus different from the hysteric and from the compulsive, differing from the former in that they have developed and continue to develop certain problem-solving activities which keep them in contact and keep them rewarded, differing from the compulsive in that they do not remain fixated at ineffective solutions, but remove those inner obstacles, muscular or psychological, that are barring adequate problem solution and remain flexibly alert to questioning and applications of possible tactics that keep them interested and other than being a compulsive robot of techniques. The dilemmatic approach can accomplish a number of such problem-solving techniques, but like all techniques it must not be captured for the neurotic purpose of avoiding, confronting, changing novelty of various demand situations and problems by insisting that dilemmatic analysis has been done and everything is possible, but nothing specifically relevant and efficacious.

Let us return then to the question of the patient that we started with: "At what point do I begin not to solve the problem? How do I prevent myself?" And now, let us lay the stress not on the moment of interruption, but on the *begin* and on the *how*. Let us contrast the non-therapeutic and the therapeutic situation. Ordinarily, the self, trying to contact some interesting present actuality, becomes aware of the boundaries of its lost functions—something of the environment or body is missing, there is not enough strength or clarity. It nevertheless presses on and tries to unify the foreground, even though the neurotic structure looms in the background as an unfinished situation, unknowable, a threat of confusion and a threat to the body. The mounting excitement is throttled, there is anxiety. Nevertheless, the self persists in the original task and allays the anxiety by further blotting out the background with reaction-formations and proceeding with less and less of its powers. In the therapy, on the contrary, it is just the point of the interruption that is now made the interesting problem, the object of concentration. The questions are: "What hinders? What does it look like? How do I feel it muscularly? Where is it in the environment? etc." The mounting anxiety is allayed by continuing excitement in this problem; what is felt is some quite different emotion, of grief, anger, disgust, fear, longing.

* * *

The neurotic begins to lose contact with the actuality; he knows it but he does not have techniques for continuing the contact; he persists in a course that gets him further from the actuality . . . to keep in contact with the shifting situation, so the interest, excitement, and growth continue, he is no longer neurotic, no matter whether his problems are "inner" or "outer." For the creative meaning of the situation is not what one thinks beforehand, but it emerges in bringing to the foreground the unfinished situations, whatever they are, and discovering-and-inventing their relevance to the apparent present lifeless situation. When in the emergency the self can keep in contact and keep going, the therapy is terminated.

In the emergency, the neurotic loses himself. To live on a little, with diminished self, he identifies with reactive feelings, a fixated interest, a fiction, a rationalization; but these in fact do not work, they do not alter the situation, release new energy and interest. He has lost something of actual life. But the patient comes to recognize that his own functioning is part of the actuality. If he has alienated some of his powers, he comes to identify with his own alienation of them as a deliberate act; he can say, "It is I who am doing this or preventing this." The final stage of experience, however, is not a subject of therapy: it is for a man to identify with his concern for the concernful and to be able to alienate what is unconcernful [Perls, Hefferline, and Goodman 1965: 464–6].

BEHAVIOR THERAPIES

Learning Theory Psychotherapy (John Dollard, Neal E. Miller)

Dollard and Miller's learning theory psychotherapy can be seen as a bridge between psychoanalytic therapy and behavior therapy. Like psychoanalytic theory it considers symptoms as the product of unconscious conflict. Like behavior therapy it applies systematic principles of learning to the understanding of the acquisition, maintenance, and modification of neurosis. Unlike modern behavior modification theory such as that of Wolpe, Lazarus, and Eysenck, Dollard and Miller do not consider neurotic symptoms to be the equivalent of neurotic personality. Like Albert Ellis, Dollard and Miller posit interference with higher mental processes, but instead of there being a set of inappropriate irrational philosophical orientations as is true for Ellis, they maintain the psychoanalytic position that repression makes fluid thinking and logical reasoning about conflicts impossible for the neurotic; therapy reverses this situation for dysphoric dilemmas. For severe neurosis, with symptoms serving to reduce underlying conflicts, as discussed by Dollard and Miller in the psychoanalytic tradition, the dilemmatic approach would not be particularly useful. It does become increasingly useful as the severity of the neurosis lessens during the course of the therapy. In addition, it should be very appropriate for the more frequent occurrence of mild neurotic problems and general problems of maladjustment or problems of crisis in otherwise normal individuals. There is something of a problem in terminology concerning neuroses. Looking back at Freud's cases such as those of the Rat Man and the Wolf Man, as well as some of the complicated hysterical cases, it might appear that Freud was dealing with what could be called either a very severe neurosis or a psychotic condition mixed with physiological dysfunctions. The need for the complicated and long, drawn-out procedures for these types of cases is understandable. Unfortunately, the same conceptual system and understanding of therapy were applied to other cases that now would be judged as mildly neurotic or maladjusted, especially to the analyses of beginning psychotherapists and psychoanalysts themselves. A mathematical scaling of the degree of neurosis or maladjustment involved would have made the problem minimal. The goal of finding, based on research and clinical experience, a therapeutic or counseling procedure suitable for each type of specific problem would have been reached sooner. It appears that each therapeutic school or approach moves out from its original base of discovery and usefulness to related areas, in which use of the method becomes far more questionable. Each therapist and each therapeutic approach (probably including present employment of the dilemmatic method) tends to be overenthusiastic and thereby goes to increase the client's or patient's belief in the system with consequent desirable benefits of increased hope and courage, but also with the inevitable accompaniment of overlooking or down-playing other factors in the individual's life and in society's problems at large.

With its concern for the higher mental processes of remembering, thinking, and reasoning, Dollard and Miller's position, as stated above, is similar to that of the dilemmatic approach. However, the dilemmatic approach offers a systematic training or education in the translation of personal case problems and situations into a standard dilemmatic form and a standard extrication route but with unique creative opportunities for resolution, differentiation, and synthesis of possible solutions freely chosen by the individual, client, or person, with or without the support of relationship assistance of a therapist or a counselor.

> If neurotic behavior is learned, it should be unlearned by some combination of the same principles by which it was taught. We believe this to be the case. Psychotherapy establishes a set of conditions by which neurotic habits may be unlearned and nonneurotic habits learned. Therefore, we view the therapist as a kind of teacher and the patient as a learner.
>
> * * *
>
> Conflict itself is no novelty. Emotional conflicts are the constant accompaniment of life at every age and social level. Conflicts differ also in strength, some producing strong and some weak stimuli. Where conflicts are strong and unconscious, the individuals afflicted keep on making the same old mistakes and getting punished in the same old way. To the degree that the conflict can be made conscious, the ingenuity and inventiveness of higher mental life can aid, in finding new ways out of the conflict situation. . . . In later life many of the strong learned drives, some quite remote from their primitive sources of reinforcement, can produce painful conflicts. "Ambition" can be pitted against "loyalty." The wish to be truthful can be pitted against "tact." Wishes for social advancement may be deterred by the fear of appearing vulgar and "pushy." Many of these complex learned drives have never been effectively described in terms of the reinforcing circumstances of life. . . . We must admit that we do not know the exact conditions under which the common conflict-producing circumstances of life generate severe conflicts in some and not so severe conflicts in others. It may be that the circumstances of life are not really "the same for normals and neurotics," that this sameness is an illusion based on poor discrimination of the actual circumstances. Therefore, it may actually be that some are less well able to use higher mental processes than others and are therefore less well able to resolve traumatic tension. It may be that some are more "predisposed" than others in that they have stronger primary drives, or stronger tendencies to inhibition, or in other unknown respects. It is quite likely that the provocative circumstances of later life which precipitate neuroses are more severe in some cases than others; or that some are exposed to just those circumstances which for them excite neurotic behavior but that others are luckier and do not come into contact with just those adverse conditions which would set them off.

* * *

As the fears motivating repression are reduced by reassurance, extinction, and discrimination, and the patient is urged to think about his problems, mental life is greatly intensified. The removal of repressions restores the higher mental processes, which in turn help with further fear-reducing discriminations, reasoning, foresight, hope, and adaptive planning.

The patient begins to try better solutions in real life as fears are reduced and planning is restored [Dollard and Miller 1950: 7, 9–11, 14].

Psychotherapy by Reciprocal Inhibition (Joseph Wolpe)

It is of interest that Wolpe's sources of anxiety, reciprocal inhibition techniques, and specific assertive sexual and relaxation techniques and others such as respiration response are all, in a way, motor responses (McDowell 1982). This would be expected since he built up his theory from treatment of cat neuroses. No doubt there are many cases labeled neuroses of that kind that Wolpe has so ably described and for whose assistance his methods are very adequate. What about, however, choice anxiety, dilemmatic anxiety, conflict anxiety of a cognitive, thoughtful, belief, moral, or planned variety? These are neither cat neuroses nor motor anxieties. This, of course, introduces the entire continuum of psychological processes from completely cognitive at one end to completely specific behavior muscle responses at the other. Can one of Frankl's patients besieged by the meaninglessness of an existential vacuum be helped by body relaxation and desensitization? Perhaps the patient should be desensitized entirely to the issue of the meaning of his life as relaxation combined with systematic desensitization might provide. There is conceivably a condition of overconcern, as well as underconcern, with the problem of meaning in life. Perhaps since Wolpe's techniques are anxiety reciprocally inhibiting, that is, reduction of tension techniques, there may be a need for an increase of tension techniques for some types of problems of existential neuroses. Similarly, problems of planning, beliefs, conflict anxiety, dilemmatic anxiety, moral, personal, and value choices, as well as others, it would appear, would be helped by therapies that are closer to the cognitive rather than the behavioral end of the described continuum. Comparative research evaluations of relative effectiveness of such different therapies for different problems should make this differentiation so that criterion issues do not become hopelessly muddled.

In cases of interpersonal anxieties, Wolpe prescribes Salter's technique with an introductory persuasive argument by example and by exhortation to the inhibited social neurotic to become more outgoing, extroverted, and even aggressive. It would appear that a necessary balancing requirement has been left out of this interpersonal situational difficulty and its recommended solution, namely, that a person can become grievously aggressive in interpersonal relations and become forced to such a high pitch of nastiness and retaliative operations that social rejection will produce anxiety that is realistically based on his own objectionable behavior. There are, after all, aggressive neurotics or boors as well as meek and hypersensitive neurotics. The former group have been well-described in the selection in the work of Alfred Adler. A dilemmatic approach might offer a balanced sensitivity that would permit the development of a flexible set of controls over assertive and nonassertive behavior. (See Chapter 5, chart on information processing. Here the dilemma of being aggressive or not being aggressive is tied to the consequences of being disliked by many people or not being a success at business.)

[Earlier I] described how neurotic cats were treated by getting them to eat in the presence of small and then gradually increasing "doses" of anxiety-evoking stimuli. The treatment was uniformly successful and I gave reasons for concluding that this was so because the anxiety responses were inhibited by the eating, which resulted on each occasion in setting up a measure of conditioned (learned) inhibition of the anxiety responses to whatever stimuli had evoked them. With repetition more and more conditioned inhibition was built up, so that the anxiety-evoking potential of the stimuli progressively diminished — eventually to zero.

The observations led to the framing of the following general principle: *If a response antagonistic to anxiety can be made to occur in the presence of anxiety-evoking stimuli so that it is accompanied by a complete or partial suppression of the anxiety responses, the bond between these stimuli and the anxiety responses will be weakened.*

* * *

The stage is now set for the introduction of deliberate methods of psychotherapy — the formal use of particular responses that, through inhibiting anxiety (or, in some instance, other neurotic responses), weaken neurotic habits. As mentioned earlier in this chapter, some weakening of these habits may already have been taking place spontaneously because in certain patients the interview situation itself evokes responses antagonistic to anxiety.

The responses at the disposal of the therapist by which therapeutic change may be *deliberately* brought about are listed below. The list certainly does not exhaust the possibilities and may be expected to acquire additions as time goes on.

1. Assertive responses
2. Sexual responses
3. Relaxation responses
4. Respiratory responses
5. "Anxiety relief" responses
6. Competitively conditioned motor responses
7. "Pleasant" responses in the life situation (with drug enhancement)
8. a) Interview-induced emotional responses
   b) Abreaction

* * *

The first problem is always, of course, to decide which of the responses can most appropriately be used to obtain reciprocal inhibition of a patient's neurotic anxiety response. This will naturally depend upon the identity of the anxiety-evoking stimuli. A good many relevant stimuli will already have been revealed by the history or by positive answers to items in the Willoughby schedule. In general, assertive responses are used for anxieties evoked in the course of direct inter-personal dealings, sexual responses for sexual anxieties, relaxation responses for anxieties arising from any source whatever but especially for stimulus configurations that do not allow of any kind of direct action (e.g., inanimate objects), and respiratory responses for pervasive ("free floating") anxiety. As will be seen from case histories given below, special circumstances may dictate an unusual choice of therapeutic responses.

* * *

Systematic use of the reciprocal inhibition principle in the life situation has so far extended to three varieties of responses, sexual responses, and the relaxation responses. Assertive responses are used against anxieties arising out of the patient's immediate relations with other individuals; sexual responses are theoretically applicable against anxieties from any source whatever; but as will be pointed out, certain practical difficulties limit their use in the life situation [Wolpe 1958: 71, 112–3, 115].

Assertion-Structured Therapy (Phillips and Weiner)

Whereas, as indicated above, Wolpe's behavior modification technique rests on reciprocal inhibition of anxiety through a new motor response, Phillips and Weiner's interference assertion theory views anxiety as a consequence of conflict based on inappropriate and overdriven assertions of assumptions and expectancies from the environment that are disconfirmed and the need for the patient to learn from the therapist's intervention a new set of assumptions and assertions that will bring a better payoff from the environment. To this extent, and in this way, interference assertion-structured therapy may be seen as somewhat closer to the dilemmatic approach in terms of information feedback from the environment and a problem-solving orientation.

5. Any problem-solving responses would be identified and encouraged. The means to this encouragement could be as pervasive and inventive as the client and therapist could contrive.
6. Undesired behavior would be prevented from occurring whenever possible, rather than being allowed to occur or studied in the hope that the analysis of it would "cure" or automatically produce behavior change. The extinction process through analysis appears, at best, to be a weak method of changing behavior.
7. The general task becomes that of finding and instituting new, desired

behavior in the place of the problem behavior. Since the new behavior is to be set up for reinforcement, the situation must be structured accordingly. In restructuring a situation for reinforcement purposes, the therapist has many procedures available, including simplifying the choices available, reducing external stimuli, and putting the individual on various schedules to ward off undesired behavior. Restructuring is essentially an experiment; as in experimental control, it must hold unwanted variables in check and allow other variables to reinforce the desired behavior.

8. The solution to most problems would be approached step by step, and not by depending upon "insightful" bursts. These gradual steps would be scheduled, with more specific ordering of behavior, setting of limits, blocking of self-defeating behavior, and similar structuring. At times the solution will appear hesitant or tentative, in the way that most habits develop.

9. Corrective behavior, whether it is only a simple act or a very large response system, would be considered to occur only on a very specific basis. The behavior that directly opposes the problem-bearing tendency would be identified and promoted through such methods as desensitization, operant conditioning and reconditioning, and aversive stimulation. Specific corrective measures could be forward-looking; they would deal with what is needed to solve the problems *now*, not with what may have caused them originally (although the original causes are probably similar to the causes of the present problems).

10. Clinical terms and descriptions, such as anxiety in most of its uses, complexes, unconscious motivational states, and most diagnostic classifications, if they are used at all, could be reduced to behavioral descriptions and *descriminable* responses. There would be no need for a separate, esoteric clinical language or explanation [Phillips and Weiner 1966: 66–8].

COGNITIVE THERAPIES

Rational Emotive Psychotherapy (Albert Ellis)

The therapist's particular belief system can help the individual to get started, on the simple or complicated maze of cognitive emotional and connotative elements of the particular structure favored by the counselor or therapist. But, ultimately, it is the goal to enable individuals to confidently feel that they can — that they have the self-confidence that is appropriately based in reality. After the individuals have succeeded where they have failed before, the particular belief system may be seen quite differently, and increasingly as an unnecessary support and eventually as something to be discarded as the individuals optimize their responsibilities, conflicts, achievements, security, and happiness.

The logical and experiential operator of negation makes submission to one belief system untenable. That belief system, whether character analysis, will therapy, client-centered, nondirective therapy, rational emotive therapy, and so on, can be modulated by the act of negation. The dilemmatic approach maximizes freedom of movement among the belief systems. The dilemma of choice among belief systems is handled like any other dilemma, minor or major, in a person's life.

The dilemma of emphasis on emotion, as in Rogerian therapy or on intellectual processes as in Ellis's approach, needs to be handled by the standard routes of extrication and reaction to these routes as described previously in this chapter and in other chapters. The dilemmatic triangle, the euphoric triangle, and the dysphoric triangle ensure the unity of cognitive and emotional processes.

The RT approach especially emphasizes the idea that human emotion does not exist as a thing in itself, has no primacy over human behavior, cannot for the most part be clearly differentiated from ideation, and is largely controllable by thinking processes.

* * *

If the hypothesis that sustained human emotion often results from or is directly associated with human thinking and self-verbalization is true, then important corollaries about the origin and perpetuation of states of emotional disturbance, or neurosis, may be drawn. For neurosis would appear to be disordered, over- or under-intensified, uncontrollable emotion; and this would seem to be the result of (and, in a sense, the very same thing as) illogical, unrealistic, irrational, inflexible, and childish thinking.

That neurotic or emotionally disturbed behavior is illogical and irrational would seem to be almost definitional. For if we define it otherwise, and label as neurotic *all* incompetent and ineffectual behavior, we will be including actions of *truly* stupid and incompetent individuals — for example, those who are mentally deficient or brain injured. The concept of neurosis only becomes meaningful, therefore, when we assume that the disturbed individual is *not* deficient or impaired but that he is theoretically capable of behaving in a more mature, more controlled, more flexible manner than he actually behaves. If however, a neurotic is essentially an individual who acts significantly below his own potential level of behaving, or who defeats his own ends though he is theoretically capable of achieving them, it would appear that he behaves in an illogical, irrational, unrealistic way. Neurosis, in other words, consists of stupid behavior by a non-stupid person.

Assuming that emotionally disturbed individuals act in irrational, illogical ways, the questions which are therapeutically relevant are: (a) How do they originally get to be illogical? (b) How do they keep perpetuating their irrational thinking? (c) How can they be helped to be less illogical, less neurotic?

* * *

More precisely, the effective therapist should continually keep unmasking his client's past and, especially, his present illogical thinking or self-defeating verbalizations by (a) bringing them to his attention or consciousness, (b) showing the client how they are causing and maintaining his disturbance and unhappiness, (c) demonstrating exactly what the illogical links in his internalized sentences are; and (d) teaching him how to rethink and reverbalize these (and other) similar sentences in a more logical, self-helping way. Moreover, before the end of the therapeutic relationship, the therapist should not only deal concretely with the client's specific illogical thinking, but should demonstrate to this client what, *in general*, are the main irrational ideas that human beings are prone to follow and what more rational philosophies of living may usually be substituted for them. Otherwise, the client who is released from one specific set of illogical notions may well wind up by falling victim to another set [Ellis 1962: 35, 37-8, 45].

Constructive Alternativism Psychotherapy (George Kelly)

Whereas Phillips and Weiner emphasize response or behavior change, Kelly emphasizes conceptual or construct change. Kelly has referred to his therapy as the thinking man's therapy. He states that he does not wish to train new responses as one would a monkey. He does not wish his counselees to learn new habits and "make like normal." Human beings are free to continually modify their constructions. In obvious ways, Kelly's system is closer than interference assertion-structured therapy to the dilemmatic approach with its emphasis on free humanistic euphoric and dysphoric constructions, extrication routes, and creative solutions. Once more, it is important not to overgeneralize a technique useful for one population group or problem to others or to denigrate a very useful set of techniques for a specific population and problems because it does not hold for other populations or problems.

We pointed out that superficial movement could be produced by sliding the client back and forth in his construct slots. For example, a client who sees people as distinguished from each other principally in terms of "kindly" versus "hostile" may be encouraged to shift himself from "kindliness" to "hostility" or vice versa. This type of therapeutic movement amounts to no more than a shifting of one of the elements in the construct context – in this case himself – from one side of the construct dimension to the other. Sometimes this kind of superficial movement is worth seeking; but, as every clinician should know, it is all too likely to end up in seesaw behavior; the client is "kindly" as long as things are going well, then he turns to "hostility," then back again, ad infinitum. . . . *Controlled elaboration* . . . is a way of bringing about reconstruction through clarification. This amounts to a reorganization of the hierarchical system of one's constructs, but not essential revision of the constructs themselves. The client is helped to work through his construct system experimentally by verbal as well as by other behavioral actions. He deals essentially with the subordination–super-ordination features of his system. He brings his constructs on line with his system as a whole. Essentially he works on the internal consistency of his system rather than attempting to make outright replacements of constructs. For example, the person who sees himself as "kindly" in a kindly–hostile dimensioned world may be helped to discover just what incidental constructs and behaviors are "kindly" and what ones are "hostile." Thus his system becomes clearly delineated whereas once it was sketchy, his superordinate constructs are tightened, and he becomes a person of greater integrity — though not necessarily a "better" man. . . . The third and most basic type of reconstruction which may take place in psychotherapy is that which changes the reference axes against which the events of life are plotted. By judiciously introducing new elements into the client's field of experience, the therapist may so change the content of the construct contexts that the axes of the client's system are rotated. The same words may be used to symbolize the constructs, but the meanings may have been subtly changed in the course of psychotherapy. For example, the client who lumps humanity as either "kindly" or "hostile" may be brought to the point of seeing that some behavior which is constricting and repressive is the sort of thing that he has been calling "kindly" and some elements which are straightforward and reliable are the sort of thing he has been calling "hostile." As this revision of contexts begins to take place, the "kindly-hostile" axis begins to rotate with respect to the rest of his system. As far as his own behavior is concerned, he sees himself confronted with alternatives which have somewhat different behavior implications. In a given situation to which the construct is applied, his *elaborative choice* will be affected. And once he has made his choice, the repertory of behaviors falling under that choice will, in turn, be revised [Kelly 1955: 938–41].

Development through Choice (Leona E. Tyler)

Tyler distinguishes the counseling that is therapy from the counseling that is choice of possibilities. The latter is more general since it involves planning of choices for individuals who may be neurotic and troubled, but also for a larger number who are simply at important choice points in their lives, such as work, education, marriage, standing alone. She develops this idea with two tools — one, that of cognitive structure relying on Piaget for description of elemental logical thinking, which she says should also hold for cognitive motives and interest in general; and, two, for an account of how it is that human development from birth to death is a matter of blocking off some areas and of selecting others. In a way, this is existential choice in general and perhaps might be related to Frankl's choice of seeking meaning and so on. Since the logic of dilemmas exhausts all possibilities, the dilemmatic method provides a set of procedures for achieving the goal that Tyler describes as structuring of choice possibilities and of development through choice.

4. Cognitive structures for organizing possibilities take a variety of forms. It will be useful to distinguish between short range structures, by means of which a person guides his moment-to-moment decisions about what to pay attention and how to respond, from long range structures that control important decisions, such as those about careers, education, and marriage. The short range structures include sets, habits, preferences and aversions, and patterns of emotional response. The long range structures are such things as ethical principles, values, attitudes, patterned interests, and self-concepts. While it is the long range variety

that holds most interest for the counselor, he must also consider the short range variety. Perhaps the distinction itself is an artificial one, and we can become accustomed to incorporating within the same frame of reference the whole range of cognitive structures individuals use as they make choices.

* * *

1. Most of the psychological structures referred to above function automatically as an individual steers his course through his own possibility world. But on occasion, they break down, and the person finds himself confused or uncertain, unable to proceed until he gets his bearings again. The difficulty may arise in any of the three areas referred to earlier — work, relationships to people, or the ability to stand alone. It may come about because of a crisis in which the person's world or his own physical or psychological equipment for dealing with it undergoes a sudden change, as happens, for instance, in the case of the death of a spouse, a serious injury, or a drastic lowering of his economic status. At such times he is more likely than at others to seek counseling. Thus persons who are troubled, anxious, conflicted or blocked in their development make up a considerable fraction of a counselor's load, a fraction that varies in magnitude from one helping agency to another. . . . The more complex society becomes and the freer individuals are from external constraints, such as poverty or a rigid class structure, the more important it is to provide opportunities for individuals to pause and survey possibilities before acting. Our society has delegated to counselors the responsibility for giving individuals this opportunity. This social function is at least equal in importance to the function set forth in the preceding paragraph. Counselors should be equipped to help not only persons whose forward movement is impeded by confusion or anxiety, but also untroubled persons who can benefit from doing some serious thinking before taking important steps in their lives [Tyler 1969: 30–1].

SUMMARY

In this chapter, we have examined at some length a large number of psychotherapeutic systems with regard to their approach to significant human dilemmas and to dilemmatic therapy. These theories are, in some respects, quite disparate among themselves with varying and sometimes clashing methods and concepts. Since psychological dilemmas are an inevitable part of the vast conflictful experience of human beings, these systems can probably all make some differential and partial contribution. As we have demonstrated elsewhere in this volume, while psychological dilemmas as just indicated are variegated, the structure of the dilemma aside from its contents has a standard logical structure and as shall be shown later, this logical structure permits a powerful method to be applied to the content of any psychological dilemma with regard to defining it, stipulating extrication routes, positively confronting creative inquiries, and suggesting possible solutions. These matters will be taken up in the next chapter on the dilemma and information theory and in the series of chapters dealing with research on the dilemma. Meanwhile, we would like to conclude this chapter with a few brief highlights of those psychotherapy systems that make some contributions, even if only partial, to the understanding and resolution of dilemmas. As will be seen, many of these are only programmatic and suggestive. Nevertheless, in the following paragraphs we shall try to describe how contemporary psychotherapies approach the dilemma, on the whole, in its euphoric and dysphoric modes and in its various structural elements.

Constructive Alternativism (George Kelly) seems to handle dilemmas by focusing on their disjunctive structural element: p or q. Thus, he suggests changing the content of the "slot" approach in construing other people from "kind–cruel" to "selfish–objective." More important, however, Kelly believes that the dilemmatic disjunction should be handled by "impermeable constructs." By this, he means that a construct of other persons' characteristics be sharply delineated to apply in certain respects behavior or situations — thus far and no further. In this respect, he resembles the general semanticist's approach that requires specific delimiting of meanings.

Freud's contributions are to demonstrate that the conscious dilemma, with which most of this book is concerned, is for a minority of persons, whom he designates "neurotics," a derivative of unconscious, unverbalized, and rigid childhood dilemmas, for example, the Oedipal complex.

Alfred Adler in his Individual Psychology appears to view all significant dilemmas as the product of a rigid and relentless pursuit of self-aggrandizement and superiority that blocks any satisfaction of social needs for significant belongingness, affection, love, and compassion. The compulsive striving toward competitive success, the dire necessity of avoiding any personal or social inferiority at all costs — these and similar dangers are salient in an Adlerian response to the dilemmatic creative inquiries of how it is that, though the last series of successes did not bring happiness, the next is sure to (euphoric dilemma) or just why it is that some failure outcome proves the person to be completely unworthy (dysphoric dilemma).

Karen Horney in her Character Analysis resembles the Adlerian approach to the dilemma though substituting concepts such as the pride system for Adler's drive toward superiority.

Albert Ellis in his Rational Psychotherapy would approach the dilemma in a manner not unsimilar to that of Horney and Adler by providing a set of 10 or more major concepts that may be seen to be derivatives of their systems, for example, "It is a dire necessity that everyone love me," or Horney's compulsive need for affection and Adler's drive toward dominance through the indirect means of neurotic submission and appreciation.

Victor Frankl in his logotherapy would seem to approach the dilemma through his concepts of paradoxical intention, de-reflection, and the search for and fulfillment of the meaning of personal existence. The negative consequences in the dysphoric dilemma (r is bad and s is bad) are reinterpreted in that a meaning for the suffering is found through exploration of specific and possible purposes that would lead the person away from what Frankl calls the fallacy of self-actualization—the self is the goal of meaning of the self (as in Rogerian psychotherapy and some varieties of humanistic psychotherapy such as Maslow's). By finding a meaning or purpose in something or someone outside of himself, he is de-reflected from the dismal aversive consequences of the dysphoric dilemma. Application of the concept of paradoxical intention in which a feared outcome is intentionally exaggerated through anticipatory irony and humor provides a useful approach to the two conditional statements of the dilemma: if p, then unhappy consequence r; and if q, then unhappy consequence s.

In this chapter, we have examined the dilemma from the approach of psychotherapy theory. In the next chapter, we shall examine the dilemma from the approach of information theory.

5

INFORMATION THEORY AND
THE DILEMMA

Information theory is a theory about choices in discrete situations. Its mathematical formulation was given by Shannon (1949), and general applications for behavioral science were suggested by Miller (1965).

Information theory stipulates certain relationships in conditions of uncertainty and conditions of its rate of reduction. While uncertainty was originally intended by Shannon to refer to interference with information transmittal over communication lines, this meaning has been extended to many binary conditions insofar as these are information conditions.

Under ordinary conditions, the individual processes information smoothly and continuously. Temporary or chronic conditions in information interruption are associated with varied types of reactive stress (Lazarus 1966). Uncertainty, therefore, can be taken as a cognitive context of anxiety. Uncertainty and anxiety can be reduced by desperate measures of information avoidance or defense mechanisms. Such measures, however, prove to be ineffective and troublesome. Uncertainty or anxiety can be reduced by information expansion (Shaw 1982) and courageous facing of threat. The dilemmatic network, as will be explained below, produces information expansion, increasing the number of choices and increasing the likelihood of a sound solution.

The dilemmatic network has the advantage of displaying the entire set of choices and their relationships. The formal dilemmatic network involves transformations from overly dysphoric or overly euphoric constructions. Thus, freedom of choice and of action is increased. Individuals are freer than they were otherwise to construe their situations in a more reasonable and balanced way, lifting inappropriate depression and toning down inappropriate ebullience. Reality of adaptation is thus achieved through individuals' own constructive actions. They are also free, if they choose, to maintain their dys-

65

phoria and in a neurotic sense enjoy their depression for a while longer. Similarly, individuals are also free to choose the ebullient pattern and to ride the wave of overconfidence and overoptimism for a while also. The system thus does not impose the requirement of a happy medium solution or of a realistic or reasonable solution on anyone. Therefore, the person has maximum psychological freedom and maximum space to exercise all degrees of discernment and caprice.

The network of operations is a kind of formula, guide, strategem, or stimulus to creativity. What it does is ask the person in the dilemma, provided he has settled down sufficiently emotionally to reason: Have you considered all the alternatives? Have you, in particular, considered, and let us consider them together, the kind of alternatives as described in the above paragraphs in the formal network? Why? Because then the entire range of possibilities will have been covered — in a dilemma, whatever the degree of emotional involvement present, one is not likely to consider all the sets of alternatives, and they should be considered. For one thing, going over each of them acts as a catalyst to further creativity in the particular problem situation. For example, the alternative "you are not limited to either p or q" in effect demands, well, what else is there — let us think, let me consider, and so on. The alternative "r is not necessarily good — being successful at business is not necessarily good," for example, stimulates surprise and questioning and the search for better and more creative solutions is stimulated. The strategems in the cognitive space of the formal network operate as a leading edge or as a catalyst — for the little time that it takes to write them out in symbolic form, the energy return and the information return are very considerable.

We give, then, no formal theory of personality development, of psychoanalytic or behavior theory and therapy methods, of other theories, methods, procedures, and so on. The only theory and goal is that of increasing the individual's freedom of choice through increasing information space by way of using the strategems in the formal network. The formal network, if carried out through writing out the symbolic operations and the specific content that the symbols stand for, can increase the thoroughness of problem appraisal and increase the likelihood of creative and uniquely fitting solutions. Will such a procedure help a moderate neurosis or maladjustment? Help — yes — in the direction of increased maturity. The reason is that it means escape from a rigid, childish conception of either-or possibilities, fantasied achievement, fantasied fears, necessary outcomes, and so on. All of these taken together are the structural elements of neurosis and immaturity. Can one simply learn to overcome longstanding neurotic habits of thought, fantasy, and action? Yes, by longstanding practice of the method described above.

We need now to come more directly to the details of the strategems with regard especially to number of alternatives.

Instead of conceiving the dilemma as if p then r and if q then s, but either p or q, therefore, r or s, let us try the following:

1. If p then r
2. r is bad (undesirable)
3. If q then s
4. s is bad (undesirable)
5. Either p or q
6. Therefore,
7. r or s
8. There is r and r is bad (undesirable) or there is s and s is bad (undesirable).

The operation of negation is now employed against points 1, 2, 3, 4, and 5 — that r follows necessarily, that it is necessarily bad (and the same for s), and that one is restricted necessarily to either p or q. All of these negations are logical and mature operations as they increase the freedom within the network and lead to the kinds of outcomes regarding creativity and such discussed in the above paragraphs.

There is another kind of negation that, operating within the arbitrary limits of the given dilemma, produces another equally arbitrary dilemma, though of a more ebullient kind; and, therefore, the person has the opportunity to see the arbitrariness of his original pessimistic dilemmatic situation. In this case, the dilemma is upended, by restricting the denial of r to a specific outcome, namely, $\bar{s}$, and obversely for the denial of s to $\bar{r}$. The steps are as follows:

1. If p then $\bar{s}$
2. $\bar{s}$ is necessarily good (desirable)
3. If q then $\bar{r}$
4. $\bar{r}$ is necessarily good (desirable)
5. But either p or q
6. Therefore,
7. $\bar{s}$ or $\bar{r}$
8. Either there is $\bar{s}$ and $\bar{s}$ is necessarily good, or there is $\bar{r}$ and $\bar{r}$ is necessarily good.

Statements numbered 8 in both lists are the complement of each other and thus the arbitrariness of the dysphoric dilemma is apparent as is the symmetrically arbitrary euphoric dilemma just described.

Note that since these two are equal as far as arbitrariness and are symmetrical, a person might sometimes, though not always, maturely decide, pending further evaluation of the other sets of alternatives and the particular details of the situation, to assume the arbitrary euphoric rather than the arbitrary dysphoric dilemma at least insofar as emphasizing the positive aspects of the dilemmatic situation are concerned. This may be only a temporary morale booster, necessary and desirable at times, but because of its arbitrariness neither efficacious nor satisfying for very long. If the person is in a real confronting dilemma, then this device despite its cheery arbitrary way is only a dodge around a mature grappling with the sets of alternatives really involved in the situation, only through which an effective solution can be found through creative problem solving as each of the strategems involved in a network serves its catalytic function (see above).

It should be possible to set up a table (see Table 5.1) indicating the above relationships in the network, the logical interrelationships and symbols, their information value in terms of bits, examples of concrete parts of cases included and all in all intended to convey the systematic organization of the network description, its application, its measurement, and its exemplification.

Table 5.1   The Dilemmatic Network and Information Theory.

Neurotic or Maladaptive Dilemma	Extrication Route**	Increase in Amount of Information in Bits
1. If p, then r	p does not necessarily lead to r	1
2. r is bad (undesirable)	r is not necessarily bad (undesirable)	1
3. If q, then s	q does not necessarily lead to s	1
4. s is bad (undesirable)	s is not necessarily bad (undesirable)	1
5. Either p or q	You are not restricted to either p or q	1
6. Therefore		
7. r or s		
8. There is r and r is bad (undesirable) or there is s and s is bad (undesirable)		-1***
1'.*If p, then $\bar{s}$	p does not necessarily lead to $\bar{s}$	1
2'. $\bar{s}$ is necessarily good (desirable)	$\bar{s}$ is not necessarily good	1
3'. If q, then $\bar{r}$	q does not necessarily lead to $\bar{r}$	1

Table 5.1 *(Continued)*

Neurotic or Maladaptive Dilemma	Extrication Route	Increase in Amount of Information in Bits
4'. $\bar{r}$ is necessarily good (desirable)	$\bar{r}$ is not necessarily good	1
5'. But either p or q	You are not restricted to either p or q	1
6'. Therefore		
7'. $\bar{s}$ or $\bar{r}$		
8'. Either there is $\bar{s}$ and $\bar{s}$ is necessarily good or there is $\bar{r}$ and $\bar{r}$ is necessarily good		-1***

Illustrative Dilemmas	Application of Extrication Routes
1. If I am aggressive, then I will be disliked by many people.	Your being aggressive does not necessarily lead to your being disliked by many people.
2. Being disliked by many people is necessarily bad (undesirable).	Being disliked by many people is not necessarily bad (undesirable).
3. If I am not aggressive, then I will not be successful at business.	Your not being aggressive does not necessarily lead to your being not successful at business.
4. Not being successful at business is necessarily bad (undesirable).	Not being successful at business is not necessarily bad (undesirable).
5. But I must either be aggressive or not aggressive.	You are not restricted to either being aggressive or not aggressive.
6. Therefore,	
7. Either I will be disliked by many people or I will not be successful in business.	
8. Either I will be disliked by many people and that is bad (undesirable) or I will not be successful at business and that is bad (undesirable).	

(continued)

Table 5.1 *(Continued)*

Illustrative Dilemmas	*Application of Extrication Routes*
1'. If I am aggressive, then I will be successful at business.	Your being aggressive does not necessarily lead to your being successful at business.
2'. Being successful at business is necessarily good (desirable).	Your being successful at business is not necessarily good (desirable).
3'. If I am not aggressive, then I will not be disliked by many people.	Your not being aggressive does not necessarily lead to your not being disliked by many people.
4'. Not being disliked by many people is necessarily good (desirable).	Your not being disliked by many people is not necessarily good (desirable).
5'. But I must either be aggressive or not aggressive.	You are not restricted to either being aggressive or not being aggressive.
6'. Therefore,	
7'. Either I must be successful at business or I must not be disliked by many people.	
8'. Either I must be successful at business and that is good (desirable) or I must not be disliked by many people and that is good (desirable).	

Creative Inquiry	*Creative Exemplifications*****
How is it that I can be aggressive and yet not be disliked by many people?	Aggression can be channeled into improving work conditions for your employees and into improving your products or services for your customers and consumers.
Just how is it that being disliked by many people is not necessarily bad?	Being disliked by many people provokes reappraisal of the mode of aggression channelization (as in one above)—is the mode that of the benevolent autocrat?
How can it be that I can be both unaggressive and yet not unsuccessful at business?	You could be assertive rather than its close relative (aggressive—in the sense of hostile and destructive) and still be successful at business.

Table 5.1 *(Continued)*

Creative Inquiry	*Creative Exemplifications*
Just how is it that being unsuccessful at business is not a bad thing?	Being unsuccessful at business could provoke reappraisal of our fear of assertion in business because of its close association with your fear of aggression.
What are the other possibilities besides being aggressive or not being aggressive?	Aggression and nonaggression can be modulated and directed with respect to time, place, object, and mode. For example, you are home now with your family and not at the business with threatening competition from an unscrupulous industrial rival.
. . .	. . .
. . .	. . .
. . .	. . .
How is it that I can be aggressive and yet not be successful at business?	You can be aggressive (in the sense of hostile and destructive) rather than its close relative—assertive—and so fail to be successful at business.
Just how is it that being successful at business is not necessarily good?	Being successful at business could provoke a reappraisal of your fear of being aggressive because of its close association with your fear of being assertive.
How can it be that I can be both unaggressive and yet not be disliked by many people?	You could fail to channelize aggression into improving work conditions for your employees and into improving your product or services for your customers or consumers.
Just how is it that not being disliked by many people is not necessarily a good thing?	Not being disliked by many people could fail to provoke reappraisal of the mode of aggression channelization (as in 3 above)—is the mode that of the benevolent autocrat?
What are the other possibilities besides being aggressive or not being aggressive?	Aggression and nonaggression can be modulated and directed with respect to time, place, object, and mode. For

(continued)

Table 5.1 *(Continued)*

Creative Inquiry	Creative Exemplifications
	example, you are home now and with your family and not at business with threatening competition from an unscrupulous industrial rival.
. . .	. . .
. . .	. . .
. . .	. . .

*The set (1'–8') is the complement of the set (1–8). Both sets are neurotic and maladaptive dilemmas, the primed set being euphoric and the unprimed set dysphoric. Since both sets are equally arbitrary and since each set can be derived from the other (as described in the text), a person might, as a temporary solution, prefer the cheery primed set, but it remains an ineffective and forced "solution" and is fragile and needs to be replaced by the strategems of the cognitive space described in the remaining columns of the table.

**The routes of extrication are produced in each case through the use of the logical operator of negation as applied to each element in the two sets.

***In the neurotic dilemmas, the disjunctive conclusion has the amount of information equal to one bit; and with the application of the logical routes of extrication, the disjunction is liquidated and a decrement of one bit results. Note that the value of -1 is entered only for row 8 and not also for row 7 since, from the perspective of the person in the neurotic dilemma, it is inevitable that 7 and 8 (though outlined separately in this table) are inextricably united. One bit is a measure of the amount of information defined as equal to the logarithm to the base two of the number of alternatives in a particular situation. Summing of column 3 yields: $(5) + (-1) + (5) + (-1) = +8$ bits of information. The number of alternatives is computed as 2^8, which equals 256 alternatives. This is in contrast to the alternative of each single dilemma (since the person in a dilemma ordinarily does not move between the dysphoric and euphoric sets but stays within one) which, for one bit of information is computed as 2^1, which equals two alternatives. In terms of amount of information, therefore, the strategems of the network of interrelationships as compared to the neurotic dilemma is in the ratio of 8 bits to one or 256 alternatives to two.

****These are creative exemplifications rather than creative exemplars. While the number of logical routes of extrication in a formal network is limited and the number of bits of information is limited, the quantity and quality of creative exemplifications is a function of meaning, a multifaceted unique characteristic of the specific human being, client, or the counselor.

The following are a list of points defining and specifying the interrelationships within the network:

1. The primed set and the unprimed set in Column 1 stand out only in the relationship of euphoric–dysphoric to each other, but it is also the case that as a set each constitutes the sixth route of extrication in Column 2.
2. Each set can be derived from the other by negating the two consequents, r and s, in Rows 1 and 3 or 1' and 3', interchanging them, and proceeding to add the premise either p or q.

3. If we now add together the two appropriate logical expressions, it may be seen that the euphoric dilemma and the dysphoric dilemma are arbitrary conjuncts of an extended conjunction, whereas the premise p or q remains constant.

4. Thus: $p \supset (r.\bar{s}).q \supset (s.\bar{r}).(p \lor q)$. This combined conjunction yields the combined conclusion $(r \lor s).(\bar{s} \lor \bar{r})$.

5. Thus the conclusions 8 and 8′ are arbitrary representations of the combined or composite conclusion.

III

RESEARCH WITH THE DILEMMA AND IMPLICATION

6

THE PSYCHOLOGICAL DILEMMA AND
LOGICAL EXTRICATION ROUTES

Since there existed no prior research on dilemmas in the psychological literature, it became necessary to develop gradually an appropriate methodology that must include, *de novo*, a delineation of the kinds of questions to be explored, possible research designs, and the creation of dilemma and case history items that would meet the requirement of being both representative of counseling practice and yet fitting for an experimental and reliable scoring for both the psychological and logical aspects of the responses or solutions that might be given by our subjects to the dilemmatic research problems.

Accordingly, this part of the chapter is divided into two main sections, the first section concerned with the creation of various possible designs and their modifications and the second concerned with a presentation of the final method used in the research.

METHOD: THE DEVELOPMENT OF POSSIBLE RESEARCH DESIGNS AND THEIR MODIFICATIONS

The Constructive Dilemma

Certain aspects of the dilemma and of routes of extrication that were presented in detail in Chapters 1 and 2 will be briefly summarized and reviewed.

AUTHOR'S NOTE: The author wishes to express his thanks for the research support provided by the Research Board of the University of Illinois. He also wishes to express strong appreciation to Thomas Leahey and Claude Cech for their assistance with experimental administration and data analysis.

In deductive reasoning, the constructive dilemma consists of the conjunction of two conditional statements as first premise and the disjunction of the two antecedents as second premise, leading to the conclusion of a disjunction of the two consequents. Symbolically: if p then r and if q then s (premise 1); p or q (premise 2); r or s (conclusion).

Possible Routes of Extrication

R does not necessarily follow from P nor does s necessarily follow from q. There are other consequents besides r and s. There are other antecedents besides p or q. p and q are very highly correlated so that there is no choice. r and s are not necessarily undesirable. r and s can be negated and reversed with respect to p and q, yielding the conclusion not s or not r.

Frequency of Selection of One of the Routes

If a single dilemmatic statement is given to a group of persons with the instructions to choose the preferred route of extrication, which routes will be chosen most frequently?

Reliability of Frequency Distribution

If a large number rather than just a single dilemma is used, how much consistency will there be over the entire array of dilemmas in the frequency distribution of most preferred routes of extrication?

Reliability of Selection over Time

If the group of subjects is called back a month or two later, and the same array of dilemmas is given with the same instructions, what will be the magnitude of the reliability coefficient for the two experimental occasions?

Type of Dilemma

Does the preferred extrication route vary with type of dilemma? Dilemmas may be of many types, but perhaps the most important dimension is the personal–emotional type versus the abstract–neutral. The personal–emotional type can be subdivided into pleasant and unpleasant varieties. The abstract–neutral can be subdivided into concrete–scientific and abstract–symbolic.

Experimental Design

A pre- and posttest design can be used. The pretest consists of 10 dilemmas, and subjects are simply instructed to write out their most preferred resolution or route of extrication. The posttest is the same except that 10 different dilemmas are used. The experimental group, but not the control group, between the pre- and posttest receives the list of 10 dilemmas together, and six alternative routes of extrication for each. The experimental group of subjects are instructed to select the preferred alternative. The control group receives the same list of 10 dilemmas.

Order of Experimental Procedures

On experimental occasion one, the pretest is given first, followed by the Maudsley Personality Test, and then followed by the forced-choice experimental condition and concluded with an experimental inquiry. A month or two later in the second experimental occasion, the posttest is administered, and the session is concluded with an experimental inquiry.

Item Number One for the Forced-Choice Dilemmas

Subjects are handed a card with the following information appearing typed on it:

Can you help this person with his problem or dilemma?

"If I am aggressive, then I am bound to be disliked by a great many people; and if I am not aggressive, then I am bound to fail in business. But I must either be aggressive or unaggressive. Therefore, I must certainly either be disliked by a great many people or a failure in business. Either way, I am miserable."

In your opinion, which one of the following alternatives would be most helpful to this person? Please select only *one* alternative and indicate your choice by placing an x at the left of one of the following six alternatives. Thank you.

_____1. Being aggressive does not necessarily lead to being disliked by a great many people.

_____2. Being unaggressive does not necessarily lead to being a failure in business.

_____3. You do not have to restrict yourself to being either aggressive or unaggressive.

_____4. Being disliked by a great many people is not necessarily bad.

_____5. Being a failure in business is not necessarily bad.

_____6. If you are aggressive, then you will not be a failure in business; and if you are not aggressive, then you will not be disliked by a great many people.

We need to construct nine additional items of this kind. In so doing, it would be best to avoid a set format in the six alternatives.

Design Modifications

The following four types of dilemmas can be used: unpleasant personal dilemmas, pleasant personal dilemmas, unpleasant scientific dilemmas, and pleasant scientific dilemmas.

For each of these four types, a control group of 20 subjects using an open-ended format and an experimental group using the forced-choice format are compared with regard to relative frequency of choice of routes of extrication from their respective dilemmas. There are thus 20 subjects times eight groups, equaling 160 subjects (see Table 6.1).

If the forced-choice format can be considered an experimental training or instructional device or even an experimental analog of a possible counseling procedure, then we are interested in the extent of transfer effects. For each of the four types of dilemmas, a 30-item test will be used. The control and experimental groups take the same 30 items in the same order. The difference is, however, that the experimental group is provided with the forced-choice format on the first 15 items and with the open-ended format on the final 15 items, which, of course, provide the material for the transfer task and its measurement (see Table 6.2).

Items for Unpleasant Personal Dilemmas

In general, we will follow the format for the card prepared, as described above, for the dilemma involving being aggressive or not being aggressive. Prepare a separate card for each item.

Considerations in Constructing the Dilemma

Careful considerations must be given to the construction of the dysphoric dilemmas. These considerations can be divided into two groups. The first group is concerned with various technical experimental requirements and the second group with psychological requirements.

The dilemma must be brief enough so that 40 or 50 can be handled effectively during an experimental session. While brief, they should be clear. They should hold intrinsic interest. They should have the form of the logical dilemma. The content of the dilemmas, however, should be natural, ordinary language. They should be written in such a way that while retaining the logical

Table 6.1 Number of Subjects by Dilemma.

Dilemma	Control Group	Experimental Group	Total
Unpleasant Personal	20	20	40
Pleasant Personal	20	20	40
Unpleasant Scientific	20	20	40
Pleasant Scientific	20	20	40
Total	80	80	160

Table 6.2 Experimental Design.

Items	Control Group	Experimental Group
Initial 15	open-ended format	forced-choice format
Final 15	open-ended format	open-ended format

form they reflect the emotional state of conflict, puzzlement, and tension of the person experiencing his personal problem. The kind of personal problem should not be beyond the understanding of the subjects in the experiment. They should range from everyday problems of normal individuals, to crisis problems of normal individuals, to problems of neurotic maladjustment. To promote empathic identification and understanding, dilemmas probably should be written in the first person. The dilemmas should sample not only the problems likely to be experienced by the subjects themselves but also some that are distinctly problems of older persons or persons in special situations; both severe and mild emotional problems should be represented, problems of special interest to men or to women should be included. An effort should be made to include representatives of the most frequent kinds of dilemmas brought by clients or patients to counselors and psychotherapists, including general personal unhappiness, general inefficiency, vocational uncertainty and dissatisfaction, problems of values and personal standards, parent and child problems, problems of identity versus conformity, problems of disproportionately low or high self-esteem, and problems of physical health and hypochondria. For comparison a few dilemmas involving problems of economics or politics might be included.

In accordance with the research design, the dilemmas would be given to both the control and experimental groups. However, the experimental, but not the control, group would receive in addition a list of six extrication routes from which they were to select the one they believed to be of most help to the person experiencing the dilemma. Each of the six routes of extrication is specially tailored to the particular dilemma, and the order of the underlying logical extrication routes should be randomized. In any research design, so far developed or to be developed, the dilemmas themselves should be randomized in their assignment to various treatments, for example, pre–post or transfer conditions.

Development of Dysphoric Dilemmas

In accordance with the considerations discussed above, 24 dysphoric dilemma problems were constructed. They were randomly distributed to three conditions called pretreatment (booklet 3), treatment (booklet 4), and posttreatment (booklet 5). For each of the 24 dilemmas, six extrication routes were worked out. Even though the extrication routes would only appear in the dilemmas of the treatment conditions (booklet 4), it was necessary to develop extrication routes for all 24 dilemma problems to permit scoring of subjects' responses (solutions) in accordance with the criteria developed in the scoring manual.

Development of Euphoric Dilemmas

After the development of the 24 dysphoric dilemmas, it was necessary to develop a parallel set of 24 euphoric dilemma problems. This was essentially accomplished by negating the dysphoric consequence, so that the resulting euphoric dilemma generally read: "If p then not r, and if q then not s; but either p or q, therefore either not r or not s." Necessary changes to facilitate smooth reading or correct grammar were made. Next, the procedures described for the dysphoric problems were followed: the development of six extrication routes for each of the 24 euphoric dilemma problems and their random assignment among the three experimental conditions—pretreatment (booklet 3), treatment (booklet 4), and posttreatment (booklet 5). In the experimental administration, these extrication routes or solutions were presented only for the treatment condition (booklet 4). The writing out of six logical solutions for each of the 24 euphoric dilemmas was necessary to meet scoring procedure criteria as discussed above.

Considerations for the Construction of Case Histories

The case history should be constructed or selected in such a way that no great clinical insight is required and yet the problem while clear is not in exact dilemmatic form. Since the subject must read, interpret, and form the dilemma in perhaps two minutes and then also give a solution, the cases must be simple, clear, and brief. They should be varied and interesting. They should range through the same kind of topics dealt with in the dilemmatic items. It would be desirable if the same case history, with suitable changes, could be used for both the distressing and ebullient condition.

The case history should vary in the salience with which the dilemma underlying the clinical case history is presented. Some of the case histories should have the dilemma practically stated for the subject, whereas in others the subject will have to do some work to discover it, and in others the dilemmatic formulation may be fairly difficult. Many of the considerations presented for the construction of dilemmas and their use in the research hold as well for the case histories, such as representativeness of case histories in usual clinical practice, randomization of case histories among the various treatment conditions, pre–post transfer conditions, and so on. The case history should be in natural language with the kinds of interrupted speech, pauses, and unclarities typical for a clinical interview, rather than a smooth, textbook case history presentation. The case history should vary in length reflecting the complexity of the issues involved.

Development of Case History Problems

In accordance with the considerations for construction of case history problems, 16 dysphoric case histories were constructed. Eight were randomly assigned to the pretreatment condition (booklet 2) and eight were randomly assigned to the posttreatment condition (booklet 6). Each of these 16 dysphoric case history problems was rewritten in an optimistic, ebullient tone in order to produce the 16 euphoric case history problems. On a random basis, eight of these were assigned to the pretreatment condition (booklet 2) and eight were assigned to the posttreatment condition (booklet 6).

Time as a Measure of Difficulty

In addition to the dependent variables of frequency of no solution response or frequency of one of the six routes of extrication response, it is possible to consider response time as an additional dependent variable. Response time may thus be used as an index of the facility with which dilemmas are solved.

Response time for phase C should be less than that for phase A in both the experimental and control groups because of practice effects. But, the experimental group should have a lower response time for phase C than would the control group. It is further expected that the experimental and control group will not differ in response time for phase A. However, analysis of covariants could equate for any initial time differences between the two groups in phase A.

"No Response Solution" or "Other (please specify)"

Various problems in coding will have to be worked out and, no doubt, a sequence of increasingly refined procedures developed that will permit precise coding specifications. One such problem is that of the no-solution or perhaps unusual solution response.

There are various ways in which the "Other (please specify)" alternative can be used. It may be used as a means of writing in a concrete recommendation or detailed operation solution in place of one of the other six alternatives that are simple negation-type responses without much content (except for the counter-dilemma alternative). If so, the response may be coded as one of the six alternatives or as a "no-response" solution if it does not fit any of these. This is the normal coding procedure to be used in Parts A and C for the experimental group and Parts A, B, and C for the control group and also for the case histories.

The "other" category may also be used by those who believe that p and q are identical or at least highly correlated so that there is no problem.

Another way would be for use by subjects who believe that there really is no realistic solution to the person's problem because of their strict adherence to the logic of the constructive dilemma.

The category may be used by those subjects who, despite the instruction to check just one alternative, wish to supplement it with some specification.

Finally, the category may be used by those subjects who simply find the task too difficult or who escape from the task by claiming that there is no solution possible.

Sequence of Experimental Administration

Pending any change produced by experience with the pilot study, the order of administration of the seven booklets is as follows: booklet of identification sheet and the Maudsley Personality Inventory, booklet of case histories for Part A, booklet of dilemmas for Part A, booklet of dilemmas for Part B, booklet of dilemmas for Part C, booklet of case histories for Part C, booklet of experimental inquiry.

Experimental Instructions

The experimental instructions for each part will be printed in the appropriate booklet. The case histories in Part A and the case histories in Part C have identical instructions. Part Two of the experimental directions for the case histories is identical with the instructions for the dilemmas of Parts A, B, and C of the control group and Parts A and C of the experimental group. Part B for the experimental group has distinctive directions.

Random Placement of Sex-Linked Items

Dilemmatic items whose content is in terms of a particular gender are randomized between the three parts of the experiment and within the 10 dilemmas of each part.

The Method Finally Chosen

We have discussed various possible designs in the order in which they were considered, modified, and rejected. Those designs which required individual administration were not accepted, and these tended generally to focus on the details of the reasoning process itself rather than on the reasoning process in interaction with personal dilemmatic situations. Those designs may be used in future research (see the Results and Discussion of this chapter).

The research method and design finally selected, it turns out, was the one that had occupied us most, as described in the method section. It will, therefore, be presented in a very succinct manner, since the background of purposes, alternatives, and other details will already have been presented.

Some of the dilemmas and some of the case histories were unchanged. Many of the others were modified to improve clarity and representativeness, and still others were rejected. New case histories and dilemmas were constructed and, together with the older ones, were subjected to scrutiny during a pilot experiment. Information was also gained during this pilot research regarding various technical matters such as time required, clarity and representativeness of directions, and so on. As a result, it was found that there would be sufficient time for only eight dilemmas or case histories per booklet rather than 10. Suitable random selection was made. The experimental inquiry expanded into a more comprehensive and, it was thought, more sensitive instrument.

Before reading the brief description of the method used in the research, it may be well for the reader to review certain of the previous sections of this chapter. At this point it would also assist the reader to turn to Appendix A, where booklets 1 to 7 are fully reproduced.

The final section of this chapter shall present the method of scoring subjects' responses to dilemmas and case histories in the form of a scoring manual. Illustrative problems in scoring are presented in full detail in Appendix B.

Subjects

The subjects were 200 Psychology 100 students.

Groups

A euphoric–dysphoric dimension was crossed with experimental control, producing four groups.

Materials

In order presented to subjects the materials were the booklets. Booklet 1 contained the Information Face Sheet — collected following data: name, identification number, sex, college, expected major, class, current grade point average (or, if freshman, high school rank quartile, except top 10%) — and the Maudsley Personality Inventory.

Booklet 2 contained a series of eight case histories, not cast in dilemmatic form but capable of being so construed. Under each item was the following frame:

If_____
then_____; and
if_____
then _____ .
But either _____
or _____
therefore either_____
or _____ .

The blanks were to be filled in by the subject in order to create an explicit dilemma from the case history. The question "What would be a realistic solution to this problem?" followed, to which subjects gave an open-ended response. Subjects were scored for whether they correctly formulated the dilemma and whether their solution was logical (see scoring manual, below). In the euphoric groups, all the dilemmas were such that both outcomes were happy ones. In the dysphoric groups, the outcomes were unhappy. This is true for all dilemmas in the two groups.

Booklet 3 contained a series of eight personal problems explicitly cast as dilemmas. Subjects made an open-ended response to the same questions as before. Booklets 2 and 3 constituted the pretests.

Booklet 4 was the therapeutic procedure booklet for the experimental groups. In these groups, booklet 4 consisted of eight items of the sort from booklet 3, except that the six logical routes of extrication were written down and subjects picked one. There was a seventh choice available, however, "Other solution." For the controls, the items were given in the same format as booklet 3.

Booklet 5 was exactly like booklet 3, except with new items.

Booklet 6 was exactly like booklet 2, except with new items.

Booklet 7 was a postexperimental inquiry; specific items will be dealt with in the Results and Discussion section of this chapter.

Procedure

Subjects were run in groups of up to 10. They were seated at a large table and handed envelopes containing the seven booklets, in order, and instructed to work their way through them following the directions on the first page of each.

A few additional oral instructions were made. First, subjects were warned that the experiment was a long one and to spend approximately five minutes on booklet 1, 15 minutes each on booklets 2 to 6, and 10 minutes on booklet 7. In order to facilitate this, the experimenter announced the time every 20 minutes and said where each subject should be.

Second, subjects were told that they were being timed. They were instructed to raise their hands when they finished each booklet, so the experimenter could note the elapsed time.

Third, subjects were told that in filling out booklet 7 they could look at any of the other booklets.

Fourth, subjects were told that even if they finished early, they would have to remain until the end, for debriefing.

The whole experiment ran about two hours.

Coding Manual

Reliable methods of coding subject's responses to dilemmas and case histories were worked out and are presented in a coding manual that lists the general and specific criteria required for assignment to particular problem solutions. A very comprehensive coding chart is presented in Appendix B. This chart presents numerous examples of kinds of responses to be coded under specific problem solution categories as well as a commentary clarifying particularly knotty coding problems. While it has been presented in Appendix B because of its length, reference to it in the course of reading criteria contained in the coding manual should prove illustrative.

RESULTS AND DISCUSSION

I. *Statistics used*
   A. Variance analyses
      1. One- and two-way analysis of covariance (ANCOVA), Chapter 12 of Myers (1972).
      2. One-way analyses of variance (ANOVA), Chapter 12 of Hays (1963).
      3. Omega-squared (percent variance accounted for by a factor) for 1 and 2 from Sec. 12.18 of Hays (1963).
   B. Post-hoc comparisons (Scheffé method), Hays (1963: Sec. 14.15).
   C. t tests, Hays (1963: Chapter 10).
   D. χ^2, λ tests, Hays (1963: Chapter 17).
II. *Variance Analysis: Differential Performance of Groups on Each Booklet*
   A. Booklet 4

An interesting place to enter the results is at booklet 4 — the training booklet for the experimental groups, just another batch of dilemmas for the control groups.

Table 6.3 summarizes two-way ANOVA on booklet 4. This analysis is for total logical solutions. Factor A is euphoric–dysphoric and Factor B is experimental–control.

The experimental control factor has a tremendous effect, accounting for 52% of the variance. The dysphoric-euphoric factor shows a moderate effect accounting for 11% of the variance, and there is a small interaction effect

Table 6.3   Analysis of Variance. *Booklet 4: Total Number of Logical Solutions*

Source	df	SS	MS	F	W^2
Total	199	995.64	—	—	—
A (E − D)	1	111.00	111.00	66.89*	.11
B (E − C)	1	528.12	528.12	318.24*	.52
AB	1	31.26	31.26	18.80*	.03
Error	196	325.26	1.65	—	—

	Means		
Factor A	Factor B		
	Experimental	Control	Total
Euphoric	6.98	2.94	4.96
Dysphoric	7.68	5.22	6.45
Total	7.33	4.08	5.705

*$p < .001$

accounting for 3% of the variance. This two-way ANOVA based on the entire sample of 200 subjects demonstrates how subjects can produce logical solutions to dilemma problems under the condition of a paradigmatic model. As indicated by the experimental directions for booklet 5, we did not seek to impose on the subjects a requirement that they solve the dilemmas of booklet 5 in accordance with the paradigmatic code. Had we done so, we would have then easily produced very powerful changes in the number of logical solutions in booklet 5 as compared to booklet 3. These effects would have been on the order of magnitude of those produced in the comparison between the experimental and control groups' performance on booklet 4. Quite similar considerations apply to booklets 2 and 6 (the case histories). Not only did the directions refrain from requiring a paradigmatic model of logical solutions, no mention was made of logical approaches, and no direction given to apply the training from booklet 4. Thus, the directions stated, "Can you find a realistic solution to help this person with his/her personal problem?"

Two-way analyses of variance (ANOVAs) for types of logical solution produced some interesting findings. The experimental–control factor for solutions of type six, the counter-dilemma solution, was significant and accounted for 22% of the variance. However, the dysphoric–euphoric factor was not significant. Yet, the counter-dilemma solution in effect transformed a dysphoric dilemma into a euphoric dilemma.

In our earlier account of the geometry of dilemmas (Figure 2.1) we had represented the euphoric and dysphoric triangles as a composite square whose diagonal constituted the second premise of both dilemma types. The sides of the square constituted the differential premise of each dilemma type. Consequently, the negation of the diagonal, as contrasted to the negation of the sides, has simultaneous extrication effects on both dilemmas. It is thereby of special interest to note that the two-way ANOVA for solutions of this type of premise (type one) revealed nonsignificant effects for the euphoric–dysphoric factor and also for the experimental–control factor.

Comparison of the means for a total number of logical solutions (Table 6.3) indicated dysphoric greater than euphoric and experimental greater than control. That subjects in response to dysphoric personal dilemmas can produce logical solutions is indicated by the experimental group's achievement of 7.68 logical solutions out of a possible 8.0.

B. Booklets 2 and 6: Case Histories

Table 6.4 summarizes two-way ANCOVA on scores for booklet 6 performance, controlled for scores on booklet 2.

This ANCOVA for total logical solutions indicates moderate effects produced by both the dysphoric–euphoric factor and the experimental–control

Table 6.4   Analysis of Covariance. *Booklets 2, 6: Total Number of Logical Solutions*

Source	df	SS	MS	F	W^2
Total	198	482.09	—	—	—
A	1	44.73	44.73	20.73*	.08
B	1	13.47	13.47	6.24**	.02
AB	1	3.15	3.15	1.46***	.00
Error	195	420.74	2.15	—	—

Factor A	Means (adjusted) Factor B		
	Experimental	Control	Total
Euphoric	2.99	2.90	2.94
Dysphoric	5.14	4.36	4.75
Total	4.16	3.63	3.85

Note: Homogeneity of variance $p < .001$
*$p < .001$
**$p < .025$
***$p < .25$
$F = 12.86$
$df = 2$

factor. The task is a difficult one, since subjects must grasp in a very brief period of time the essential dilemma and then find a realistic solution, without a direction for either recalling or applying the dilemmatic extrication routes of booklet 4. Many extralogical solutions, especially arbitrary solutions, were given.

C. Booklets 3 and 5: Dilemmas

Table 6.5 summarizes two-way ANCOVA on scores for booklet 5, controlled by scores on booklet 3. The interesting finding here is that in this ANCOVA for total number of logical solutions, there is a pronounced dysphoric–euphoric effect accounting for 29% of the variance and a nonsignificant experimental–control factor. The latter results suggest that, left to themselves, subjects find the solution of dilemmas a difficult task and that more extended practice with the kind of paradigmatic model given in booklet 4 with specific directions to apply such a model to dilemmas of booklet 5 would be required to overcome task difficulty and raise dilemmatic solution performance close to the level of that for solution performance on booklet 4 dilemmas. The powerful dysphoric-euphoric effect suggests the possibility that subjects may not be perceiving euphoric dilemmas as symmetric with dysphoric dilemmas except for polarity. Rather, it would seem that rather than solving euphoric dilemmas, subjects first translate them into dysphoric dilemmas and then proceed to solve these.

Table 6.5 Analysis of Covariance. *Booklets 3, 5: Total Number of Logical Solutions*

Source	df	SS	MS	F	W^2
Total	198	600.39	—	—	—
A	1	180.77	180.77	85.36	.29*
B	1	1.90	1.90	1	0
AB	1	4.80	4.80	2.26**	.05
Error	195	412.92	2.11	—	—

Factor A	Means (adjusted) Factor B		
	Experimental	Control	Total
Euphoric	4.15	3.62	3.88
Dysphoric	5.45	4.80	5.13
Total	4.80	4.21	4.51

Note: Homogeneity of variance F = .14
 *p < .001
**p < .20

III. Pre–Post Improvement

Table 6.6 shows the results of matched pairs t tests carried out on all booklets pairs (2, 6 and 3, 5) for all solution types possible, also broken down within personality type logical solutions only. The difference used was pre–post, so a *negative* result indicates an increase in number of solutions of whatever type. Excluding the personality analyses, dilemma formulation, and "total nonlogical solutions," 69 tests were executed, of which 25 were significant, 11 in the direction of improvement.

On the surface, the pattern of treatment group mean changes from booklet 2 through booklet 6 or from booklet 3 to booklet 5 defies a simple organization. The findings are somewhat better organized when personality types are considered in interaction with treatment groups. Thus, in each of the treatment groups, it is the stable introvert personality group alone that demonstrates systematic improvement in total number of logical solutions. This is also the personality group that does best on correct dilemmatic formulation for the case history. Finally, it should be noted that all four groups significantly improved their dilemmatic formulation performance, suggesting a possible coherence between correctness of dilemmatic formulation and correctness of logical case history solution. This possibility was investigated through a series of analyses reported next.

IV. The Relation of Formulation and Logicality

Table 6.7 shows the results of chi-square (χ^2) and lambda (λ) analyses of the contingency between case histories formulated correctly or not and logically solved or not. Lambda is a measure of predictive association in a contingency table, indicating the degree to which one can predict one category from knowledge of the other; it takes values between 0 and $+1$. Correctly formulated dilemmas are often more logically solved than those formulated incorrectly.

Illustrative is the finding in the chi-square analysis for the precondition (booklet 2) across all four treatment groups, that the concomitant frequency of correct formulation and logical solution was 281 whereas the concomitant frequency for incorrect formulation and nonlogical solution was 593.

V. Item Analysis

Table 6.8 shows the number of subjects giving a logical solution to each item throughout the entire task, broken down by groups. Table 6.9 shows a similar analysis for dilemma formulation. It is of interest to comment briefly on those items that subjects found particularly difficult. The commentary will be organized sequentially for each treatment group across booklets.

B. Group A (Experimental Euphoric)

Only seven subjects out of 50 provided a logical solution to item 8 of booklet 2. Many subjects perceived this item as a dysphoric problem, proceeded to formulate it as a dilemma, and then solved it as a dysphoric problem.

Table 6.6 t-Test Results, Pre-Post.

	df	A	df	B	df	C	df	D	actual used df	df
Booklets 2, 6	7|0 2|1			4|1 5|2		2|1 7|2		1|0 7|2	49	40
Total logical		−0.08		−0.77		0.32		2.20****		
Total Nonlogical		0.93		0.65		−0.45		−2.28****		
1		−0.62		2.05****		0.09		1.94		
2		−1.59		−2.39****		0.66		*1.93		
3		3.29**		1.24		5.03*		0.33		
4		1.28		0.57		0.88		1.69		
5		−1.36		2.96**		−1.88		0		
7		0.35		−1.66		2.11****		1.73		
9		0.30		1.29		−2.09*****		−1.34		
Personality Types										
I N. I. (55)	14	−1.74	12	−0.12	12	−1.74	13	0		
II. S.I. (45)	7	−2.54****	11	−2.87***	12	−0.10	11	2.48****		
III. N.E. (45)	11	0.73	8	0.66	13	1.09	10	2.94***		
IV. S.E. (55)	14	0.41	16	0.25	9	1.12	13	1.04		
Dilemma Form										
Overall		−3.60*		−7.63*		−3.41**		−4.29*	49	40
I. N.I.		−1.21		−2.78***		1.62		−4.04**		
II. S.I.		−3.05***		−4.28**		−11.87*		−1.90		
III. N.E.		−1.43		−5.70*		−1.32		−1.61		

	−3.20**	−3.58**	−1.39	−1.62	49	40
IV. S.E.						
Booklets 3, 5						
Total Logical	−3.82*	0.23	−1.63	0.09		
Total Nonlogical	3.82*	−0.23	1.63	−0.09		
0	—	—	−1.0	—		
1	−1.62	1.21	−2.29****	−2.29****		
2	4.73*	0.74	−3.27**	−3.89*		
3	−2.92**	−4.40*	−0.90	−1.54		
4	3.06**	4.34*	1.32	3.71*		
5	2.21****	−0.77	2.28****	−0.63		
6	—	−1.0	−1.42	—		
7	−1.03	−1.51	−3.86*	−3.59*		
9	4.69*	1.59	4.22*	1.74		
10	1.35	—	−1.42	—		
Personality Types						40
I. N.I.	0.32	0.73	−1.35	2.61****		
II. S.I.	* −2.29	−0.80	0.88	−0.12		
III. N.E.	−2.56****	−1.35	* −1.98	0.63		
IV. S.E.	−4.06**	0.83	−0.40	−0.58		

Note: N.I. = nonstable introvert; S.I. = stable introvert; N.E. = nonstable extrovert; and S.E. = stable extrovert.

  *p < .001
  **p < .01
  ***p < .02
  ****p < .05

93

Table 6.7 χ^2 **Results: Contingencies between Logical Solutions versus Formulation.**

Variable	A Pre	Post	B Pre	Post	C Pre	Post	D Pre	Post
χ^2	4.54***	6.52**	6.00**	1.30	10.17*	1.67	.84	13.96*
$\phi = \phi'$	.11	.13	0	.06	.16	.06	.05	.19
C	.01	.13	0	.06	.16	.06	.05	.18
λ_{log}	0	0	0	0	0	0	0	0
λ_{form}	0	.07	0	0	0	0	0	.19
$\lambda_{log, form}$	0	.04	0	0	0	0	0	.10

Test	χ^2	$\phi = \phi'$	Overall C_{AB}	λ_{form}	λ_{log}	λ_{both}
Pre	12.0*	.08	.08	0	.65	.39
Post	23.0*	.20	.11	.11	.07	.09

*p < .005
**p < .025
***p < .05

Item six of booklet 3 has a frequency of only five correct logical solutions. For this item, the repetition of "Divorce" and "Failure" cast a dysphoric shadow, though denied by the frequent employment of negation. These frequent "nots" probably provided another source of difficulty.

Since for all items in booklet 4 (Experimental Treatment Booklet) logical solution frequency ranged between 38 and 48, the difficulty of casting a euphoric item as a euphoric dilemma rather than reducing it to a dysphoric problem and the difficulty of responding to double or triple negation are not insurmountable.

Item two of booklet 5 has a frequency of 43 correct logical solutions in contrast to some other euphoric items. Antecedents of this item are pleasant, even humorous: "If they laugh at my jokes" versus "If I get a divorce."

Item seven of booklet 6 has a frequency of seven logical solutions. From the beginning, this item has a serious, agitated quality and it is only at the very end that a hasty and shallow ebullience appears: "It's no big problem — no big problem, I tell you."

C. Group B (Experimental Dysphoric)

For booklet 4 (Experimental Treatment Booklet) the frequency of logical solutions ranged from 46 to 50 (n = 50). When presented with a list of possible logical solutions, subjects overwhelmingly prefer one of these to alternative "7," some other preferred solutions of their own. In future research, it may

Table 6.8 Item Analysis—Performance of All Groups by Items—Number of Subjects Giving a Logical Solution.

	Overall		A		B		C		D	
	Booklet 2, 6	Booklet 3, 5	Booklet 2, 6	Booklet 3, 5	Booklet 2, 6	Booklet 3, 5	Booklet 2, 6	Booklet 3, 5	Booklet 2, 6	Booklet 3, 5
Pre 2, 3	118	121	21	17	37	39	18	25	42	40
	131	104	15	10	49	42	19	7	48	45
	126	124	19	31	36	41	30	28	41	24
	85	104	19	21	29	36	16	12	21	35
	111	111	13	12	43	43	12	12	43	44
	104	75	11	5	43	39	9	5	41	26
	51	92	11	11	16	38	9	13	15	30
	55	112	7	26	21	30	10	30	17	26
Treatment 4	145			48	50			18	29	
	162			48	46			29	39	
	128			38	49			7	31	
	144			40	49			22	38	
	188			48	49			42	49	
	135			45	47			13	30	
	139			42	48			11	38	
	102			41	46			5	10	
Post 5, 6	77	73	20	9	22	31	19	9	16	24
	90	166	10	43	35	47	12	30	33	46
	122	92	27	18	39	33	22	16	34	25
	100	120	15	19	39	45	14	16	32	40
	78	149	17	37	25	36	9	37	27	39
	88	92	16	15	36	38	8	12	28	27
	90	126	7	26	36	45	14	15	33	40
	116	75	12	14	48	32	19	10	37	19

Table 6.9 Item Analysis—Number of Subjects Correctly Casting Each Case History as a Dilemma.

	A	B	C	D	Overall
Booklet 2	25	4	23	7	59
	25	8	25	11	69
	27	25	23	23	98
	6	21	4	16	47
	3	15	6	15	39
	13	29	6	26	74
	16	19	13	18	66
	12	17	15	15	59
Booklet 6	27	26	35	24	112
	26	31	25	26	108
	23	34	25	25	107
	12	26	9	19	66
	32	21	34	18	105
	33	29	21	31	114
	10	38	16	29	93
	17	37	13	30	97

be of interest to vary the factor of presented solutions by providing a list of six nonlogical solutions, together with alternative "7."

In booklet 6, item one has a frequency of 22 whereas item eight has a frequency of 48 correct logical solutions. It is strange that the frequency of item one should be less than half of that for item eight, since item one concludes with the dilemmatic choice already formulated for the subject: "I have to either hurt my mother or hurt myself," whereas the dilemmatic choice formulation is not presented verbatim in item eight. But item one is a very long case, contains a number of centrifugal themes and issues whereas for item eight the issue of flying or not flying and their consequences is highly focused. Experimental research in which variations in focus of issue or number of issues is systematically manipulated should prove illuminating.

D. Group C (Control Euphoric)

Item eight of booklet 4 has a frequency of only five correct solutions. Possible explanations of this low frequency are (1) it is very brief, almost contentless, somewhat abstract and (2) unless juxtaposed with its dysphoric counterpart (Group D Control Dysphoric), its jaunty ebullience might be misperceived.

Item six of booklet 6 has a frequency of eight. Apparently, subjects did not accept the protective self-assurance expressed by the person in the case history and, incorrectly, responded to the item as though it were dysphoric.

E. Group D (Control Dysphoric)

Two items of booklet 4 are of interest. Item five has a frequency of 49 correct logical solutions, almost a perfect score. This item is succinct, but concrete and familiar. "Eating sweets — getting fat." Item eight with a frequency of 10 correct logical solutions was discussed in the previous paragraph, under the control-euphoric group, as being brief but relatively contentless and abstract: "Dare I do it?", "Miss an opportunity or take advantage." It is also possible that the "Dare I do it?" stimulated personal misgivings that interfered with smooth problem solving.

Item two of booklet 5 has a frequency of 46 correct logical solutions. This same item also had a very high solution frequency under the euphoric condition. Apparently, as constructed it has close symmetry of mood polarity. It is also brief, concrete, and familiar.

VI. Impressionistic Results

This section will report impressions as given by subjects informally to the experimenter or as part of the postexperimental inquiry as well as observations of the experimenter made during the course of the experiment. Some of these impressions are in the form of data gleaned from the experimental inquiry and subjected to statistical tests while others remain distinctly qualitative. Reflection on these quantitative and qualitative impressions stimulated new and interesting research problems and innovations.

Booklet 7 Analyses

Question I, 1 inquired as to how easy or difficult it was for subjects to formulate the case histories of booklet 2 as dilemmas (see Appendix A for exact form of the question). Time measures taken by the experimenter indicated that booklet 2 required the most time for completion. Subjects reported spending a great deal of time on the first one or two of these case histories. Apparently, the task initially was novel and difficult. It is, therefore, of interest to compare difficulty of dilemmatic formulation for the case histories of booklet 2 with the case histories of booklet 6.

The following comparative data suggest that subjects found the dilemmatic formulation task much easier for booklet 6 than for booklet 2. For booklet 2, 23 subjects found it very easy. For booklet 6, 42 did. On booklet 2, 47 subjects found it moderately easy, 87 on booklet 6. There were 51 people on booklet 2 who found it equally as difficult, only 45 did on booklet 6. And 53 people found it moderately difficult on booklet 2, only 24 found it moderately difficult on booklet 6. Finally, 26 people found it very difficult on booklet 2, only two people reported the task very difficult on booklet 6.

Question III, 4a refers to whether the subjects believed their solutions to the case histories of booklet 6 were adequate (see Appendix A for exact wording). In general, subjects did believe their solutions were adequate. Comparison with the corresponding data for the case histories of booklet 2 indicates increased satisfaction with adequacy of problem solution from booklet 2 to booklet 6. For booklet 2, 93 people said yes, the solutions were adequate, 118 said so on booklet 6. On booklet 2, 43 people said no; 30 people said no on booklet 6. Plus, 64 had no opinion on booklet 2; 52 had no opinion on booklet 6.

Question IV, 5 asked whether dilemmatic formulation was arbitrary and artificial or whether it was realistic. A majority asserted that it was realistic: 52 said that it was arbitrary, 114 people said it was realistic, and 31 people had no opinion.

Question IV, 6 stated, "The essence of a true logical dilemma is that there is no way out unless you change one or other of the conditions, that is, negate it. Otherwise what must follow can only be the unfolding of the logical alternatives as stated in the conditions of the dilemma. Would you say that the problems encountered by the individuals were true logical dilemmas? Yes, no, don't know." There were 97 people who said they were true dilemmas, 71 said no, and 32 did not say.

In summary, most persons in the experiment believed that the problems were true dilemmas, that dilemmatic formulation of case histories is realistic, that the difficulty of formulating case histories into dilemmas decreased from booklet 2 to booklet 6, and that the adequacy of their solutions to the problems increased from booklet 2 to booklet 6.

An interesting comment was made by one subject in the experimental debriefing: "Yes, after I got through booklet 4 and into booklet 6 I understood what you wanted. But in that case the tag line should have read 'What would be a logical solution?' rather than a realistic solution." To study the effect of this change in instruction, 10 new subjects were selected and administered the same case histories, but with the instruction to provide a "logical" solution to the person's problems. These subjects' dilemmatic formulations and problem solutions did not appear to differ from those produced under the standard experimental instruction.

Some particular types of dilemmatic formulation errors were noted especially for group A subjects (experimental–euphoric) who formulated the dilemmas as "if p then r, if r then t, but either p or q, therefore, either r or t." For example, "If I am aggressive, then I will be successful; and if I am successful, then I can go into business for myself, but either aggressive or not aggressive . . . therefore either successful or business for myself."

Some subjects commented that they felt more satisfied with their solutions to the case histories than to the dilemmas (booklets 3 and 5) because they seemed to have more information or seemed more direct and serious.

As compared with the dysphoric groups, subjects in the two euphoric groups seemed more uncertain about their dilemmatic formulations and frequently constructed a dysphoric dilemma instead of a euphoric dilemma.

Sometimes, though correctly constructing the euphoric dilemma, they proceeded to a dysphoric-type solution. One of these subjects commented that solution six was not a solution but a restatement of a dysphoric dilemma.

Many subjects evaluating the dilemmatic form as realistic indicated that they were unable to reach solutions because of insufficient information in the case histories. These subjects felt frustrated by what they perceived as insufficient information. Lack of intellectual competence to formulate dilemmas might, by some subjects, be rationalized as need for further information. Perhaps careful isolation of essentials in a case is associated with the stable introvert personality. There is some research indicating that diagnostic decision making frequently is not enhanced and sometimes suffers from the provision of additional information. It may be of interest to refer to the section on Item Analysis with regard to the relationship between case history or dilemma problem length and correct dilemmatic formulation or correct logical solution. Finally, a new experiment could vary case history length systematically. It may be anticipated that in such research, excessive length would be associated with the presence of several rather than one central dilemma, but that there is some minimal length or information detail required. If so, there might be an adverse U-shaped function between case history length and optimal dilemmatic formulation and problem solution.

One subject mentioned that he had a conflict between regarding the problem as restrictive to the universe of what was given as opposed to the universe of problems in general. He felt conflicted over restricting himself to the specific given information in the problem or of using experience he had obtained in the course of dealing with similar general problems in himself or in others. He was one of these subjects who was attributing various details, circumstances, and value judgments to the problems that were not so specified. In this connection, many journeymen, psychotherapists, and counselors have the problem of restricting themselves to just what it is that the client is describing, saying, or experiencing. Inattentive listening, inaccurate perception, and ascription of various conditions, values, or aspects to the client's situation or even of personality theories or research they are currently reading are persistent problems of beginning therapists.

Some subjects reported becoming fatigued after completion of the first three booklets and felt that there should have been an overall reduction in the number of items. Subjects did have a total of 40 items, 16 case histories, and 24 dilemma problems. In future research, these numbers might be cut in half. In an alternate design, booklets 2 and 3 might be eliminated with booklets 4, 5, and 6 retained in their present length.

An interesting experimental variation would be to reverse the order of the case history booklet and the dilemma problem booklet (booklets 2 and 3) to check for the effect of putting case histories into dilemmatic form and vice-versa. This variation was stimulated by the spontaneous comments of some subjects that if they had been given one of the dilemma booklets first, then at least they would know how to put the case history booklet items into dilemmatic form. Another possibility, already mentioned above, would be to give subjects booklet 4 first.

Some subjects mentioned that because it had been such a long experiment with so many items, toward the end they became rather weary and got haphazard or sloppy in their responding. This can effect certain aspects of pre–post difference.

In studying the paradigm effects of booklet 4 on the response of the two experimental groups to the dilemma problems of booklet 5, it was noted that in the case of some subjects the stylistic form of solutions of booklet 4 would be incorrectly adopted in booklet 5. For example: If p then not necessarily r would be transformed into something like if p then not necessarily s. This kind of partial learning suggests the need for more practice with logical solutions of the type in booklet 4 and also, at the theoretical level, another example of Piaget's contention that cognitive structures in general and logical structures in particular are assimilated only quite gradually.

7

THE COMPARATIVE EFFECTS OF DIDACTIC CORRECTION AND SELF-CONTRADICTION ON FALLACIOUS SCIENTIFIC AND PERSONAL REASONING

SUMMARY

The relative power of two methods of changing fallacious reasoning was investigated in 160 male and female undergraduate university students. Subjects (Ss) were randomized among three experimental conditions: didactic correction method, self-contradiction method, and control. Resistance to committing the fallacies of affirmation of the consequent and denial of the antecedent was studied in an experimental reasoning task. The didactic correction method was significantly ($p < .001$) more effective than the self-contradiction method for both types of logical fallacies and for both scientific reasoning problems and personal reasoning problems. On a transfer task concerned with a reduction of errors in drawing logical inferences, the didactic correction method was significantly ($p < .01$) more effective than the self-contradiction method. It was concluded that the didactic correction method, based on repetitive cognitive information feedback procedures, was more effective in reducing fallacious reasoning than the self-contradiction method, based on self-recognition of inconsistency in inferential behavior. It was recommended that the comparative efficacy of the didactic correction and self-contradiction methods be studied in a fixed array rather than in a trial-by-trial paradigm in order to reduce memory load and that generality of method effectiveness be studied with types of logical fallacies beyond the affirmation of the consequent and the denial of the antecedent.

AUTHOR'S NOTE: The author wishes to express his thanks for the research support provided by the Graduate College of the University of Illinois. He also wishes to express strong appreciation to Richard Sadilek for his assistance with administration and data analysis.

INTRODUCTION

A distinction can be drawn between the approach of psychology and the approach of logic in the study of reasoning. Psychology is concerned with describing how people reason and perhaps why, but not with whether they reason correctly. Logic (Terrell 1967) attempts to provide systematically the laws or principles that distinguish correct from incorrect reasoning. The science of psychology (Wason and Johnson-Laird 1972) is concerned with how people reason and with establishing scientific laws descriptive or explanatory of that reasoning behavior.

Reasoning that violates a rule of logic is invalid or fallacious. A subclass of fallacious reasoning consists of informal fallacies in which the violation of the rule of logic results from certain linguistic or psychological factors that tend to deceive the person into believing that he is reasoning accurately. The fallacies of amphibology, composition, and division depend upon linguistic ambiguity (Johnson-Laird 1969). The fallacies of appeal to force, pity, authority, and similar emotional appeals depend on psychological rationalization (Feather 1967). The abstract character of the terms involved in reasoning (Wilkins 1928) may lead to invalid conclusions and encourage the fallacy of the illicit conversion (Simpson and Johnson 1966).

For the most part, psychological research on fallacious reasoning has been concerned with group or individual differences in response to tests of logical reasoning (Morgan 1956; Sharma 1960) or with isolating the psychological processes responsible (Chapman and Chapman 1959; Janis and Frick 1943; Sells 1936). The present study is concerned with the possibility of the modification of fallacious reasoning.

In an exploratory investigation, Wason (1964) found that the fallacious inferences involved in the affirmation of the consequent and denial of the antecedent could be inhibited by an experimental design that created a self-contradictory or *reductio ad absurdum* situation. Wason (1964) wondered whether this method had any generality or any superiority to a method resembling teaching-machine procedures. The present investigation (1) compared a didactic correction method with the self-contradiction method, (2) tested generality across content varying in personal–emotional or scientific–abstract significance, (3) tested for transfer to an extraexperimental criterion, and (4) attempted to take some account of individual differences.

Principles of logical inference in deductive reasoning (Terrell 1967) stipulate that in a conditional statement having the form if p, then q, that if p is true, then q is a correct inference; and if q is false, then p must be false. It is, however, fallacious to conclude that if p is false, then q must be false, or if q is true, then p must be true. Both fallacies proceed from an inductive or probabilistic approach rather than from a deductive approach which requires that a drawn inference must be certain. Thus, whether inferences drawn from a conditional statement are valid or fallacious depends on whether the formal rules of deductive reasoning or the everyday rules of inductive reasoning are followed. In the present experiment, as in Wason's (1964) investigation, Ss were presented with specific information regarding a rule that holds without exception and permits the drawing of either valid or fallacious inferences. The fallacious inferences drawn by Ss can involve either the affirmation of the consequent or the denial of the antecedent.

METHOD

Subjects and Design

The Ss were 160 students who participated in the experiment as part of their introductory psychology course research obligations. They were randomly assigned to eight equal groups: for the antecedent condition, a self-contradiction, a didactic correction, and a control group; for the consequent condition, a self-contradiction, a didactic correction, and a control group; and two control groups for the test of logical inference, one for the antecedent form of the test and one for the consequent form.

The order of administration of experimental materials for Ss in the self-contradiction, didactic correction, and control groups of the antecedent (or consequent) condition was the Maudsley Personality Inventory (Eysenck 1959), the antecedent (or consequent) form of the pretest of logical inference, the main experimental task, and the antecedent (or consequent) form of the posttest of logical inference.

Each S was randomly assigned to one of the permutations of the order of the four types of material (Types A, B, C, and D). All procedures were individually administered and were completed in a two-hour period.

Measures

Test of Logical Inference

To test for possible transfer effects of the methods of self-contradiction and didactic correction, a pre- and postlogical inference measure was administered. Printed in a booklet, the items of this test had a form that consisted of two premise statements, followed by a space in which the conclusion was to be written. Half of the items had personal–emotional significance and half were neutral–scientific in character. The personal–emotional items dealt with intelligence, grades, dating, physical attractiveness, and other personal, family, or vocational problems. The neutral–scientific items dealt with mechanics, economics, statistics, astronomy, meteorology, and anthropology.

Four forms of the test of logical inference were used: a pre- and postform for the antecedent task and a pre- and postform for the consequent task. Each form contained 20 items, two permitting valid and 18 permitting fallacious inferences. For the antecedent task, the valid items were of the form: (1) if p, then q, (2) p, (3) therefore. . . . The fallacious items had the form: (1) if p, then q, (2) not p, (3) therefore. . . . For the consequent task, the valid items had the form: (1) if p, then q, (2) not q, (3) therefore. . . . The fallacious items had the form: (1) if p, then q, (2) q, (3) therefore. . . .

Control Group for the Logical Inference Test

The antecedent and consequent forms of the test of logical inference were administered to two control groups of Ss who, between pre- and postadministration of this test, took a test of common information. This test consisted of 65 items and covered everyday information in the fields of sports, art, music, science, literature, history, and current events. The intent was to control for experimental task time.

Personality Measures

To provide some information about individual differences, the Maudsley Personality Inventory (Eysenck 1959), with its broadly defined factors of neuroticism and extraversion, was administered at the beginning of the experiment.

Procedure

The Ss were verbally instructed as follows:

> Your task is to try to find out the critical, or missing, grade point average (number of dates, age, q variable) in the rule. I will show you the IQs (ratings, distances, p variables) of a number of students (students, stars, x's), one at a time. After examining the particulars of each, you will have to answer two questions about the critical grade point average (number of dates, ages, q variables) and then give your estimate of it. You will not be timed. Do you have any questions?

If S responded fallaciously on the first trial of a given type of material, he was queried until he gave a valid response. This procedure was not followed on successive trials. The S was permitted to keep the slip with the particulars of trial one, his answers to the two questions, and his estimates of the critical value missing in the rule so that he might have them for reference as he studied the particulars of trial two. After completing his answers and estimate to trial two, the slip for trial one was collected and S was permitted to keep the slip for trial two while he studied that of trial three, and so on for the remaining trials of a given type of material.

At each trial, S was required to answer two questions about the relationship between particulars of that trial. The estimate of the critical value missing in the rule was intended to motivate Ss and to furnish an index for the possibility that S might be drawing inferences in a haphazard or random fashion.

For the antecedent task, the following two questions were posed on each slip: "Could x be less than the critical grade point average (frequency of dating, age of star, q value) missing in the rule? Could x be more than the critical grade point average (frequency of dating, age of star, q value) missing in the rule?" Here, x represented the particular grade point average (frequency of dating, age of star, q value) on a given trial.

For the consequent task, the following two questions were asked: "Could x be more than the critical IQ (physical attractiveness rating, distance from the earth, p value) missing in the rule? Could x be less than the critical IQ (physical attractiveness rating, distance from the earth, p value) missing in the rule?"

For the even-numbered trials, the first of this pair of questions discriminated a valid inference, and the second a fallacious inference. A no response to these questions indicated that a fallacious inference has been drawn, since it eliminated one of two possibilities. A yes response to these questions did not exclude either possibility and was, therefore, the correct answer when the information permitted a fallacious inference to be drawn.

Antecedent Task

In the antecedent task, designed to encourage the fallacy of denial of the antecedent, Ss were given the following instructions verbally: "This is a reasoning task that requires a lot of concentration and careful thought. It begins like this: 'In a certain university, the following relationship between intellectual aptitude and grade point average held without exception.'" Ss were shown a card on which was printed the following rule: "All students with an IQ of 130 or more earned a grade point average of at least_____." In a series of 10 trials, Ss were shown the IQs and grade point averages of particular students from the university for which the rule held. Each trial consisted of a separate slip of paper that contained the following information (1) the IQ and grade point average for the particular student; (2) two questions that asked Ss to determine whether the particular grade point average on the slip could be higher or lower than the grade point average missing in the rule; and (3) a statement that asked Ss to estimate the grade point average missing in the rule. On the first four trials, the grade point averages of students with IQs above 130 were all higher than those of students with IQs below 130. It would be valid to infer that the grade point average missing in the rule could not be higher than that of any student whose IQ was more than 130, but fallacious to infer that it could not be less than that of any student having an IQ below 130.

Self-Contradiction

Beginning with the fifth trial and continuing through the 10th trial, the grade point averages of students were steadily dropped. This permitted a valid inference to be made on trials five, seven, and nine and permitted a fallacious inference to be made on trials six, eight, and 10. For example, on trial four, a student having an IQ of 128 had a grade point average of 3.7, but on trial five a student with an IQ of 135 had a grade point average of 3.5. Thus, the valid inference on trial five that the critical grade point average (the grade point average missing in the rule) could not be more than 3.5 contradicted the fallacious inference on trial four that the critical grade point average must be more than 3.7. But, on trial six a student with an IQ of 122 had a grade point average 3.37. The fallacious inference on this trial that the critical grade point average could not be less than 3.37 was consistent with the valid inference on trial five that the critical grade point average could not be more than 3.5. Thus, the valid inferences on trials five, seven, and nine were consistent with the fallacious inferences on trials that succeeded them but inconsistent with fallacious inferences that preceded them.

Consequent Task

In the consequent task, Ss were presented with the following rule: "All students with an IQ of _____ or more earned a grade point average of at least 4.0." It would be valid to infer that all students with a grade point average of less than 4.0 must have an IQ less than that of the critical IQ. It would be fallacious to infer that all students with a grade point average more than 4.0 must have an IQ higher than that of the critical IQ. On each of 10 trials, Ss were presented with the IQ and grade point average of a specific student and were required to answer two questions regarding the limits of the critical IQ, as well as to give their correct estimate of it. On trials one, two, three, and four, the IQs of students with grade point averages over 4.0 were all higher than those of students with grade point averages below 4.0. Thus, valid and fallacious inferences on these trials were consistent with each other. Trials one and three permitted valid inferences, and trials two and four, fallacious inferences.

Self-Contradiction

Beginning with trial five, however, the IQs on successive trials were steadily increased. Thus, on trial four, a student with a grade point average of 4.1 had an IQ of 132, but on trial five, a student with a grade point average of 3.9 had an IQ of 136. The valid inference on this trial that the critical IQ could not be less than 136 contradicted the fallacious inference on trial four, that the critical IQ could not be more than 132. On trial six, however, a student with a grade point average of 3.7 had an IQ of 138. The fallacious inference, on this trial, that the critical IQ could not be more than 138 was consistent with the valid inference on trial five that the critical IQ could not be less than 136. Thus, valid inferences on trials five, seven, and nine were consistent with the fallacious inferences that followed them but inconsistent with fallacious inferences that preceded them.

Control Group

A control group of Ss was used in both the antecedent and consequent tasks. They differed from the experimental Ss in that the information presented on all 10 trials permitted consistency between valid and fallacious inference.

Didactic Correction Method

The Ss in the didactic correction method received the same 10 trials as Ss in the control groups; however, in addition, following their response to trial four, they were provided with an explanation of valid or fallacious conclusions for that trial. In the antecedent task, following S's response to trials four, six, eight, and 10, a card was presented with the following information printed on it:

> The rule *does not say* that a student with an IQ *less* than 130 must have a grade point average *less* than that of a student whose IQ is more than 130. The rule, in fact, says nothing about a student who has an IQ *less than 130*. For a student who does have an IQ less than 130, his grade point average *can be either higher or lower* than the critical grade point average for the rule.

Following trials five, seven, and nine, the following information was presented on a card, "Since the IQ on the slip of paper is above 130, the grade point average on the slip of paper *must be above* the grade point average for the rule."

In the consequent task, following trials four, six, eight, and 10, the following information was presented on a card: "The rule *does not say* that a student with a grade point average above 4.0 *must have an IQ higher than that for the rule*. For a student with a grade point average above 4.0, his IQ *can be either higher or lower* than the critical IQ for the rule."

Following trials five, seven, and nine, the following information was presented on a card, "Since the grade point average on the slip of paper is less than 4.0, the IQ on the slip of paper *must be less* than the IQ for the rule."

Material

Personal–Emotional Material (Types A and B)

The generality of the self-contradiction and didactic correction methods was tested across material varying in personal–emotional and scientific–abstract content. Type A material dealt with the relationship between IQ and grade point average and has been described. Type B was concerned with the relationship between ratings of physical attractiveness and frequency of dating. In a certain university, the following relationship between physical attractiveness and frequency of dating held without exception, "All men (women) with a physical attractiveness rating of 80% or higher went out on dates at least _____ times a month." For the consequent task, the following rule was used, "All men (women) with a physical attractiveness rating _____% or higher went out on dates at least 20 times a month.

Scientific–Abstract Material (Types C and D)

In a certain scientific study, the following relationship between a star's distance from the earth and star's age held without exception, "All stars which are 1,000 light years or more from the earth are at least _____ years old." In the consequent task, the rule was as follows, "All stars that are _____ light years or more from the earth are at least 3 billion years old."

Type D material involved symbolic and mathematical relationships: A certain group of mathematicians found that the following relationship between variables p and q held without exception, "All x's with a variable p equal to 150 or more had a q variable of at least _____." In the consequent task, the rule was as follows, "All x's with a variable p equal to _____ or more had a q variable of at least 5,000."

RESULTS

Comparative Effectiveness of Didactic Correction and Self-Contradiction in Inhibiting Fallacious Inferences

The frequency distribution of "resist making fallacious inferences" (Table 7.1) was analyzed with the use of Whitfield's tau (Whitfield 1947). The major findings were that the didactic correction method was significantly ($p < .001$) more effective than the self-contradiction method, which, in turn, was significantly ($p < .01$) more effective than the control group in inhibiting fallacious reasoning (Table 7.1) whether the reasoning task involved scientific reasoning problems or personal reasoning problems.

Comparison of Treatment Groups on Pre–Post Test of Logical Inference

An ANCOVA was performed on the eight treatment groups, with the postscore on the logical inference test as the dependent variable and the prescore as the covariable. Adjusted mean scores (correct inferences) were as follows: didactic correction (antecedent fallacy) group equaled 15.23, didactic correction (consequent fallacy) group equaled 14.59, self-contradiction (antecedent fallacy) group equaled 7.14, self-contradiction (consequent fallacy) group equaled 6.91, control (antecedent fallacy) group equaled 6.13, control (consequent fallacy) group equaled 5.18, pre–post control (antecedent fallacy) group equaled 6.13, and pre–post control (consequent fallacy) group equaled 5.71. The result of the ANCOVA was $F(7, 149) = 8.13$, $p < .01$. Tukey pairwise test comparisons indicated that the two didactic correction groups were significantly ($p < .01$) different from the other six groups. Subsequent separate analyses of scientific versus personal logical inference test items did not change the pattern of findings reported for the total test score.

Personality Type Performance on Logical Inference Test

Four personality type groups were formed by the median intersection of the orthogonal neuroticism and extraversion scales of the Maudsley Personality Inventory (Eysenck 1959): neurotic extraverts, stable extraverts, neurotic introverts, stable introverts. Within each of these personality type groups ($N = 40$), an ANCOVA was done for the four treatment groups, with the use of the postlogical inference test score as the dependent variable and the prelogical inference test score as the covariable. Four treatment groups were produced by combining the original eight treatment groups: didactic correction (combined antecedent and consequent) group, self-contradiction (combined antecedent and consequent) group, control (combined antecedent and consequent) group, pre–post control (combined antecedent and consequent) group.

The ANCOVAs for the neurotic introvert and stable introvert groups were not significant. The ANCOVA for the neurotic extravert group resulted in $F(3, 33) = 7.19$, $p < .01$. Adjusted mean scores (correct inferences) were as follows: didactic correction group = 15.12, self-contradiction group = 7.18, control group = 6.93, pre–post control group = 5.81. Scheffé pairwise contrasts indicated a significant ($p < .01$) difference between the didactic correction group and each of the other groups. In the case of the stable extravert personality type group, the ANCOVA indicated $F(3, 33) = 6.93$, $p < .01$. Adjusted mean scores (correct inferences) were as follows: didactic correction group = 13.73, self-contradiction group = 8.17, control group = 7.39, pre–post control group = 5.97. Scheffé pairwise contrast test indicated a significant

Table 7.1 Number of Subjects Initially Susceptible to Making Fallacious Inferences Who Resisted Making Subsequent Fallacious Inferences at Different Stages of the Task or Made the Maximum Number of Fallacious Inferences: I.E., Made No Corrections for Combined Types A, B, C, and D Materials.

Group	Antecedent Task Resist	Antecedent Task No rev.	Consequent Task Resist	Consequent Task No rev.	Combined Antec. and Conseq. Tasks Resist	Combined Antec. and Conseq. Tasks No rev.
Self-contradiction						
Number susceptible	42		52		94	
Sixth trial	7	6	2	0	9	6
Eighth trial	10	2	6	3	16	5
Tenth trial	8	0	4	0	12	0
No. Making No Corrections	31		45		76	

Control						
Number susceptible		59		73		132
Sixth trial	1	1	0	0	1	1
Eighth trial	1	0	1	0	2	0
Tenth trial	1	0	0	0	1	0
No. Making No Corrections		58		72		130
Didactic correction						
Number susceptible		16		32		48
Sixth trial	6	5	22	19	28	24
Eighth trial	7	2	25	5	32	7
Tenth trial	8	0	27	1	35	1
No. Making No Corrections		8		4		12

Note: Resist refers to Ss who resisted on individual trials; No rev. refers to Ss who did not revert to fallacious reasoning.

(p < .05) difference between the didactic correction group and all the other groups.

The results would seem to suggest that the personality type groups characterized as extraverted (neurotic extraverts and stable extraverts) responded differentially to the didactic correction and self-contradiction methods, but that personality type groups characterized as introverted (neurotic introverts and stable introverts) responded equivalently to the two methods.

DISCUSSION

Comparison of Didactic Correction Versus Self-Contradiction Method

The didactic correction method proved to be a very effective procedure for reducing fallacious reasoning. Its effectiveness was dependent on a cognitive information feedback procedure. In a study concerned with the modification of fallacious reasoning with implication (if, then) logical problems, Leahey and Wagman (1974) also found a cognitive information feedback procedure especially effective. In both the Leahey and Wagman (1974) study and in the present investigation, it was demonstrated that effectiveness in modifying fallacious reasoning transferred to an external task. The self-contradiction method, though not as effective as the didactic correction method, did significantly reduce fallacious reasoning, as compared with control group performance. The method, however, was dependent on the self-recognition of inconsistency in response and the ability to avoid such self-contradiction in future reasoning responses. Such intellectual competence may well have been an excessive cognitive load for most research participants, and certainly was more cognitively demanding than being repeatedly reminded by a printed card concerning what were valid and fallacious responses (didactic correction method).

Wason (1964), after demonstrating the effectiveness of the self-contradiction procedure, wondered whether the method would have generality and whether a method based on a teaching machine analogy might prove as effective. The present research demonstrated the generality of the self-contradiction method across reasoning problems with varying personal and scientific content. It also demonstrated the greater effectiveness of a method based on a teaching machine analogy, that is, didactic correction method.

Wason's (1964) data indicated for his combined antecedent and consequent conditions that out of 14 susceptible Ss in the self-contradiction group, five failed to make any corrections, while out of 16 susceptible Ss in his control group, 12 failed to make any corrections. The respective percentages were 35.7% for the self-contradiction group and 75% for the control group. In the present research, for all types of material combined and for the antece-

dent and consequent conditions combined, there were 76 Ss out of 94 susceptible in the self-contradiction group who failed to make any corrections; 12
out of 48 in the didactic correction group; and 130 out of 132 susceptible in
the control group (Table 7.1). Respective percentages were found for self-contradiction (81%), didactic correction (25%), and control group (98.5%).

The Ss did not perform as well as Wason's Ss in the self-contradiction
and control condition. But Ss in the didactic correction condition performed
substantially better than Ss in Wason's self-contradiction condition. The fore-
going suggested that the task was especially difficult, 75% of Wason's control group and 98.5% of the present control group failed to make any corrections of fallacious reasoning.

Reverting to Fallacious Reasoning

Wason found that most of his Ss who, though initially susceptible to
making fallacious inferences, successfully resisted making a fallacious inference on trial six or eight tended to resist making fallacious inferences on the
subsequent trials of this 10-trial experiment. In the present research, Ss responded to a total of 40 trials and, more particularly, to 10 trials for each
of the four types of material. It is of interest to learn whether Ss behaved like
Wason's Ss with respect to reverting or not reverting to fallacious reasoning.
For this purpose, the data were tabulated (Table 7.1) with respect to the number of Ss who, after their initial correction of fallacious reasoning on a particular trial, continued to resist fallacious reasoning.

Wason's findings were confirmed for the self-contradiction group and
the didactic correction group. Thus, for all four types of material combined
and for antecedent and consequent conditions combined (Table 7.1), the appropriate frequencies for trials six, eight, and 10, respectively, were as follows: self-contradiction — 6, 5, and 0; didactic correction — 24, 7, and 1; control group — 1, 0, 0. It would thus be a moot point as to whether these data
support Wason's claim of "insight" by his nonreverting self-contradiction
group Ss or whether they refute the claim and replace it by a "one-trial learning" explanation common to both self-contradiction and didactic correction
procedures.

Test of Logical Inference

While the discussion has so far emphasized the clear superiority of the
didactic correction method to the self-contradiction method in inhibiting fallacious inferences, it was of special interest to note what happened when the
support given to the didactic correction group by the presence of an explanatory correction card on each trial was removed during the administration
of the test of logical inference. The didactic correction group maintained its

superior effectiveness, as compared to the self-contradiction method, for both antecedent and consequent reasoning fallacies and for both personal and scientific reasoning content. This finding was unexpected. It had been thought that without the support of the cognitive feedback procedure, the didactic correction group would revert to fallacious reasoning and would thereby drop below the performance level of the self-contradiction group whose insight into fallacious reasoning, developed by a *reductio ad absurdum* procedure, should be well-transferred to performance on the logical inference test.

Future Research

The present research has compared the relative effectiveness of two methods for modifying fallacious reasoning. These methods were tested in a trial-by-trial experimental paradigm that required participants to retain information from previous trials. This memory load may have been especially disadvantageous to the self-contradiction method, as reported by several Ss in the postexperimental inquiry. Replacement of the trial-by-trial paradigm with an information array paradigm would eliminate the memory load and thus make possible a clearer competition between a method based on self-recognition and self-correction of inconsistency versus a method based on repetitive cognitive information feedback. It would also be valuable to extend the comparative effectiveness of the two methods to logical fallacies beyond those of denial of the antecedent and affirmation of the consequent.

EXPERIMENTAL INQUIRY–QUALITATIVE ASPECTS

The experimenter (E) administered a standard experimental inquiry to each S in an effort to learn more about qualitative differences in approach to the tasks, in reasoning strategies and in the effect of content on performance.

S-10: Didactic Correction Consequent Group

This S failed to follow the straightforward information given on the didactic correction cards and is a good example of rationalizing her inability to cope with the task demands by insisting that the didactic correction cards were incorrect.

> E: Did the instructions given to you on the second task effect your performance on that task?
>> S-10: I wasn't sure if the [didactic correction] cards were right.
> E: This is the correct reasoning for this task.

S-10: Are you trying to trick me or something? I think the cards are confusing. They make it [the task] more confusing rather than making it easier.

The E noted that this S was one of the skeptical ones; she was one of the few who failed to get the didactic correction right. She missed all the ones on that task because she did not understand the cards or she did not think they were right.

S-8: Didactic Correction Consequent Group

The E's notes describe for this S the increased task difficulty produced by the interacting effect of the type of material and the fact of its being administered initially.

E: Did the content have any effect on your answers to the two questions and to the estimates?
S-8: Somewhat. [The E noted that it was mainly Type C, his first type of material, that had a negative effect.] I didn't understand the stars very well.

In general, most people thought that the first type of material had a confusing effect and the content had some effect on their answers. It was particularly hard to understand when p's and q's were administered first.

S-13: Didactic Correction Consequent Group

This S illustrates failure of transfer from the didactic correction procedure to the posttest of logical inference and a S for whom the concrete literal instructions on the didactic correction cards could not provide a general enough cognitive structure that would enable her to perceive the common logical inferential pattern involved in both the experimental task and the transfer task. The E noted that this S got the ABDC permutation, got all the pre- and posttest wrong, and "got it" on trial eight of Type A — which was the easiest. The S stated that the pretest had no effect on the posttest and had no effect on the experimental task and the experimental task had no effect on the posttest.

S-6: Self-Contradiction Antecedent Group

This is one of the few Ss who demonstrated excellent reasoning in the self-contradiction task and who gave a good explanation of her cognitive processes and of perceiving that, beginning with trial five, consequent values were steadily increased and that for antecedent values below the critical value that the consequent value could be either more or less than the critical value missing in the rule. Apparently, then, self-contradiction served effectively to inhibit the drawing of fallacious inferences for all her subsequent experimental trials.

E: Did you have any difficulty in answering either or both of the questions ["Could it be more" and "Could it be less"] on the slip of paper on the experimental task?

S-6: I used the idea that there could be an exception. [This means that when she saw these contradictions, she considered those to be exceptions. A few other Ss also did this.] I think it was easier to answer the questions than it was to give the estimates. [The E noted that this was rather unusual—most people thought the reverse.] I think I estimated them pretty accurately and answered the questions well.

E: Was there anything strange about the numbers given on the 10-trial reasoning tasks?

S-6: Yes, on D [p's and q's, which was her third type of material]. Lower variables changed to higher variables. The p's and q's were the most difficult to reason about, but memory played a large part in the experimental task. I think I did better on the later 10-trial sequences—especially the last two.

E: Did the first 10 trials have any effect on the next 10 trials [the Wason task]?

S-6: It decided the way I graded the next ones. [So it did have some effect.]

E: What process of reasoning did you use?

S-6: The ones that were less than what was needed were yes–yes. [She "got it" on the eighth trial of the first type of B.]

S-16: Self-Contradiction Antecedent Group

In contrast to the previous S, this S, while he performs very well, is not able to give a very lucid account.

S-16: There was no effect of any of the tasks on each other.

E: Were you aware of any contradictions on the 10 trials?

S-16: Yes, with the contradictions I worked down to a certain point with the estimates.

E: Did the contradictions have any effect on your answers to the two questions and on your estimate of the critical values?

S-16: Yes.

E: What do you think the task was getting at?

S-16: Logic—a reaction from a situation from something prior. [The S missed *some*. He was not very lucid about his speech, but he did quite well.]

S-3: Self-Contradiction Antecedent Group

A very interesting and very frequent phenomenon was the tendency to average data of the 10 trials and of sequential estimates, which interacted negatively with the effects of contradiction as illustrated in the protocol below.

E: Was there anything strange about the numbers given on the ten-trial reasoning task?

S-3: I couldn't pick out the average. [Several Ss wanted to average the numbers together in order to find out an estimate; but, of course, there was no average.] I thought there was a contradiction on the first 10, but not on the rest of the three types. [This was because he got it right after the first 10 and he did not see any contradictions.]

E: What did the contradictions mean to you?

S-3: I was looking for an average. After you [E] explained the first one on the Type C [his second type of material] to me, I got it. [The E queried Type C and explained the first one; E noted that evidently his explanation gave S a clue.]

S-18: Self-Contradiction Antecedent Group

This S, though she gave little in the way of explanation of her reasoning processes, performed perfectly on all trials for all four types of material and also responded correctly to both the pre- and posttest of logical inference and was able to grasp the logical similarity of the three reasoning tasks. The E noted that this woman was not susceptible; she had had little math and no logic in her educational background. She got everything right on the Wason task.

S-18: I already knew how to do it [i.e., the instructions did not effect her performance].

E: Did the first task have any effect on the second task?

S-18: It used the same form—if-then.

E: Did content have any effect on your reasoning?

S-18: Some. The stars effected my reasoning a little bit because it was harder to think in light years.

S-9: Self-Contradiction Antecedent Group

The protocol summary exemplifies a type of S best described as a "concrete responder." The E noted this man got the permutation CADB (stars first). He "got it" on the fourth type of material, which was the dating, but S experienced some difficulty before he mastered it. The E queried C and D.

S-9: The first task made me more careful when I was reasoning on the second task. [The E noted that nothing else had any effect.] I didn't notice any contradictions on the experimental task.

[The E explained to S what was contradictory.]

E: What effect, if any, did the contradictions have on your estimate of the critical values?

S-9: I couldn't figure some of it out, but I figured it out on the last type. The dating was more understandable. The content had a large effect.

E: Did the content have any effect later on?

S-9: Definitely. The stars and the p's and q's confused me.

S-23: Self-Contradiction Antecedent Group

The protocol for this S illustrates very well the effect of contradiction on fallacious reasoning. The E's notes also indicate that this S was very well-motivated and very much involved in the task, perhaps a requirement more than a desideratum for effectiveness on the contradiction procedure.

E: Did the contradictions on the experimental task effect your reasoning?

S-23: I noticed the contradictions on trial six or seven of the Type D material [his first type].

E: What effect, if any, did the contradictions have on your answers to the two questions?

S-23: It reversed the yes–no in some cases and the yes–yes in others.

E: What effects did the contradictions have on your estimates – on your critical values?

S-23: It decreased them. [The E noted that this was the case.] After the first four trials, something seemed to click and I understood what was going on.

S-22: Self-Contradiction Antecedent Group

The inappropriate imposition of a mathematical structure on the particulars of each trial throws this S way off and blocks the working of contradiction. This S had the DCBA permutation – really the hardest in reverse order. The E included in his notes: "Well-motivated – cynical – thought he knew everything about math." The S tried to convince the E that the entire experiment was set up wrong. The E had to argue at length with the S before he would even take the test.

The S got the Type D first, which played right into his hands because it was the math type. The trials were numbered X1, X2, X3, X4, . . . , X10, which is simply numbering the trials. It said for an X1 with a p variable equal to _____, it had a q variable equal to _____. The S was worried that X1 had to be less than X2.

E: Just forget the X's and just start the trials.

S-22: You can't forget the X's – they're an integral part of the whole thing. [The E noted that even though S did not think he did, this S got it all wrong.] The first test had a little bit of effect on the third test, but none of the other things had any effect.

E: Were you aware of any contradictions on the 10 trials?

S-22: Not actually contradictory; the values were misarranged.

E: At what point did you notice that?

S-22: On the first series [Type D], it didn't bother me. Then I changed my answers.

E: What process of reasoning did you use to answer the two questions on the task?

S-22: Nothing would ever be less than the critical value—no relationship was ever established. [The E noted that the S was evidently looking for some mathematical relationship.]

S-11: Self-Contradiction Antecedent Group

The effect of self-contradiction in requiring the S to change her reasoning is indicated in the following protocol summary. The E's notes stated that S did "almost okay—got quite a few right on the Wason task." The E noted that S had a little logic and some math courses in high school.

E: What would you say was the effect of the first task on the second task?

S-11: It was just like syllogisms on both. It did have some effect [the first on the second task]. The other tasks did not have any effect on each other. I noticed the contradictions on the second task on the Type C material [which was the second type she got].

E: What did the contradiction mean to you?

S-11: It forced me to reason correctly [which is what we wanted her to say].

E: Did the content have any effect on your answers to the two questions and on your estimates?

S-11: Yes, the Type C material [stars] was the only one that had an effect. [The E did not have to query her at all. She got all of Type B right, which was the last type, and all of Type A right also, which was the second from the last. She got almost everything right except the first type, that is, she did correct herself.]

S-1: Control Antecedent Group

This S was able to bypass the diverse content in the four types of material and to respond to their univocal logical structure. This S was "not susceptible on the Wason task; consequently, he got all the Wason task correct." The E noted that S knew a lot about logic, but he had had no course in it.

S-1: I don't think any of the tasks had any effect on any of the other tasks.

E: What did you think the task was getting at? [The E observed that S was able to explain this question relatively well.]

S-1: I think I made some mistakes on the second question [the second type of material. However, he did not.].

E: What was the effect of content on your answers to the two questions on the estimates?

S-1: Content had no effect. There was a pattern, and they were all logically the same — all the four types. [Evidently, he considered only the logical relationships.]

S-15: Control Antecedent Group

This protocol illustrates the case of a S who reverts to fallacious reasoning and does so by reinterpreting relationships in the rule.

E: Did the first 10 trials on the experimental task [Type B material] have any effect on the next 10, and those on the next 10, and so forth?

S-15: I didn't pay much attention on the second, third, and fourth types.

E: Why did you change from the yes–yes [the correct answer on the first type] to yes–no?

S-15: Because I reinterpreted the rule to mean no one with less than 80 percent rating could go out on more than the critical number of dates [i.e., she reverted to fallacious reasoning].

S-14: Control Antecedent Group

This S's protocol portrays the deleterious intrusion of personal feeling about the content of the task material into her reasoning processes. This S had the CBAD permutation.

E: What effect did the first task have on the third task?

S-14: I left more blanks on the first one. I was worried about personal feelings. It was hard to write down an answer if you didn't agree with it, so I based most of my answers on common sense. [The E deduced that she had a more logical approach on the posttest since she did not leave as many blank, but her logic was wrong.]

E: What process of reasoning did you use to answer the two questions on the experimental task?

S-14: I really didn't see what you wanted. [Then, E explained and queried her on the Type B, which was her second type of material. She failed to understand the stars (her first type); she answered no–no to quite a few questions on it.] I inferred things [which refers to her personal feelings toward the dating type of material. She did not give any real explanation for the process of reasoning.] The content of the A [grade point average] and B [dating] types influenced my reasoning.

S-17: Control Antecedent Group

In contrast to the previous S, the protocol of this S indicates a detachment of content from logical operations and insight into the structure of valid and fallacious inferential behavior.

E: Did the second reasoning task have any effect on the last?

S-17: Yes, it confirmed my initial opinions. [Evidently, the "it" refers to the logic of the task.]

E: What would you say was the effect of the first task on the second task?

S-17: The first task gave me the impression that you shouldn't jump to conclusions. [The E noted that this seemed to be good insight.] I didn't think that the first task had any effect on the last.

E: Did the first 10 trials have any effect on the next 10?

S-17: Not as far as the questions; but with the estimates, yes, there was an effect. There definitely was a pattern involved. There never was a distinct lower value for q [on the Type D material]. Values can always be more than the critical number, but it could sometimes — in certain causes — be less. [The E observed that S was not susceptible. He knew what he was doing all through the experimental task.]

E: Did content enter into your reasoning?

S-17: No, not on a logical basis.

S-19: Control Antecedent Group

In contrast to both the previous Ss, this S declares that content is of no significance in her reasoning, is highly confident that she was reasoning very well during the experiment, and, despite the fact that she had had a recent university semester course in logic, failed completely the logical requirements of the experimental task. The E had to query her on the first type of material, and she failed to get any of the answers right all through the experimental task, even though she did have a logic course.

S-19: "I didn't think the questions on the slips of paper were very important. I thought the estimates were more so. I didn't have any difficulty reasoning about anything. The first ten trials made it easier for the next ten trials on the experimental task." E noted that content had no effect on her reasoning. She seemed to be relatively confident about what she was doing, but she got them all wrong.

S-21: Didactic Correction Antecedent Group

An example of cognitive rigidity is given in the following protocol summary of a S who, rather than modifying her inferential behavior, chose to defend it by defying the explanations on the didactic correction cards. The E observed that this S got the experimental task completely wrong. Her background included some logic and only a small amount of math in high school.

E: Did you have any difficulty in answering either or both of the questions on the slips of paper on the experimental task?

S-21: Yes, I believed the instructions, but defied the instructions. Still, I thought it would be less. I read the instructions thinking it could be either more or less, but I had it in my mind that the number could be less than the critical value, or would have to be less than the critical value, and so I didn't change my reasoning. [The E indicated in his notes that she got everything wrong.] The p's and q's were the most difficult to reason about.

E: Did the didactic correction instructions effect your performance on the third task?

S-21: I disregarded them. They were presented too many times. [The E explained that they were presented after each trial, so she evidently tired of them.]

S-7: Didactic Correction Antecedent Group

The protocol notes for this S indicate an unusual grasp of the common logical structure of the three reasoning tasks and the associated disregard of content. This male S was run with the CDBA permutation. He had had a lot of math in college, including differential equations; however, he had had no logic. The E included in his notes that this man got it immediately on the experimental task. He seemed to really understand the pre- and posttests and the experimental task.

E: What effect did the experimental task have on the third task?

S-7: It was boring. There was no effect of the first on the second [the pre on the post] on the second time [the posttest]. I didn't read after p. I read only p, then q—not p. I only read as far as p, then looked at the second line to see if there was a not-p; and, if there was, I left it blank. [The E noted that S got those right.]

E: Did the instructions given on the experimental task [the didactic correction instructions] effect your performance on that task?

S-7: It was the same logic as on the first test.

E: Did the content have any effect on your answers?

S-7: It was ridiculous! I was looking for a formula for the estimates throughout the four types of material. [Some of the people persisted, especially with the Type D, in looking for a formula all the way to the end. Later, on asking the E whether there was a mathematical relationship between the two, some Ss were rather surprised to find out there was not; but most of these were the ones who got it wrong. Most people who concentrated on the estimates seemed to get it wrong, but those who knew what they were doing did not spend much time on the estimates—they put down the same estimate almost throughout. The E queried this S on Type C (his first type of material). The E noted, however, that after S got the instructions, he got it immediately on the sixth trial.]

S-25: Didactic Correction Antecedent Group

A curious "reasoning by extremes" procedure is described in the following protocol summary for this S.

E: What process of reasoning did you use to answer the two questions on the experimental task?

S-25: I looked at the extremes. It couldn't be less, or more, or whatever. [The E observed that S fell into the pattern yes–no, no–yes, and reasoned it out in this manner, which was, of course, wrong.]

E: What did you think the task was getting at?

S-25: How well you can predict that one number will be given others.

E: Did content have any effect on your reasoning?

S-25: Only on the grade point average (Type A). [The E noted that S got them all wrong on the last one.]

S-4: Control Consequent Group

The essential structuring given to the rule by the words "at least" is ignored by this S, and she fails on all trials.

E: What process of reasoning did you use?

S-4: I looked at the extreme values and eliminated them.

E: Did you notice any key words in the rules that were essential to the understanding of the problem?

S-4: No. [The E explained that the words noticed should be "at least" or "or more," and that most persons recognized at least one of the two possibilities. Content had no effect on this S's reasoning. The E recorded that this was a typical control S. Also, she did not get anything right on the experimental task.]

S-24: Self-Contradiction Consequent Group

This protocol illustrates a S who, as distinct from many others, could both perceive inconsistency in the "strangeness" of the sequencing of information and respond to the inconsistency with a correct resolution.

E: Was there anything strange about the numbers that were given on the 10-trial sequences in the experimental task?

S-24: They set you up for a low number and then threw in a high number.

E: What process of reasoning did you use to answer the two questions on the task?

S-24: On the star material, if the particular number was above the limit, then I answered yes–yes. If the distance was less than 40 million light years, then it was less than the represented amount.

S-29: Self-Contradiction Consequent Group

In contrast to the previous S, this S recognizes the inconsistency in the presented information, but is unable to resolve it.

E: Was there anything strange about the numbers given on the 10-trial sequences on the experimental task?

S-29: There could be a high IQ with a low grade point average, and high rating with low dating. [The E noted that S evidently saw these numbers as something strange and contradictory.] I thought the p's and q's were the most difficult to reason about, because they were mathematical and because they were given first. I think I did the best on the dating type.

E: Did the first 10 trials have any effect on the next 10?

S-29: Yes, they were confusing.

E: Was there a pattern involved — generally? Was there a pattern in your yes–no responses, no–yes, or yes–yes, in your answers to the questions?

S-29: Not until the last 10 (Type B material). [However, the E noted that she got the last type wrong anyway.]

E: Did you notice any key words in the rules that were essential to the understanding of the problem?

S-29: Yes, "at least" or "or more."

E: Did you find what might be thought of as a solution or general statement you could make to summarize the main problems on the task? [The E asked either this question or "what was the process of reasoning you used."]

S-29: No. The A and B type material was easier. [The E observed that she did not get anything right, had good motivation, good concentration, and was friendly.]

S-12: Self-Contradiction Consequent Group

The following is a protocol of a S who had two semesters of university calculus, perceived the common logical structure of the three experimental tasks, recognized the critical importance of "at least" or "more than," recognized the presence of changes in the consequent values, and, yet, failed completely to take account of the contradictions implied and consequently failed all trials. The E indicated in his notes that this S had no previous logic, got the ABCD permutation, and did not get any right on the experimental task. The E queried him on the first type of material (Type B).

E: Did the experimental task have any effect on the third task? Did the first task have any effect on the second task?

S-12: No, from the first to the third, there was a collective process. [The E noted that S must have meant some sort of practice effect.] The third was easier. The first introduced you to the third.

E: To what degree were tasks one and two related?

S-12: To a high degree. Also, the experimental and the third to a high degree. One and three [the pre and post] were the same.

E: How important did you feel the two questions on each slip of paper were on the experimental task?

S-12: The importance was to see how my opinion could change. [The E noted that S was thinking in ratios, which was wrong. In fact, S even remarked that this was wrong on the first type of material, Type A.]

E: Did you have any difficulty in answering either or both the questions on the slips of paper?

S-12: No, not after Type A. [Nevertheless, S did get them all wrong.]

E: Was there anything strange about the numbers on the 10-trial sequences?

S-12: Some seemed completely extreme exceptions to the rule.

E: Were you aware of any contradictions on the 10 trials? What was contradictory?

S-12: The extremes.

E: What did the contradictions mean to you?

S-12: I took them as meaning an exception.

E: What effects, if any, did the contradictions have on your answers to the two questions?

S-12: None.

E: What effect, if any, did they have on your estimates?

S-12: None. I disregarded the extremes as exceptions.

E: What process of reasoning did you use in answering the two questions on the task?

S-12: I answered the questions from the estimates. I made the estimate first, then answered the question from that [which was a dangerous way to go about it].

E: Did there seem to be a pattern involved?

S-12: Yes, the last five got to be real high values.

E: How big a part would you say memory played in the experimental task?

S-12: Pretty big part — I had to remember the first. The dating was the most difficult to reason about. P's and q's were the easiest. All the materials were the same in the logical sense.

E: Did the first 10 trials have any effect on the next 10?

S-12: Yes, they familiarized me with the material.

E: What do you think the task was getting at?

S-12: How good a gin player you are. You can draw conclusions from certain facts.

E: Did you notice any key words in the rules that were essential to the understanding of the problem?

S-12: At least and or more.

E: Did my correction of your answer in the first trial help you later in the task? [Earlier S had asked E if this was an average and E replied no.]

S-12: That helped.

E: Did the content have any effect on your reasoning?

S-12: On Type A it did — on Type D maybe. I started comparing my own grade point average with the ones in the tasks. [The S did not get any right.]

S-28: Self-Contradiction Consequent Group

The following protocol illustrates a S for whom self-contradiction worked very effectively at an early point in the experimental trials and who, apparently, transferred this learning successfully to the posttest of logical inference. For this S, E's notes indicate that S corrected his reasoning on trial eight of his first type of material (Type C) and got them correct from there on; E did not query him at all. This S had two weeks of logic in high school and calculus and differential equations in college.

E: Did the experimental task have any effect on the third task?

S-28: I remembered the logic I had on the second task, and it helped me on the third. The first test had no effect on the experimental, and the first test had no effect on the third.

E: Was there anything strange about the numbers given on the 10-trial sequences?

S-28: Yes—high–low and 5. [The E noted that from trial four to trial five S noticed the contradiction of the high number with the low corresponding number.] It was the same on all the trials—one that fit, one that didn't.

E: Were you aware of any contradictions and what was contradictory?

S-28: On the first type there was a contradiction. [The E noted that, evidently, S did not notice any after that because he corrected his reasoning, that is, he noticed a contradiction of the first type and corrected his reasoning; from then on, there would not have been any contradictions.]

TEST OF LOGICAL INFERENCE

Following are the four booklets of the test of logical inference. They are: antecedent pretest, antecedent posttest, consequent pretest, and consequent posttest.

Preceding each individual booklet were the following instructions:

The following test contains a series of items designed to test reasoning ability. In each case two statements are given, followed by "Therefore, _____."

In the blank after "Therefore," you are to write what *necessarily* follows (if anything) from the given statement.

Do not turn back. Keep going until you finish.

Proceed immediately to the test.

The Antecedent Pretest

1. If John has good ability and studies hard, he will get good grades.
   John has good ability and studies hard.
   Therefore, _____.

2. If Mary keeps herself looking attractive, she will have many dates.
   Mary does not keep herself looking attractive.
   Therefore, _____.

3. If Bill plans his career in line with his abilities and interests, then he will have a successful career.
   Bill does not plan his career in line with his abilities and interests.
   Therefore, _____.

4. If Marilyn disagrees with her parents on many significant issues, then she will have a stressful and unhappy life.
Marilyn agrees with her parents on many significant issues.
Therefore, _____.

5. If the hinge is kept well-oiled, the door will not squeak.
The hinge is kept well-oiled.
Therefore, _____.

6. If Bob dresses differently than everyone else, then he will feel tense.
Bob does not dress differently than everyone else.
Therefore, _____.

7. If the variety of automobile styles increases, then there will be an increase in the number of car sales.
The variety of automobile styles has not increased.
Therefore, _____.

8. If the temperature rises, then we shall all feel uncomfortable.
The temperature has fallen.
Therefore, _____.

9. If the volume of sound is reduced, the bass tones will have to be increased.
The volume of sound has been increased.
Therefore, _____.

10. If the reduction in railroad passenger service is not halted, there will be a rise in the level of airplane passenger service.
Reduction in railroad passenger service has been halted.
Therefore, _____.

11. If this poem is in the style of Shakespeare's writings, then it was written by Shakespeare.
This poem is not in the style of Shakespeare's writings.
Therefore, _____.

12. If Eskimos do not use snowmobiles, then the breed of Husky dogs will not die out.
Eskimos do use snowmobiles.
Therefore, _____.

13. If the heart pumps faster, then blood pressure will be raised.
The heart is not pumping faster.
Therefore, _____.

14. If Social Security benefits are increased, then older people will be better off.
Social Security benefits are not increased.
Therefore, _____.

15. If the annual temperature of large cities is increasing, then the Earth must be getting closer to the Sun.
The annual temperature of large cities is not increasing.

Therefore, _____.

16. If the child gets everything he wants, then he will become a spoiled brat.
The child does not get everything that he wants.
Therefore, _____.

17. If Mr. Jones does not get a job promotion, then Mrs. Jones will be a discontented wife.
Mr. Jones does get a job promotion.
Therefore, _____.

18. If Mr. Roberts buys his wife a fur coat, then she will become a better housewife.
Mr. Roberts does not buy his wife a fur coat.
Therefore, _____.

19. If Peter's mother comes to live with them, then his wife will insist on leaving him and the children.
Peter's mother does not come to live with them.
Therefore, _____.

20. If these two young people are of the same religion, then they will have a successful and happy marriage.
These two young people are not of the same religion.
Therefore, _____.

The Antecedent Posttest

1. If Carl is aggressive, then he will be successful in business.
Carl is not aggressive.
Therefore, _____.

2. If Ralph does poorly in his studies, then he will have feelings of intellectual inadequacy.
Ralph does poorly at his studies.
Therefore, _____.

3. If Kathleen does not compete with anyone, then she will have only friends.
Kathleen does compete with many people.
Therefore, _____.

4. If Lucy is pleasant in her interpersonal relations, then she will be liked by everyone.
Lucy is pleasant in her interpersonal relations.
Therefore, _____.

5. If Jerry seeks both competitive success and dependent love, he will be quite unhappy.
Jerry does not seek both competitive success and dependent love.
Therefore, _____.

6. If Betty chooses an engineering career because of her excellent mathematical ability

and scientific interest, then she is likely to be less personally attractive to men.
Betty does not choose an engineering career.
Therefore,
_____.

7. If the light level in the room should increase, the camera shutter speed will be reduced.
The light level in the room has decreased.
Therefore,
_____.

8. If the annual rainfall this year stays below 20 inches, it will be good for the trees.
The annual rainfall this year has not stayed below 20 inches.
Therefore,
_____.

9. If this retail hardware storeowner is charged more by the wholesaler, then he will have to raise his prices.
This retail hardware storeowner is not charged more by the wholesaler.
Therefore,
_____.

10. If solar storms occur this year, radio communication will become poorer.
Solar storms did not occur this year.
Therefore,
_____.

11. If they quarrel at breakfast, then Mr. Robinson will be inefficient all day at work.
They do not quarrel at breakfast.
Therefore,
_____.

12. If this man hides his epileptic condition, then he will secure a job.
This man does not hide his epileptic condition.
Therefore,
_____.

13. If he agrees with her, then he has no mind of his own.
He does not agree with her.
Therefore,
_____.

14. If the war continues, then inflation will increase.
The war does not continue.
Therefore,
_____.

15. If information is unavailable, then people will not stop smoking.
Information is available.
Therefore,
_____.

16. If it is snowing outside, then it probably is not July.
It is not snowing outside.
Therefore,
_____.

17. If this mouse has brown eyes, then its grandmother had brown eyes.
This mouse does not have brown eyes.
Therefore,
_____.

18. If this piece of Peruvian pottery is similar to Polynesian pottery, then ancient Polynesians probably settled Peru.
This piece of Peruvian pottery is not similar to Polynesian pottery.

Therefore,
_____

19. If Mr. Thomas does not reduce the cholesterol level of his diet, then he will have a heart attack.
Mr. Thomas does reduce the cholesterol level of his diet.
Therefore,
_____

20. If Mr. Rodney does not reduce his business activity, he will develop a duodenal ulcer.
Mr. Rodney does reduce his business activity.
Therefore,
_____

The Consequent Pretest

1. If John has good ability and studies hard, he will get good grades.
John does not get good grades.
Therefore,
_____

2. If Mary keeps herself looking attractive, she will have many dates.
Mary has many dates.
Therefore,
_____

3. If Bill plans his career in line with his abilities and interests, then he will have a successful career.
Bill has a successful career.
Therefore,
_____

4. If Marilyn disagrees with her parents on many significant issues, then she will have a stressful and unhappy life.
Marilyn has a stressful and unhappy life.
Therefore,
_____

5. If the hinge is kept well-oiled, the door will not squeak.
The door does squeak.
Therefore,
_____

6. If Bob dresses differently than everyone else, then he will feel tense.
Bob feels tense.
Therefore,
_____

7. If the variety of automobile styles increases, then there will be an increase in the number of car sales.
There is an increase in the number of car sales.
Therefore,
_____

8. If the temperature rises, then we shall all feel uncomfortable.
We all feel uncomfortable.
Therefore,
_____

9. If the volume of sound is reduced, the bass tones will have to be increased.

The bass tones have to be increased.
Therefore,

_____.

10. If the reduction in railroad passenger service is not halted, there will be a rise in the level of airplane passenger service.
There is a rise in the level of airplane passenger service.
Therefore,

_____.

11. If this poem is in the style of Shakespeare's writings, then it was written by Shakespeare.
This poem was written by Shakespeare.
Therefore,

_____.

12. If Eskimos do not use snowmobiles, then the breed of Husky dogs will not die out.
The breed of Husky dogs has not died out.
Therefore,

_____.

13. If the heart pumps faster, then blood pressure will be raised.
The blood pressure is raised.
Therefore,

_____.

14. If Social Security benefits are increased, then older people will be better off.
Older people are better off.
Therefore,

_____.

15. If the annual temperature of large cities is increasing, then the Earth must be getting closer to the Sun.
The Earth is getting closer to the Sun.
Therefore,

_____.

16. If the child gets everything he wants, then he will become a spoiled brat.
The child has become a spoiled brat.
Therefore,

_____.

17. If Mr. Jones does not get a job promotion, then Mrs. Jones will be a discontented wife.
Mrs. Jones is a discontented wife.
Therefore,

_____.

18. If Mr. Roberts buys his wife a fur coat, then she will become a better housewife.
Mrs. Roberts has become a better housewife.
Therefore,

_____.

19. If Peter's mother comes to live with them, then his wife will insist on leaving him and the children.
Peter's wife insists on leaving him and the children.
Therefore,

_____.

20. If these two young people are of the same religion, then they will have a successful and happy marriage.
They have a successful and happy marriage.
Therefore,

_____.

The Consequent Posttest

1. If Ralph does poorly in his studies, then he will have feelings of intellectual inadequacy.
   Ralph does not have feelings of intellectual inadequacy.
   Therefore,
   _____.

2. If Carl is aggressive, then he will be successful in business.
   Carl is successful in business.
   Therefore,
   _____.

3. If Lucy is pleasant in her interpersonal relations, then she will be liked by everyone.
   Lucy is not liked by everyone.
   Therefore,
   _____.

4. If Kathleen does not compete with anyone, then she will have only friends.
   Kathleen has only friends.
   Therefore,
   _____.

5. If Jerry seeks both competitive success and dependent love, he will be quite unhappy.
   Jerry is quite unhappy.
   Therefore,
   _____.

6. If Betty chooses an engineering career because of her excellent mathematical ability and scientific interest, then she is likely to be less personally attractive to men.
   Betty is less personally attractive to men.
   Therefore,
   _____.

7. If the light level in the room should increase, the camera shutter speed will be reduced.
   The camera shutter speed has been reduced.
   Therefore,
   _____.

8. If the annual rainfall this year stays below 20 inches, it will be good for the trees.
   The annual rainfall this year has been good for the trees.
   Therefore,
   _____.

9. If this retail hardware storeowner is charged more by the wholesaler, then he will have to raise his prices.
   This retail hardware storeowner has had to raise his prices.
   Therefore,
   _____.

10. If solar storms occur this year, radio communication will become poorer.
    Radio communication has become poorer.
    Therefore,
    _____.

11. If they quarrel at breakfast, then Mr. Robinson will be inefficient all day at work.
    Mr. Robinson is inefficient all day at work.
    Therefore,
    _____.

12. If this man hides his epileptic condition, then he will secure a job.
    He has secured a job.
    Therefore, _____.

13. If he agrees with her, then he has no mind of his own.
    He has no mind of his own.
    Therefore, _____.

14. If the war continues, then inflation will increase.
    Inflation has increased.
    Therefore, _____.

15. If information is unavailable, then people will not stop smoking.
    People have not stopped smoking.
    Therefore, _____.

16. If it is snowing outside, then it probably is not July.
    It is not July.
    Therefore, _____.

17. If this mouse has brown eyes, then its grandmother probably had brown eyes.
    This mouse's grandmother probably had brown eyes.
    Therefore, _____.

18. If this piece of Peruvian pottery is similar to Polynesian pottery, then ancient Polynesians probably settled Peru.
    Ancient Polynesians probably settled Peru.
    Therefore, _____.

19. If Mr. Thomas does not reduce the cholesterol level of his diet, then he will have a heart attack.
    Mr. Thomas had a heart attack.
    Therefore, _____.

20. If Mr. Rodney does not reduce his business activity, he will develop a duodenal ulcer.
    Mr. Rodney developed a duodenal ulcer.
    Therefore, _____.

IV

RESEARCH WITH
THE DILEMMA,
THE COUNSELOR,
AND THE COMPUTER

8

SYSTEMATIC DILEMMA COUNSELING: THEORY, METHOD, RESEARCH

SUMMARY

Dilemma counseling—with its theoretical base in cognitive structure research and with systematic method of dilemma formulation, extrication route, creative inquiry, and solution generation—is intended for ubiquitous and highly troubling avoidance–avoidance conflict cases (psychological dilemmas). In an exploratory experiment, 120 undergraduate students with highly troubling psychological dilemmas were randomized among three conditions: dilemma counseling, eclectic counseling, and control. Individual counseling occurred in a single intensive two-hour session. Dependent measures of quality of solution were taken at termination of counseling and measures of outcome a week later. Dilemma counseling, compared with eclectic counseling, produced significantly greater reduction in problem troublesomeness, and each treatment produced significantly more improvement than did the control condition. Dilemma counseling achieved significantly better solutions and more solutions than did eclectic counseling. There was significant rank concordance of quality of solution between clients and independent professional psychologists. Number of solutions was positively correlated with extraversion in eclectic counseling but negatively correlated with extraversion in dilemma counseling. Correlation coefficients differed significantly. Dilemma counseling was compared with other cognitive counseling approaches, and research in dilemma counseling was discussed.

AUTHOR'S NOTE: The author wishes to express his gratitude to Augustine Baron, Kenneth W. Kerber, and Thomas H. Leahey for their assistance in various aspects of the research. The research project was supported by a grant from the University of Illinois Research Board.

Ever since Hebb (1949) described the growing emphasis on cognitive orientation as the second revolution in general psychology, there has been a rapid acceleration of interest in many subareas of psychology, including personality and clinical psychology. Thus, Mischel (1973, 1977) presents a cognitive reconceptualization of the social learning approach to personality, and Mahoney (1977) describes a revolution in clinical and counseling psychology that gives primacy to cognitive processes, especially logic and reasoning. Lazarus (1977) a creative leader in the development of behavior therapy, recommends a fundamental replacement of animal-based conditioning models with cognitive and information-processing models.

At the level of technique, the new emphasis in counseling and therapy is on cognition, logic, and problem solving (D'Zurilla and Goldfried 1971; Mahoney 1974; Beck 1970; Ellis 1962; Meichenbaum 1977; Raimy 1975).

Cognitive misinterpretations illustrative of the paradigm "I think, therefore I feel" are given by Lazarus (1971), Ellis (1962), and Beck (1976). Beck (1976) discusses several categories of cognitive misinterpretations. "Arbitrary inference" involves the drawing of a conclusion although the evidence is lacking, insufficient, or even contrary to the conclusion. An example is the fixed interpretation of an unanswered letter as having the exclusive meaning of personal rejection. In "overgeneralization," a single event spreads to become a fixed rule, for example, failure in one intimate relationship inevitably means total interpersonal incompetence. "Magnification" is the tendency to overexaggerate the meaning of a particular event in the over-all life of a person.

Lazarus (1971) points out the common cognitive distortions involved in "dichotomous reasoning" and "oversocialization." In "dichotomous reasoning" the individual evaluates an event in binary fashion (good–bad) rather than recognizing degrees or mixes of evaluations of personal experience and meaning. In "oversocialization," there is a failure to analyze at a mature level early acquired prescriptive and proscriptive belief systems. The category "oversocialization" is also pointed out as a prevalent cognitive dysfunction, along with several other categories of illogical thought by Ellis (1962).

In the present chapter, a systematic approach is taken toward the many modes of cognitive misinterpretation or distortion involved in the psychology of the dilemma. Attention will be given to the logical and psychological conditions of persons whose thought patterns and consequent feelings about themselves and others have become rigid and dysphoric. Systematic dilemma counseling is both a conceptual system that organizes the many categories of cognitive misinterpretations discussed above, as well as others, within the framework of dilemmatic thinking or psychological conflict and a counseling system that organizes modes of modifying faulty thought patterns and methods for generating solutions to psychological dilemmas.

This chapter has four general purposes. First, a systematic description is given of the theory of dilemma counseling. The theoretical account covers the cognitive processes concerned with the dilemma as a psychological problem. Second, the innovative methods of dilemma counseling are presented. Dilemma counseling methods are described and exemplified, and a representative list of types of psychological dilemmas are presented. Third, an exploratory investigation of the efficacy of dilemma counseling is reported. Finally, implications of the theory, method, and efficacy of dilemma counseling are discussed, and suggestions for further research and clinical application are offered.

DILEMMA COUNSELING THEORY

The work of Wason and Johnson-Laird (Johnson-Laird and Wason 1971; Wason 1964, 1968; Wason and Johnson-Laird 1972) has clearly demonstrated that people have difficulty in reasoning correctly with implication, a key operator in the Piagetian formal level (Inhelder and Piaget 1958). In their research, Wason and Johnson-Laird (1972) demonstrated that subjects evaluate an implication "if p, then r" to be meaningless when p is false, true when p and r are true, and false when both p and r are false, rather than false only when p is true and r is false. Thus, subjects frequently commit the fallacy of affirmation of the consequent: if p, then r; r, therefore p. Also, the valid argument *modus tollens* (if p, then r; not r, therefore, not p) is frequently rejected by subjects. Yet, implication is a proven reasoning tool of considerable scope and power. Therefore, it would be valuable to develop methods for teaching its correct use. The correct utilization of implication can be of value in evaluating persuasive arguments, in scientific reasoning, and, as will be shown, in working through complex personal problems.

Leahey and Wagman (1974) developed a set of informational feedback procedures that produced the following benefits in subjects' ability to reason with implication: (1) correctly distinguishing between implication and the biconditional (if p, then r and if r, then p); (2) correctly rejecting the fallacy of affirmation of the consequent (if p, then r; r, therefore p) and denial of the antecedent (if p, then r; not p, therefore not r); and (3) correctly employing the valid inferential forms of *modus tollens* (if p, then r; not r, therefore not p) and *modus ponens* (if p, then r; p, therefore r).

Wagman (1978) compared the efficacy of self-contradiction versus didactic correction (teaching machine analogy) as methods for the modification of fallacious personal and scientific reasoning with implication problems. While both methods were superior to those of a control group that received no specific experimental instruction or manipulation, the didactic correction method, which depended on direct cognitive feedback, was superior to the self-contradiction procedure, which relied on subjects' weak ability to recognize that they were reasoning inconsistently and thus to correct self-contradictory deductions. Thus, this research finding, like that of Leahey and Wagman (1974), demonstrates (1) that unaided subjects had great difficulty in reasoning with implication whether the content was personal reasoning or scientific reasoning and (2) that cognitive feedback procedures effectively improved competence in reasoning.

A dilemma is composed (Terrell 1967) of two implications: if p, then r; and if q, then s, together with the exclusive disjunction, either p or q. As discussed above, an implication is false only when p is true and r is false. Therefore, it is necessary to negate the consequents r and s either as forms of action or with respect to their quality. This generates the first four of five dilemma extrication routes as presented in Table 8.1. The fifth extrication route leads out from negation of the exclusive disjunction (see row 5 of Table 8.1). At a more abstract level, therefore, all five extrication routes for dilemmas depend on the formal operation of negation, one of the four main logical operators in Piaget's (1970: 703-32) group of involuted logical operations (identity, negation, reciprocity, correlative).

An individual in a personal dilemma experiences the problem as inescapable and himself bound helpless between the horns of the dilemma. This is especially likely to happen when persons are in an anxious or depressed mood with associated obsessive thought (Lazarus 1966). At these times, the necessity of their plight seems absolutely inescapable.

Unpleasant dilemmas usually have the quality of necessity or "mustness." The person feels driven, blocked, and helpless between, if not on, the horns of the dilemma. He feels trapped between what he believes are necessary evils. The emotional state of conflict, puzzlement, and tension is further intensified and complicated by the difficulty of reasoning competently with dilemmas, as discussed above. Counselors and psychotherapists see many clients who are involved in personal life-choice problems, problems that, in the phraseology of topological theroy, can be considered avoidance–avoidance problems. For the avoidance–avoidance type, the problems in general read as follows: If I make a decision for action p, then unhappy consequence r will occur; and if I make a decision for action q, then unhappy consequence s will occur. But, I must do either p or q, and so one of these unhappy consequences, r or s, must occur.

DILEMMA COUNSELING METHOD

Dilemma Example

Dilemmas are very common and take many forms. Of the dilemmas treated in the research project to be described, some were simple and focused and others were intricate and complex. Some concerned personally significant

Table 8.1 Generalized Dilemma Formulation and Dilemma Matrix.

If I do action p, then unhappy consequence r will occur. And if I do action q, then unhappy consequence s will occur. But I must do action p or action q, and therefore unhappy consequence r or s will occur.

Dilemma Components	Route of Extrication	Creative Inquiry
1. If I do action p, then unhappy consequence r will occur.	Doing action p won't necessarily lead to unhappy consequence r.	How is it that doing action p won't necessarily lead to unhappy consequence r?
2. r is bad (aversive).	r isn't necessarily bad (aversive).	How is it that r isn't necessarily bad (aversive)?
3. If I do action q, then unhappy consequence s will occur.	Doing action q won't necessarily lead to unhappy consequence s.	How is it that doing action q won't necessarily lead to unhappy consequence s?
4. s is bad (aversive).	s isn't necessarily bad (aversive).	How is it that s isn't necessarily bad (aversive)?
5. I must do either action p or action q.	There are other alternatives besides action p or action q.	What other alternatives are there besides action p or q?

but limited cognitive life-choice problems while others showed general existential concerns. The following example written by a research subject is an existential dilemma. Just as the example illustrates one variety of dilemma, so the dilemma counseling techniques used for this example do not illustrate all procedures available in systematic dilemma counseling (Wagman 1978).

"I have trouble believing in anything really lasting as far as other people are involved. I can believe in myself but it's hard to believe in others. Every time a relationship get serious, I'm in constant fear of being possessed by someone and I end up breaking it off. It is probably because of the relationships I've had in the past where I really have gotten involved and been disappointed, but anymore I really don't want to get involved and it is surprising me. Everybody at home keeps telling me to meet some new girl and settle down (typical?) but I keep seeing myself as unhappy as my friends who have. I'm only 21 and I'm not ready to settle down yet, but still their constant urgings don't tend to make life peaceful around home—so as a result, I don't go home much anymore even though I'd like to be friends with my parents."

Dilemma counseling method covers a number of specific techniques. Before describing these specific techniques, several general characteristics of the method are briefly presented.

Overview of the Dilemma Counseling Method

Application of the dilemma counseling method to a psychological case problem requires the careful formulation of the case as a psychological dilemma and the resolution of the dilemma through the dilemma matrix method (Table 8.1).

In addition to the difficulty in reasoning with implications, the logical structure of the avoidance–avoidance problem seems to impose the inescapable necessity of enduring aversive consequences. The person feels trapped in the dilemma and helpless in the face of the negative outcomes. These difficulties are often intensified by the confused emotional state of the person who experiences the conflict.

Application of the dilemma counseling method to an avoidance–avoidance problem first involves the careful formulation of the problem as a psychological dilemma as shown in Table 8.1. The first column of the matrix presents five components of the dilemma formulation. These components represent a restatement of the basic assumptions of the problem. The second column of the matrix presents five extrication routes corresponding to the five dilemma components. The extrication routes force the client to negate the various assumptions of his problem. The third column of the matrix presents five creative inquiries. The creative inquiries challenge the client to develop alternatives (new perspectives, means–ends, correction of cognitive and existential misinterpretations, etc.) that are more realistic and more optimistic with respect to the consequences of the problem. These alternatives represent solutions to the original dilemma by eliminating the necessity of enduring aversive consequences.

Examination of the rows of the dilemma matrix will help to clarify the nature of the dilemma counseling method. The first dilemma component (row one of the matrix) states: If I do action p, then unhappy consequence r will occur. This component is merely a repetition of the first if–then statement in the dilemma formulation. The extrication route states: Doing action p will *not* necessarily lead to unhappy consequence r. Here the client is asked to reexamine what *appears* to be the inescapable relationship between action p and consequence r. The creative inquiry encourages the client to reexamine this relationship with the question: How is it that doing action p won't necessarily lead to unhappy consequence r? Arguments in response to this question extricate the client from the dilemma by removing the necessity of enduring the first aversive consequence. Row three of the matrix is identical to row one except that it deals with the second if–then statement in the dilemma formulation.

The second dilemma component (row two of the matrix) states: Unhappy consequence r is bad. This statement is an implicit assumption of an avoidance-avoidance dilemma. The extrication route states: Unhappy consequence r is not necessarily bad. Here the client is asked to examine features of consequence r that may not have been considered previously. The creative inquiry encourages this process with the question: How is it that unhappy consequence r is not necessarily bad? Arguments in response to this question extricate the client from the dilemma by accentuating the more favorable features of consequence r. Row four of the matrix is identical to row two except that it deals with the second consequence in the dilemma formulation.

The fifth dilemma component (row five of the matrix) states: I must do either action p or action q. Again, this statement is an implicit assumption of the dilemma. The extrication route states: There are other alternatives besides action p or action q. Here the client is asked to consider if in fact he or she has only two courses of action. The creative inquiry asks the question: What other alternatives are there besides action p or action q? Arguments in response to this question extricate the client from the dilemma by suggesting nonaversive measures to replace the original aversive actions. Therefore, each row of the dilemma matrix offers possible solutions to the client's problem by emphasizing the inappropriateness of the basic assumptions of the dilemma.

It should be made clear that while the presentation of the dilemma counseling method has been made via logical symbols (p, q, r, s), correct formulation of the dilemma and of the dilemma matrix requires that the specific case content be used in place of the logical symbols. In this way, both the counselor and the client have the advantage of the powerful logical structure of the dilemma method while simultaneously working on the case problem in its own unique and confronting terms.

Once the psychological case has been formulated as a dilemma, the structural procedures of (1) the dilemma differentiation into five dilemma components, (2) application of the standard extrication route for each component, and (3) generation of the appropriate creative inquiry can be used on any dilemma.

The dilemma counseling method, due to its logical structure, provides a complete set of perspectives. General counseling procedures may get caught up or bogged down in only one or two of the five possible perspectives as well as fail to take full account of their combinations and interactions. By reducing rigidity in thinking and in expectations, the extrication routes provide a hopeful set of cognitive operations. The creative inquiry, in socratic or other style, in a dialogue with the content of the extrication route, acts as a catalyst in the generation of specific and uniquely appropriate solutions. This set will contain at least five solutions (at least one for each of the creative inquiries) and the counselor and client may compare their ranked quality of solutions, terminating with the generation of the optimal solution. Both counselor and client should then feel that they have rigorously and creatively worked through the client's confronting psychological dilemma.

Dilemma counseling techniques can be grouped into five sequenced and interrelated processes. These processes may be listed as: (1) formulating the original problem as a psychological dilemma, (2) formulating the extrication route for each component, (3) formulating the creative inquiry for each extrication route, (4) generating solutions for each creative inquiry, and (5) ranking and evaluating solutions.

Formulating the Original Case as a Psychological Dilemma

It is a rare client who brings a perfectly articulated psychological dilemma to a dilemma counselor. Typically, the presenting problem is somewhat jumbled, and salient themes with antecedent and consequent conditions certainly need to be delineated by the counselor. The formulation of the case into a psychological dilemma is crucial since the sequence steps of extrication route, creative inquiry, and solution generation depend on the correct formulation of the five dilemma components. The dilemma counselor should set forth the dilemma and dilemma components clearly to the client asking, in effect, "Does this pretty well represent your situation?" A negative answer by the client or a half-hearted assent should stimulate the dilemma counselor to involve the client in a better formulation. The dilemma formulation resulting from such a counselor–client interaction is illustrated in Table 8.2 for the research subject whose existential dilemma was given above. The components of this dilemma are presented in the first column of Table 8.2. In

Table 8.2 Dilemma Formulation and Matrix for Case Example.

If I get involved, I get disappointed. If I don't get involved, I have to face my parents' constant urgings to settle down. But I must get involved or not get involved, and, therefore, I will either get disappointed or have to face my parents' constant urgings to settle down.

Dilemma	Extrication Route	Creative Inquiry
1. If I get involved, I get disappointed.	Getting involved will not necessarily lead to getting disappointed.	How can it be that getting involved will not necessarily lead to getting disappointed?
2. Getting disappointed is bad.	Getting disappointed is not necessarily bad.	How can it be that getting disappointed is not necessarily bad?
3. If I don't get involved, I have to face my parents' constant urgings to settle down.	Not getting involved will not necessarily lead to having to face my parents' constant urgings to settle down.	How can it be that not getting involved will not necessarily lead to having to face my parents' constant urgings to settle down?
4. Having to face my parents' constant urgings to settle down is bad.	Having to face my parents' constant urgings to settle down is not necessarily bad.	How can it be that having to face my parents' constant urgings to settle down is not necessarily bad?
5. But I must either get involved or not get involved.	I am not restricted to getting involved or not getting involved.	How can it be that I am not restricted to getting involved or not getting involved?

145

general, we have found the following list of criteria to be quite useful for good formulation.

First, does the formulated dilemma sharply focus on the central conflict of the psychological case problem? Second, does the formulation clearly contain two choices (p, q)? Third, does the formulation clearly contain two resulting aversive consequences (r, s)? Fourth, are the choices (p, q) and the consequences (r, s) correctly ordered (if p then r and if q then s)? Fifth, are the two choices in correct format (but either p or q)? Sixth, are the two aversive consequences in correct conclusion format (therefore either r or s)?

Formulating the Extrication Route for Each Dilemma Component

As indicated above, components of dilemma and the dilemma as a whole seem to exert an inescapable binding force on the client. To free the client, the counselor uses a standard extrication procedure. From the perspective of the logic of implication, the logical operator of negation is applied to the implicates and their quality. The result of applying this extrication procedure to each dilemma component of the dilemma example is presented in the second column of Table 8.2. As explained earlier, the process would involve completing (dilemma component — extrication route — creative inquiry — solutions) the first row of the dilemma matrix, followed by completion of each of the other four rows in turn. The effect of the extrication procedure is to ameliorate the client's feeling of being trapped between aversive consequences. As one client put it, "*Not necessarily* is a great booster." The client begins to feel a little more optimistic but quickly begins to wonder "how this could be."

We have found it useful for the counselor to stimulate and involve the client by asking him, after presenting the extrication route, "What do you think of that?" or "do you agree or disagree?"

Formulating the Creative Inquiry for Each Extrication Route

The extrication route was designed to break a rigid psychological set. The creativity inquiry is designed to expand psychological possibilities along the opened route of extrication. The counselor helps to phrase the creative inquiry (Table 8.2) but the client is strongly encouraged to be an active participant in the consideration of creative possibilities. We have found that this active involvement by the client redirects his attention and thinking around his personal impasse and brings about an accompanying reduction in his feelings of futility. The result of the creative inquiry process for the dilemma example is shown in the third column of Table 8.2. The creative inquiry has been directed to the extrication route for each row of the dilemma matrix, in turn.

Generating Solutions to Each Creative Inquiry

The client and counselor work together in the generation of solutions. The counselor keeps in mind the advantage of having the client learn a general method of solving his future dilemmas as well as resolving his current psychological problem. Therefore, we have found it helpful to have the client fill in a dilemma matrix like that of Table 8.2 for his own problem and to write down solutions generated for each creative inquiry. This writing procedure keeps the client actively involved with the counselor and provides a handy study guide for the client's future use.

While the process of generating solutions for creative inquiry is always something of a free art, we have found certain principles and specific tactics especially useful. Where should the counselor and client start in hunting for helpful ideas? Thanks to the previous formulation of dilemmas, extrication route, and creative inquiry, the principal parts of the problem have been distinctly arranged and fully conceived (Table 8.2). Next, the counselor and client should (1) consider the problem from various sides, (2) emphasize different parts, (3) examine varying details, (4) examine the same details reiteratively but in different ways, (5) combine the different details differently, (6) look for a new meaning in the details and in their combinations, for example, pointing out specific cognitive misinterpretations, (7) strive to discover some new meaning of the whole dilemma, for example, pointing out general cognitive or existential misinterpretations, (8) try to think of what helped in similar situations in the past, (9) try to recognize something familiar in the case problem, and (10) try to make use of these recognized familiarities. These activities of counselor and client may result in immediate good solutions, but even hazy and incomplete ideas may make their conception of the problem more complete and more coherent, more integrated or better balanced. Some of these incomplete or nearly complete ideas might be considered, and if they appear valid, then the situation should be reconsidered in light of this more reliable and penetrating idea. With this new idea, the situation will have changed, and the counselor and client should consider this new situation from various sides. The soundest of these solutions should then be written down for each row of the dilemma matrix (Table 8.3) in turn. Proposed solutions to the creative inquiries for the dilemma example matrix (Table 8.2) are given in Table 8.3.

After solutions are written down for each of the creative inquiries, there remains the important task of rank ordering them with respect to quality. It is our experience that decisions about quality of solution should be left to the client. The counselor has made his input throughout the process of formulation, extrication route, creative inquiry, and generation of solution. It is now up to the client to consider the solutions against the standard of his own

Table 8.3 Proposed Solutions for Dilemma Case Example.

Solutions

1. (a) Past difficulties do not have to be repeated in the future. Just because I have had some disappointing relationships in the past does not mean that I am doomed to forever. Sooner or later the right woman will come along.
   (b) Often solutions work themselves out in the doing. Knowing the kinds of personality traits of a woman that will disappoint me, I can be alerted to break off before becoming too involved.
2. (a) Badness is a relative term. Getting disappointed by a woman is not the worst thing in the world that can happen to someone. I can think of a lot worse things.
   (b) We learn from our mistakes. Maybe I can figure out what I do that might encourage certain women to be possessive.
   (c) Difficulties can serve to motivate us to change our behavior. I might profit from my disappointments and try out other ways of relating to women that might prove more satisfactory.
   (d) You are not alone in feeling the way you do. Most people in the course of their development have disappointments in intimate relations. It is not at all unusual to have such experiences.
3. (a) Good communication can often solve problems. Maybe if I sat down and had a long talk with my parents I would convince them that there's nothing so great about settling down for a person my age.
   (b) Feelings can change over time. Maybe my parents will come to feel differently about any urgency in my settling down. I might come to feel that they are less pressuring me than concerned about my happiness.
4. (a) You are not alone in feeling the way you do. All parents seem to have their little pet gripes to their kids. So my parents have theirs, too.
   (b) Increasing independence from parents is an important part of growing up. Maybe I can handle their gripes without getting too upset and still not give in to their nagging about settling down, and maybe then I could go home more often to see them.
5. (a) Given two unfavorable alternatives, one doesn't necessarily have to do either. I could just go out in order to have fun and not worry about either becoming involved or not involved.
   (b) Decisions about relationships do not have to be made immediately—trial periods are possible. I could go out with a woman for a while and postpone any decisions to a later time.

idiosyncratic personal life values. The client's determination of solution quality also extends to evaluating how satisfactory or how adequate the best of these solutions is for solving his problem. Finally, it may be noted that the question of the client's ability to discern good- from poor-quality solutions is discussed in a research context below.

Types of Psychological Dilemmas Treated

Dilemma counseling has been applied to the type of problem usually brought to a university counseling center or clinic. Such problems typically represent current adaptational concern at a moderate level of intensity, requiring a brief course of counseling or psychotherapy. Thus, the dilemma counseling method is directed toward most moderately serious counseling problems rather than toward the small fraction of cases requiring intensive and extensive treatment approaches.

EXPLORATORY RESEARCH: METHOD

Participants

An initial group of 200 undergraduate participants completed the Maudsley Personality Inventory and then read a set of eight "typical" life-choice dilemmas selected from psychological problems written by other introductory psychology students in a previous pilot project. Next, participants were asked to write down four of their own personal problems.

For each of their problems, participants were asked to rate on an eight-point scale how troublesome the particular problem was for him, with ratings ranging from not at all troublesome (1) to extremely troublesome, interfering with my life (8).

Two graduate research assistants read through each participant's personal problems after the initial group session and selected those participants with at least one problem that fit a dilemma (avoidance–avoidance) formulation. Priority was given to problems whose rating of troublesomeness was in the six to eight range (up to extremely troublesome, interfering with my life). The interrater reliability was high ($r = .85$), with the selected problems resembling quite closely those seen by clinical psychologists in a university counseling center. Types of psychological problems included interpersonal, personal, vocational, marital, and educational cases.

Procedure

Once participants with suitable problems had been selected, they were randomly assigned to one of three experimental conditions: individual dilemma counseling, individual eclectic counseling, or control, with 40 participants in each condition. Participants in the control condition were seen only for the purpose of taking dependent measures at the time of the follow-up session.

Participants in the individual dilemma counseling condition and in the individual eclectic counseling condition were treated in a single intensive two-hour session. One week later, dependent measures were collected in a follow-up session. The measures were collected by a graduate research assistant both for the participants who had been treated the previous week and for an equal number of control participants. During the same week, the described staggered procedure was begun again and with new participants in the individual dilemma counseling condition and in the individual eclectic counseling condition with their follow-up scheduled for the succeeding week. Elapsed time between initially writing down their problems and the taking of dependent measures was thus matched for participants in the treatment and no-contact control conditions.

Participants in individual dilemma counseling were treated by an intern in advanced clinical psychology who used the method described above. Participants in individual eclectic counseling were treated by another similar intern who used whatever procedures seemed appropriate for the particular case. Techniques included reflection of the client's feelings of frustration about being in the dilemma, relaxation, reassurance, and persuasion procedures, and provision of relevant suggestions and information. At the conclusion of the single two-hour treatment session, each participant wrote down his solutions to his psychological problem, ranked them according to quality, and, for the cardinal solution, rated its degree of adequacy for solving his problem on an eight-point scale from not at all adequate for solving my problem (1) to completely adequate for solving my problem (8).

Psychologists' Ranking of Quality of Solution

Four professional psychologists who had no knowledge of the purpose of the research rank-ordered each participant's set of solutions with respect to quality. Each psychologist was given a booklet that contained for each code-numbered participant a typed copy of the participant's case, a typed copy of the participant's solutions with the order of solution randomized, and a form for entering their rankings of participant's solutions. The booklet contained the described materials for all participants in each of the two treatment conditions. The order of arrangement of participants' materials within the booklet was completely randomized.

Personality Factors

To explore possible interactions between general personality factors and counseling effects, the factor-analytic Maudsley Personality Inventory (Eysenck 1963) was administered to all participants at the beginning of the experiment. The Maudsley Personality Inventory contains two orthogonal personality factor scales, neuroticism-stability and extraversion-introversion.

Statistical Procedures

The major statistical procedures included ANOVA and ANCOVA to determine treatment effects and correlation methods to study psychologists' rankings of quality of solutions and to estimate relationships between treatment effects and the personality factors of neuroticism and extraversion. Analyses were performed at the University of Illinois digital computer laboratory on an IBM 360/75 computer.

RESULTS

Number of Solutions Generated

Dilemma counseling participants generated significantly more solutions to their psychological dilemmas than did eclectic counseling participants ($F = 5.23$, $p < .02$). Mean solutions were 6.23 ($SD = 1.19$) for dilemma counseling and 2.54 solutions ($SD = 0.56$) for eclectic counseling.

Adequacy of Best Solution

Dilemma counseling participants rated their best solutions as significantly more adequate than did eclectic counseling students ($F = 5.71$, $p < .02$). Mean ratings of adequacy were 6.89 ($SD = 1.26$) for dilemma counseling and 4.12 ($SD = 0.78$) for eclectic counseling on an eight-point rating scale; $8.00 =$ solution is completely adequate, $1.00 =$ solution is completely inadequate.

Quality of Solution as Ranked by Psychologists

Table 8.4 presents mean correlations between rankings of quality of solution by subjects and professional psychologists. As noted, the intercorrelation among psychologists is significant ($r = .43$, $W = .55$, $p < .001$) as is the intercorrelation between the subjects and psychologists ($r = .45$, $W = .57$, $p < .001$).

Reduction in Troublesomeness of Problems

An ANCOVA for the dilemma counseling, eclectic counseling, and control conditions was done on the rating of troublesomeness of problems, using the rating at the time of follow-up as the dependent measure and that at the time of writing down the problem initially as the covariable. For this analysis ($F = 5.96$, $p < .01$), adjusted means were 2.83 for dilemma counseling, 3.92 for eclectic counseling, and 4.98 for controls. Scheffé pairwise contrasts in-

Table 8.4 Intercorrelations of Solution Quality Rankings by Psychologists and Subjects: Average r (Weighted Mean r).

Variable	Psychologist A	Psychologist B	Psychologist C	Psychologist D
Subject	.50	.41	.37	.39
Psychologist A		.39	.56	.62
Psychologist B			.23	.31
Psychologist C				.50

Note: Average intercorrelation among the psychologists = .43, W = .55, p < .001. Average intercorrelation among the psychologists and subjects = .45, W = .57, p < .001.

dicated significantly (p < .05) more reduction in troublesomeness with the dilemma counseling than with the eclectic counseling and significantly (p < .01) more reduction in problem troublesomeness in the eclectic counseling condition than in the control condition.

Personality Measures

Scores on the Maudsley Personality Inventory (neuroticism, extraversion, and their interactions) were intercorrelated among themselves and with the number of solutions, subjects' rating of their best solutions, and the average psychologists' rankings of the subjects' best solutions. This was done for each experimental group separately and for all combined.

There was no general effect across all groups. However, extraverted subjects tended to produce more solutions in the eclectic counseling condition, but fewer in the dilemma counseling condition (eclectic counseling: r = .61, n = 34, p < .01; dilemma counseling: r = − .29, n = 36, p < .10). There was a significant difference between the two correlation coefficients (z = 4.03, p < .01).

DISCUSSION

Effects of Systematic Dilemma Counseling

The findings of this exploratory experiment are supportive of the dilemma counseling method. Participants who were treated this way reduced the troublesomeness of their psychological dilemmas significantly more than did no-contact control participants. Such a gain over spontaneous recovery is important. In addition, the results indicate that participants in dilemma counseling, as compared with those in eclectic counseling (1) generated significantly more solutions, (2) evaluated their best solutions as significantly more adequate, and (3) applied their best solutions to their problem, producing significantly greater reduction in troublesomeness. This provides further evidence on efficacy of systematic dilemma counseling.

Personality Variables and Systematic Dilemma Counseling

Findings indicate complex relationships between personality variables and systematic dilemma counseling. The neuroticism–stability factor was unrelated to any counseling effects. However, the extraversion–introversion factor did appear to be related. Introverted subjects tended to produce more solutions in the systematic dilemma counseling condition than in the eclectic counseling condition.

As described in the manual (Eysenck 1963), introverted personalities tend to be thoughtful and organized. Perhaps, then, there was a match between subject's personality and counseling method. Extraverted subjects, described by the manual as expressive and relationship-seeking, tended to produce more solutions in the eclectic counseling condition. These interactions of personality factor–counseling method are given some further support by a psychotherapy-personality study (DiLoreto 1971) in which introverts benefited most from rational therapy and extraverts benefited most from client-centered therapy. A specific method (systematic dilemma counseling) for a particular personality type (introverted personality) having specific psychological problems (dilemma type problem) is consistent with current research in counseling and psychotherapy (Mahoney 1977) that stresses a match of procedures, persons, and problems.

Competence in Judging Solutions to Dilemmas

It has been indicated earlier that the dilemma counselor and the participant actively shared in working through the stages of the systematic dilemma problem-solving method (formulation of dilemma, extrication route, creative inquiry, and generation of solution) and that the participant, after writing down all solutions for all five dilemma components, was independently responsible for comparing the quality of the solutions within the generated set. To determine how well the participant carried out such an evaluative task, given his own involvement in his problem, four clinical psychologists independently rank-ordered the participants' set of solutions. Conventional wisdom believes that clinical psychologists, while not always in complete agreement with each other concerning solutions to clinical problems, do share a modicum of expert consensus. It was, therefore, interesting to find out that the intercorrelations among psychologists A, B, C, and D were all significantly different from zero and were all in the moderate range. The finding that subjects agree with the independent clinical psychologists concerning the relative quality of different solutions to their problems about as well as psychologists agree with each other strengthens confidence in the ability of unsophisticated subjects to discern poor from good solutions to their psychological dilemmas. Such discernment by clients is important, since 90% of the participants reported that they had, following the treatment session, applied their top-ranked solutions to their troubling psychological problems. Such competence in judging quality of solution will become significant when an autonomous self-help form of systematic dilemma counseling is developed.

Systematic Dilemma Counseling and General Problem Solving

These findings suggest that the dilemma counseling method can meet the requirements for general problem solving as well as the requirements for solving psychological dilemmas: (1) the discovery of a set of possible dilemma solutions and (2) evaluative selection of the optimal solutions.

D'Zurilla and Goldfried (1971), following their intensive review of problem-solving methods, described the general stages or elements in problem solving. The dilemma counseling system is a specialized set of techniques intended for dilemma-type problems but possessing the necessary characteristics of the general parameters described by D'Zurilla and Goldfried (1971): (1) the generation of a general problem-solving set or orientation (description of systematic dilemma counseling as given by dilemma counselor to client at beginning of session), (2) definition of the problem (use of checklist of dilemma formulation to epitomize the case problem as a psychological dilemma), (3) generation of alternative solutions (use of the dilemma matrix, extrication route, and creative inquiry to produce dilemma solutions), (4) tentative selection of a solution (ranking solutions within the generated set and rating the adequacy of the best solution), and (5) the testing of that solution (client tries out the most adequate dilemma solution and returns to the process if needed).

Cognitive Approach of Systematic Dilemma Counseling

Reasoning with personal dilemmas is perplexing since they involve dealing with implication, which often is handled fallaciously by many people as indicated earlier (Wagman 1978, Leahey and Wagman 1974, Wason and Johnson-Laird 1972). In addition, the logical structure of the dilemma itself seems to impose an inescapable necessity on a psychological problem. These two factors of difficulty in reasoning with implication and logical necessity require a specific and potent method of dilemmatic extrication. Such a method has been described in this article and schematically depicted in Table 8.1. The counseling method is a set of specific strategies designed for cases seen by a counselor or psychotherapist and assessed to be in the form of a confronting dilemma or can readily be put into such a form. There are other types of cases, for example, phobias, which may be met by other specific methods such as the behavior modification technique of desensitization. The dilemma method, and its theoretical background (Wagman 1978), is more nearly cognitive (Kelly 1955) and existential (Frankl 1963, May 1967) than behavioristic, insofar as general distinctions can be made (Mischel 1973).

Psychological dilemmas are prevalent in everyone's life. Their ubiquity is accompanied by diversity in personal circumstance and in personal meaning. However, as indicated in the theory and method sections of this article, diverse psychological dilemmas have a standard underlying logical structure, and dilemma counseling provides a set of powerful general procedures for working with any particular dilemma.

Future Research in Systematic Dilemma Counseling

Dollard and Miller (1950), in their learning-based psychotherapy, assert the central importance of dilemmas and conflicts in everyone's life (including those who have neurosis) but admit that the ways in which the higher processes of logical reasoning and thinking can be brought to bear on dilemma resolution have not been systematically explored by psychology, in the research laboratory, in the family and school environment, or in the psychotherapeutic relationship.

Future research in systematic dilemma counseling can usefully be focused in two general areas. First, the psychological dilemma as a logical cognitive structure (Piaget 1970; Miller, Galanter, and Pribram 1960; Simon 1957) needs further exploration in both a laboratory and a clinical setting. Second, the cognitive processes that facilitate (Osborn 1963, Mowrer 1960, D'Zurilla and Goldfried 1971) and block (Bloom and Broder 1950; Johnson, Parrott, and Stratton 1968) reasoning and problem solving with dilemmas should be studied. Variables such as cognitive complexity of the client (Harvey, Hunt, and Schroeder 1961), decisional conflict styles (Janis and Mann 1976), and type of dilemma should be interesting and useful research areas. Comparative efficacy research designs should help to delineate the most salient areas of clinical application for dilemma counseling.

Finally, systematic dilemma counseling is useful not only for solving a current problem but also may be taught by the counselor or possibly by a self-instructional module for the purpose of increasing the client's independence and competence in solving future dilemmas. Research on such possibilities of developing autonomous systematic problem-solving procedures would be in direct line with the increasing research activity in self-treatment or self-control (Goldfried and Merbaum 1973) methods.

9

PLATO DCS:
AN INTERACTIVE COMPUTER SYSTEM
FOR PERSONAL COUNSELING

SUMMARY

The concepts, rationale, potential, and methods of the self-paced inter-active PLATO® computer-based Dilemma Counseling System (PLATO DCS) are presented first.* Display figures demonstrate the interaction modes and sequences by which the computer counsels a client and teaches a generic method of personal problem solving applicable to the client's future psychological dilemmas. Next, a large-scale pre-postexploratory experimental test of PLATO DCS is described. Findings indicate that PLATO DCS counseling resulted in greater improvement in the clients than did a control condition. Solutions generated by PLATO DCS were generally of high quality. Neuroticism was positively correlated with greater problem improvement, remaining involved with the computer, and more favorable evaluation of PLATO DCS. Most subjects evaluated PLATO DCS as interesting and not too impersonal. Many subjects enjoyed the independence granted by solving personal problems on a computer. PLATO DCS is in use for research and service applications at numerous colleges and universities.

The age of the computer has come with such startling rapidity and has had such a widespread impact on society and on the individual that it is ap-propriately described as the electronics revolution (Abelson and Hammond 1977), comparable in significance to the industrial revolution. Increasingly, computers are valued as research and professional tools in medicine, the be-havioral sciences, and education.

---

*The PLATO system is a development of the University of Illinois. PLATO® is a service mark of Control Data Corporation.

Computers in Educational and Vocational Guidance

Computer applications in educational and vocational guidance have been explored by a number of investigators. Lowry (1966), in collaboration with System Development Corporation (Zagorski 1974), developed AUTO-COUN, a computer program that successfully modeled counselor behavior in assisting ninth-grade Palo Alto, California, students to select appropriate high school courses. Price (1974), using outcome criteria of grade point average and number of courses changed, found no difference between a computer-based system and a counselor-based system in junior high school educational guidance effectiveness.

A computer-based vocational guidance system (Melhus, Hershenson, and Vermillion 1973) was as effective in producing vocational choice outcomes as traditional counseling for high-readiness students but not for low-readiness students, for whom live counseling was more effective. The highly significant and interesting theme of differential and joint effects of computer and counselor in various career and educational guidance settings is examined by Super (1970) and Harris (1974) for high school and college students and by Farmer (1976) for adult clients.

Computers in Personal Interviewing and Counseling

Various attempts have been made to extend computer applications beyond guidance and testing to the more intimate realms of personal interviewing and counseling. Greist, Klein, and Erdman (1976) developed a computer program to interview suicidal patients. The computer interview produced a summary of the patient's clinical state and a prediction of whether the patient would make a suicide attempt. Findings indicated that suicidal patients preferred the computer interview to talking to a psychiatrist. It was also found that the computer was more accurate than experienced clinicians in predicting suicide attempts.

Two computer interview programs, ELIZA and DOCTOR, were developed by Weizenbaum (1965, 1976) as demonstrations of the client-centered technique of reflection of feeling. Colby, Watt, and Gilbert (1966) and others (e.g., Taylor 1970) have also developed brief demonstration projects of computer simulation of selected aspects of psychoanalytic interviewing. These projects, as well as that of Slack and Slack (1974), involved only simple demonstration possibilities rather than the development of a completely computer-based personal counseling system.

Several points should be made about the use of computers in guidance, testing, and personal interviewing or counseling. First, there does seem to be evidence that computers used in the broad range of situations from educational guidance to psychiatric interviewing are accepted by students, clients, and patients. Second, development and evaluation seem more advanced in testing and guidance than in counseling and psychotherapy. The attempts at computer applications in counseling and psychotherapy have met with a number of formidable problems. The difficulties will be discussed next, and an attempt to solve them will be briefly presented.

PROBLEMS IN THE DEVELOPMENT OF A COMPUTER AS A PERSONAL COUNSELOR

Previous Approaches

Part of the difficulty in accomplishing the goal of developing a computer as a personal counselor has been that research has proceeded much too directly without due attention to the problems of match between computer communication logic (Cotton 1982; Quintanar et al. 1982) and psychotherapy communications. Thus, Colby, Watt, and Gilbert (1966) found it very difficult to assimilate into the binary logic of computers the multilogic or nonlogic of free association in psychoanalytic communication. A second difficulty was that researchers began the difficult process of developing computer-based personal counseling with the most complex and sophisticated forms of psychotherapy rather than with the simplest forms. A third difficulty was that predominantly affective (Colby, Watt, and Gilbert 1966; Taylor 1970; Weizenbaum 1965) rather than predominantly cognitive types of counseling or psychotherapy were chosen. A fourth difficulty was that the computer technology of the 1960s was not sufficiently sophisticated with respect to speed, flexibility, memory, and individual interaction capability to be used effectively in personal counseling.

The Present Approach

In planning for the development of what ultimately came to be the PLATO DCS, a careful rationale was employed to approach and overcome these difficulties. A method of simple interactive cognitive counseling was invented in which communication logic was commensurate with the computer's logic. A sophisticated computer system and computer network were fortunately available at the University of Illinois Urbana-Champaign campus.

The PLATO DCS Computer System

The PLATO DCS computer system at the University of Illinois at Urbana-Champaign (Alpert and Bitzer 1970; Smith and Sherwood 1976) links over 1,200 graphical display terminals to a Control Data Corporation Cyber

73 computer. The terminals are located at various colleges, universities, government, and business organizations in the United States and Canada, Australia, and the United Kingdom (Holt 1983). Therefore, thousands of clients could potentially be served by a personal counseling procedure developed and made available over the PLATO DCS system.

PLATO DCS Display and Terminal

Each terminal is composed of a keyset that transmits the user's input to the central computer and of a display screen that shows computer-generated information. The keyset is composed of the standard typewriter characters plus special function keys by which the user controls the flow of PLATO DCS materials. The display screen shows letters, figures, drawings, graphs, and other information typed by the user or produced by the central computer. Writing speed on the display screen is 180 characters per second with a display capacity of 2,048 characters. Response time from user input to computer response is 0.2 second.

Dialogue with PLATO DCS

In their simplest form, materials presented on the PLATO DCS display screen consist of a repeating sequence, that is, a display on the user's screen followed by the user's response to that display. The user reacts to each display by pressing a single key to move to new material or by typing a word, sentence, or other expression. A user's response might also be a question or a command to PLATO DCS to respond with a particular type of display. Authors of PLATO DCS materials provide enough details about possible user responses so that PLATO DCS can maintain a dialogue with each user. Thus, the PLATO DCS system allows for individualized interaction sequences between the user and the computer.

SYSTEMATIC DILEMMA COUNSELING

Concepts of Dilemma Counseling

Unpleasant dilemmas usually have the quality of inevitability or necessity. The person feels driven, blocked, and helpless, between — if not on — the horns of the dilemma. The person feels trapped between what he or she believes are necessary evils. The emotional state of conflict, puzzlement, and tension of the person experiencing a personal dilemma is further intensified and complicated by the difficulty of reasoning competently with dilemmas (Leahey and Wagman 1974; Wagman 1978; Wason 1964).

Counselors and psychotherapists see many clients who are involved in personal-choice problems that can be considered avoidance–avoidance problems according to topological theory. In general, the problems read as follows:

> If I make a decision for action p, then unhappy consequence r will occur; and if I make a decision for action q, then unhappy consequence s will occur. But, I must do either p or q, and so one of these unhappy consequences, r or s, must occur.

Techniques of Dilemma Counseling

Application of the dilemma counseling method to a psychological case problem requires the careful formulation of the case as a psychological dilemma and the resolution of the dilemma through the dilemma matrix method.

Dilemma counseling techniques can be grouped into five sequenced and interrelated processes. These processes may be listed as (1) formulating the original case problems as a psychological dilemma, (2) formulating the extrication route for each dilemma component, (3) formulating the creative inquiry for each extrication route, (4) generating solutions for each creative inquiry, and (5) ranking and evaluating solutions.

Originally developed and shown to be effective (Wagman 1979) in a counselor-treated mode, dilemma counseling was modified in two successive experiments to a semiautonomous treatment mode (Wagman 1980b) and then to a fully autonomous form that was shown to be effective (Wagman 1981). The autonomous form of systematic dilemma counseling consisted of (1) a self-help booklet that provided examples, practice, and guidance in learning how to solve psychological dilemmas and (2) an accompanying set of cassette recordings that contained a running text of supportive counselor commentary. Following this experiment, it was felt that autonomous dilemma counseling could be greatly improved through the use of a personal interactive computer that would provide a more vivid and self-paced method for solving a current psychological dilemma and for learning how to solve future ones.

INTEGRATING SYSTEMATIC DILEMMA COUNSELING AND THE PLATO DCS SYSTEM

Rationale

Computer-based counseling is a frontier of scientific thought. Previous attempts to develop computerized client-centered counseling (Weizenbaum 1965) or computerized psychoanalytic counseling (Colby, Watt, and Gilbert 1966) have floundered because of the incommensurability of the precise logic of the computer and the free-flowing associations of counseling. Computer-based dilemma counseling has solved this problem by developing a highly structured set of strategies based on the logic of implication, which is also the logic of computers in their "if, then" operation sequencing.

The functions of a computer-based education system that provides a medium for presenting a method of self-help counseling can be explored by viewing PLATO DCS in three different roles: that of teacher, counselor, and researcher.

PLATO DCS as Teacher of the Dilemma Counseling Method

PLATO DCS allows for individualized teaching whereby students can work at their own pace, review material of their own choosing, and seek help when the necessity arises. Also, the judging capabilities of PLATO DCS allow for a continuous monitoring of student responses, with instantaneous feedback regarding appropriate or inappropriate student input.

PLATO DCS as Counselor for Psychological Dilemmas

In individualized counseling, each person can tailor the use of PLATO DCS materials to his or her own problems. Clients can work at their own pace and can seek help when needed. PLATO DCS can provide praise and encouragement contingent on specific responses, much as a human counselor might do. Also, PLATO DCS could potentially make suggestions regarding specific and generalized solutions to psychological problems via a wealth of material that could be stored in the memory of the computer.

PLATO DCS can be instructed to remember all or part of any interaction with an individual for reference at a later time by the individual or by a counselor. Finally, the accessibility of material on PLATO DCS would allow persons who are already familiar with PLATO DCS to return on later occasions to solve minor psychological problems and perhaps more serious ones, thereby relieving counselors and psychotherapists for work on more serious cases.

PLATO DCS as a Researcher in Dilemma Counseling

All types of PLATO DCS parameters—such as number of attempts to answer a particular question, number of requests for additional materials, amount of review, and time spent in a particular portion of PLATO DCS—can be stored simultaneously for many users and can be referenced on-line or via hard-copy printouts. Such PLATO DCS parameters can be utilized to improve materials in light of PLATO DCS effectiveness. It would also be possible to change the structure of PLATO DCS for research purposes to test the effectiveness of different methods of presenting the same material.

DESCRIPTION OF PLATO DCS

To convey an adequate description of the development and use of PLATO DCS, displays similar to the display prints of the system will be included in the textual discussion. The following is a display of the six main parts of PLATO DCS. As the student finishes reading each paragraph, he or she merely presses the NEXT key on the PLATO DCS keyset to move to sequential displays.

Dilemma Counseling System

This system has six major parts. The first part is a general introduction to the dilemma counseling method. The second and third parts give you practice in phrasing problems as dilemmas. The fourth and fifth parts give you practice in generating solutions to these dilemmas. The final part allows you to apply the dilemma counseling method to a problem of your own.

Select the appropriate number for the part of the Dilemma Counseling System that you wish to see.

1. Introduction
2. Dilemma Phrasing Example Problems
3. Dilemma Phrasing Practice Problems
4. Dilemma Matrix Example Problems
5. Dilemma Matrix Practice Problems
6. Your Own Problem

A final press of the NEXT key on this initial display erases the introductory material and presents a new display entitled Dilemma Phrasing Checklist. This checklist provides criteria for constructing the dilemma phrasing for various examples of practice and personal problems:

Dilemma Phrasing Checklist

1. Have you determined the central theme of the problem? That is, have you determined the two choices that must be made and the unhappy or aversive consequences for this problem?
2. Does the dilemma formulation contain two choices, that is, choice p and choice q?
3. Do the two choices result in two unhappy or aversive consequences?
4. Are the two choices and their consequences in the "if, then" and "either, or" phrasing?
5. Are any inferences that you have made about the choices or about the unhappy consequences that are present consistent with the problem as stated by the person?

For each of the dilemma phrasing example problems, the process is as follows: (1) The original wording of a problem is written on the screen, (2) a press of the NEXT key displays a poor dilemma phrasing comment below the poor dilemma phrasing, (3) a third NEXT instruction to the computer erases the poor dilemma phrasing and the instructional comment while retaining the original wording of the problem, and (4) a better dilemma formulation is displayed. The following is the initial display for dilemma phrasing Example Problem 1. Notice that the directive at the end of the display reminds the client that he or she can again see the dilemma phrasing checklist by simply pressing the HELP key on the PLATO DCS keyset.

Example 1

This is the way the person wrote the problem originally:
I just don't know what to do. I have to choose a major, and I can't decide whether to go into business or into some branch of science. There are some good and bad things about both fields. I can make more money being in business but there's nothing very intellectually rewarding about it. On the other hand, scientists do have intellectually rewarding jobs, but they don't make very much money. So what do I do?
A poor dilemma phrasing might be:
If I have a limited income, then I will be unhappy. And if I have limited intellectual satisfaction, then I'll also be unhappy. But either I have to have a limited income or limited intellectual satisfaction, and therefore I will be unhappy.
Comment:
While this is probably true as far as the subject is concerned, it doesn't take into account the choices that he is trying to make, that is, being a scientist or in business. Consequently, the trapped choice situation is not captured in the formulation above. The phrasing does not meet Criteria 1 and 2 in the Dilemma Phrasing Checklist.
Press HELP to see the Dilemma Phrasing Checklist.
The next display is also from dilemma phrasing Example Problem 1. In this display, the poor dilemma phrasing and the comment from the previous display have been replaced by a better phrasing formulation and by an appropriate comment. Reference to the dilemma phrasing checklist is still possible. Dilemma phrasing Example Problems 2 and 3 consist of displays that are similar to those for Example Problem 1.

Example 1

This is the way the person wrote the problem originally:
I just don't know what to do. I have to choose a major, and I can't decide whether to go into business or into some branch of science. There are some good and bad things about both fields. I can make more money being in business but there is nothing very intellectually rewarding about it. On the other

hand, scientists do have intellectually rewarding jobs, but they don't make very much money. So what do I do?

A better formulation would be:

If I become a scientist, then I will have a limited income, and if I go into business, then I will have limited intellectual satisfaction. But I must either become a scientist or go into business, and, therefore, I will either have a limited income or I will have limited intellectual satisfaction.

Comment:

Now we have the trapped choice situation with the person having a clear idea of what choices he or she sees and the unhappy consequences of each.

Press HELP to see the Dilemma Phrasing Checklist

Thus, a student practices the formation of the dilemma phrasing for each of three problems in the following manner. An arrow appears on the display screen for each dilemma part, one at a time and in sequence. For each arrow, the student types in the appropriate phrasing by referring to the original wording of the problem, which is also displayed on the screen. On completion of his or her response for each dilemma part, the student's phrasing is examined by the computer for the presence of a specific key word or of several key words. If the word(s) is(are) present, the student moves on to the next dilemma part; if not, the student is asked to retype his or her response to include the specified key word(s). As each dilemma part for a particular problem is completed, it remains on the screen for later reference. The following display from dilemma phrasing Practice Problem 1 demonstrates what happens if a client does *not* include the appropriate word for one of the dilemma parts.

Original Wording

I have a very domineering mother. She interferes with my life constantly. She says that since I am still at home, she can tell me to do anything and I have to obey. If I say that I don't want to, she threatens to stop paying for my education and kick me out of the house. She won't let me buy a motorcycle or car with my own money. She won't let me visit my girlfriend's parents, at their invitation. She even bosses my stepfather around. He may agree with me on some matters but will not cross my mother.

Dilemma Phrasing

If I obey my mother, *then* I will not be able to do what I want.

If I do not obey my mother, then she will stop paying for my education.

But *either* I obey my mother or do what I want.

Therefore *either*_____.

*or*_____.

Press NEXT and try this phrase again.

Use the keyword *obey* in your answer.

Press LAB to start over the dilemma phrasing for this problem.

Press NEXT to continue.

When the student has successfully filled in all of the eight dilemma parts for a specific problem, he or she is then asked a series of five questions based on the dilemma phrasing checklist. Each of the questions deals with a specific criterion for the formulation of a good dilemma phrasing.

Finally, the student can compare his or her dilemma formulation to a previously prepared good dilemma formulation for each problem. The original wording of each problem is erased from the screen and is replaced by the good dilemma phrasing while the student's phrasing remains on the screen. A comment is also displayed at this time to point out any characteristics of the process of formulating the dilemma for this particular problem, which might generalize to the formulation of other dilemmas.

The student is now introduced to the components of the dilemma matrix by an example problem. The following is the dilemma phrasing and first matrix row for Example Problem 1. A comment is displayed with an arrow pointing to the center cell of the matrix row. Successive displays that are similar to this one review each row of the dilemma matrix for this problem. A comment is given about *each* cell of *each* matrix row. After the comment for the third cell of each row of the matrix, a sample solution is displayed that is appropriate for the creative inquiry in that row of the matrix.

Example 1

If I become a scientist, then I will have a limited income; and if I become a businessman, then I will have limited intellectual satisfaction. But I must either become a scientist or go into business, and, therefore, I will either have a limited income or I will have limited intellectual satisfaction.

Dilemma	Route of Extrication	Creative Inquiry
If I become a scientist, then I will have a limited income.	Becoming a scientist will not necessarily lead to having a limited income.	How is it that I can become a scientist and yet not have a limited income?

We can phrase this a little more positively by adding key words such as *not necessarily lead to*. The extrication route then takes the general form: Doing action p won't necessarily lead to unhappy consequence r.

The following is a display of all five of the sample solutions for matrix Example Problem 1. On this display, clients are asked to rank the quality of the solutions from 1 (best) to 5 (worst). In a succeeding display, the student is shown his or her ranking of the five solutions and must respond to the display by rating how adequate the best solution is on a scale from 1 (not at all adequate) to 8 (completely adequate).

Example 1

Rank 2

While many scientists are on a limited salary, many also derive income from industrial and technical consultations and from writing and publishing.

Rank 1

Though your income as a scientist may be limited, it would still enable you to live quite comfortably, since scientific incomes are in the top 10% of general population income.

Rank 3

Intellectual satisfaction is derivable from intellectual activities and participation outside of business hours. Also, many aspects of business make great demands on intellectual imagination and acumen.

Rank_____

A person seeking unlimited intellectual satisfaction in his business may soon find that the necessary, practical everyday business activities are being neglected.

Rank_____

You could combine business and science as in director of research, director of scientific personnel, marketing and advertising of scientific technology and products, pharmaceutical sales manager, and so on.

Please rank the solutions from 1 (best) to 5 (worst).

The student is next introduced to the structural components of the generalized dilemma matrix (see Table 8.1). The user is instructed how to make use of the structural components as a general guide when working with specific problems. The following is a display from the dilemma matrix Practice Problem 1. This shows that when the student correctly completes the matrix row (as judged by PLATO DCS), the row from the generalized dilemma matrix is erased. It is replaced by (1) the completed row of the matrix for the current problem as filled out by a dilemma counselor and (2) a space for the student's solution for this row of the matrix. Thus, a student can compare his or her version of the matrix row with that of an expert in the dilemma counseling method, and he or she can gain experience in generating creative solutions for the dilemma-type problems. The other four rows of the matrix for Practice Problem 1 are completed by using displays that are analogous to those of the first matrix row. Dilemma matrix Practice Problem 2 consists of displays that are very similar to those for Practice Problem 1.

Practice Problem

If I stay in finance, then I may continue having trouble. If I don't stay in finance, then it might take a longer time to graduate and upset my parents. But I must either stay in finance or not stay in finance, and therefore I may either continue having trouble or take a longer period of time to graduate and upset my parents.

Dilemma	Route of Extrication	Creative Inquiry
If I stay in finance, then I will continue having trouble.	Staying in finance will not necessarily lead to having trouble.	·How can it be that staying in finance will not necessarily lead to having trouble?

Dilemma	Route of Extrication	Creative Inquiry
If I stay in finance, I may continue having trouble.	Staying in finance will not necessarily lead to having trouble.	·How can it be that this is not necessarily the case?

Now type in a solution for this row of the matrix table.
It may be that other finance courses will be much less difficult for me.

In summary, a client learns the dilemma counseling method on PLATO DCS by constructing the dilemma formulation and the dilemma matrix for several sample problems. The client is also required to generate possible solutions to the sample problems. The computer provides feedback to the client regarding the appropriateness of his or her work.

A client applies the dilemma counseling method to his or her own problems by using the techniques that were learned in the first portion of the material on PLATO DCS. The first step in applying the method is for the client to type a description of his or her problem onto PLATO DCS. This initial description is in paragraph form.

Next, the client is asked to generate the dilemma formulation for his or her problem. The original wording of the problem remains on the PLATO DCS screen while the client formulates the dilemma. Instructions on the screen remind the client that he or she may redo the formulation, if necessary, to make changes or corrections.

On completion of the dilemma formulation, the original wording of the client's problem is erased from the screen. The dilemma formulation is retained on PLATO DCS while the client completes each row of the dilemma matrix. The dilemma component, route of extrication, and creative inquiry are completed with regard to the client's specific problem by referring to the corresponding row of the generalized dilemma matrix shown at the bottom of the screen.

On completion of each row of the matrix, the client is asked to generate answers to the creative inquiry. The dilemma formulation and the current row of the matrix for the client's problem remain on the screen while the client responds to the creative inquiry. As mentioned earlier, responses to the creative inquiry represent possible solutions to the client's problem.

The final display on PLATO DCS presents the solutions generated by the client for his or her problem. The client ranks these solutions from best to worst and then considers the adequacy of the best solution.

A more complete description of the PLATO DCS can be found in Wagman and Kerber (1979, 1980).

Exploration of reactions to PLATO DCS concerns users' evaluations regarding (1) personal acceptance of computer counseling, (2) effectiveness of PLATO DCS as a teacher of a method for solving psychological problems, and (3) effectiveness of PLATO DCS as a counselor for a current troubling psychological dilemma. The method for carrying out this exploratory study of users' attitudes and evaluations of PLATO DCS will now be described.

EXPLORATORY RESEARCH: METHOD

Students who were experiencing troublesome psychological dilemmas were randomly assigned to a PLATO DCS group or to a no-contact control group. After two sessions on the computer, subjects in the PLATO DCS group completed a questionnaire in which they evaluated PLATO DCS. Subjects in both groups responded to a series of self-report measures of problem improvement at a one-week follow-up session.

Subjects

There were 77 male and female undergraduate students at the University of Illinois at Urbana-Champaign who served as subjects in connection with course requirements. These participants were selected from a larger group of 160 students on the basis of the criteria described below.

Procedure

In an initial large group session, 160 subjects first responded to the Maudsley Personality Inventory (Eysenck 1959). Subjects then read a booklet that contained a series of eight typical psychological problems faced by university students. Next, subjects were asked to write in the booklet at least four of their own personally troubling psychological problems. They also rated each problem on an 8-point problem troublesomeness scale.

The problems written by subjects were typed and then evaluated by two research assistants to determine whether they met specified selection criteria. To be selected, a problem had to be sufficiently detailed and conflictful to be dilemma formulable. The second criterion was that the problem was rated by the subject at or above 6 on the problem troublesomeness scale, where 1 meant not at all troublesome and 8 meant extremely troublesome, interfering with my life. The reliability coefficient between the two research assistants was $r = .92$. There were 90 subjects, each of whom had one problem meeting both criteria, who were selected for further participation in the study.

Each participant was randomly assigned either to the PLATO DCS condition or to the control condition. Scheduling problems reduced the number of subjects in the PLATO DCS $(n = 41)$ and control $(n = 36)$ groups. Participants in the PLATO DCS condition interacted individually with the computer system during two sessions. There was a three-day interval between the two sessions. In the first session, participants spent up to two hours learning the dilemma counseling method. In the second session, participants spent up to one hour applying the learned method to their own psychological dilemmas. At the conclusion of the second session, subjects rated on an 8-point scale the adequacy of the best solution they generated for their problem (1 = completely inadequate for solving this dilemma and 8 = perfectly adequate for solving this dilemma) and responded to a questionnaire in which they evaluated PLATO DCS. During a one-week follow-up session, problem improvement was assessed with several self-report scales.

Participants in the control condition had no contact with PLATO DCS. In addition to participating in the initial group session, these subjects responded during a follow-up session to the same problem improvement scales taken by participants in the PLATO DCS condition. The amount of time from the initial group session to the follow-up session was matched for PLATO DCS and control subjects.

Evaluation Measures

After completing their interaction with PLATO DCS, subjects responded to a nine-page questionnaire in which they evaluated the system. There were 22 items. Eight items related to personal acceptance of the computer system.

Each of these items (e.g., "too impersonal") was rated on a 5-point scale, in which 1 meant strongly disagree and 5 meant strongly agree. These personal acceptance items are further described in the Results section of the present study.

Eight items related to the teaching effectiveness of PLATO DCS. Each of these items (e.g., "the dilemma practice problems") was rated on a 5-point scale, in which 1 meant not at all useful and 5 meant extremely useful.

Six items related to the counseling effectiveness of PLATO DCS. Each of these items (e.g., "applying the method to my own problem") was rated on a 5-point scale, in which 1 meant not at all helpful and 5 meant extremely helpful. Examples of specific items concerned with PLATO DCS counseling and teaching effectiveness as well as several global evaluation items are given in the Results section.

Performance Measures

In addition to its role as counselor and teacher, PLATO DCS functioned as a researcher by collecting data on each subject's performance as he or she worked through the practice problems and his or her own problem. Such performance data as time to complete own problem versus time to complete practice problems for both dilemma formulation and dilemma matrix were registered by the computer as objective measures of subjects' learning.

Correctness of Dilemma Formulation and Dilemma Matrix

Each subject's input for his or her own problems and practice problems was printed out in hard copy. A trained rater then scored the accuracy with which each subject completed the dilemma formulation and dilemma matrix for his or her own problem and for one practice problem. The rater was trained by use of the PLATO DCS dilemma phrasing checklist and by conferences with the author. Further description of rater training is given in Wagman and Kerber (1979).

Follow-Up Measures

The PLATO DCS participants and the control participants were assessed on two measures of problem improvement for the one-week follow-up session. On the first scale, participants rated the overall degree of improvement in their problems (1 = extremely improved and 8 = extremely worse). On the second scale, participants rated the troublesomeness of the problem (1 = not at all troublesome and 8 = extremely troublesome, interfering with my life). The solutions that had been generated a week earlier during computer interaction were also rated by PLATO DCS participants as to how the solutions applied to their problems (1 = extremely helpful and 8 = extremely harmful).

RESULTS

There were 42 subjects who completed the PLATO DCS Evaluation Questionnaire. With respect to the global item, 21% of the subjects felt that PLATO DCS was considerably or extremely helpful in finding solutions to their problems; 69% thought that PLATO DCS was slightly or somewhat helpful. Only 10% of the subjects thought that PLATO DCS was not at all helpful in finding solutions to their problems. Table 9.1 summarizes the responses of the subjects to additional items that pertain to PLATO DCS.

Subjects in the PLATO DCS group responded to 22 items concerning their evaluation of the dilemma counseling system. A principal-components analysis was performed on the responses to these items. On the basis of a plot of the eigenvalues and on the basis of interpretability, three components were extracted that accounted for 55% of the variance. A varimax rotation was employed to yield three orthogonal components. Each item was identified with the component on which it loaded most highly.

Component 1 (30% of the variance) dealt with the evaluation of PLATO DCS as a teacher. Items that loaded highly on this component included ques-

Table 9.1   Evaluation of PLATO Dilemma Counseling System (PLATO DCS).

Item	% Disagree	% Neutral	% Agree
Interesting to work on	10	29	62
Rather use a printed booklet	83	7	10
Learned the method quite well	2	12	86
Would use lesson again	40	21	38
Too impersonal	56	15	29
Feel more at ease on PLATO DCS than if I saw a counselor	34	24	42
Useful to see counselor *and* use PLATO DCS	14	21	64
Feel more satisfaction in solving my problem on PLATO DCS than if I saw a counselor	21	33	45

Note: The disagree category consists of ratings of 1 or 2 and the agree category of ratings of 4 or 5 on a scale in which 1 meant "disagree" and 5 meant "agree." Values in the table are rounded to the nearest whole percentage.

tions about specific parts of the dilemma counseling system (e.g., the dilemma phrasing problems and the generalized dilemma matrix). Subjects with high scores on this component thought that the various parts of the system were useful when learning the dilemma counseling method. They also indicated that they learned the method quite well by using PLATO DCS.

Component 2 (15% of the variance) dealt with the evaluation of PLATO DCS as a counselor. Subjects with high scores on this component thought that PLATO DCS was helpful in solving their problems, desired to use PLATO DCS again in order to solve a problem, and felt that PLATO DCS was not too impersonal. They also felt that they were more at ease and that they experienced greater satisfaction when they used PLATO DCS to solve a problem as opposed to when they saw a counselor.

Finally, Component 3 (9% of the variance) dealt with satisfaction in the use of PLATO DCS. Subjects with high scores on this component thought that PLATO DCS was interesting to work on and stated that they would rather not use a printed booklet in place of PLATO DCS in order to learn the dilemma counseling method. They also felt that it did not take too much time to complete PLATO DCS and that there was not too much typing to do in PLATO DCS.

Performance Measures

Reductions in the amount of time to complete successive dilemma phrasing problems, dilemma matrix problems, and solutions for the matrix problems may in part be an indication of the teaching effectiveness of PLATO DCS. Therefore, several analyses were conducted on the amount of time (Table 9.2) required for each subject to complete his/her problems. Findings indicated that subjects improved in their ability as they progressed from practice problems to their own problems.[1] Complete analyses for all performance variables are given in Wagman and Kerber (1979).

Correctness of Dilemma Formulation and Dilemma Matrix

The dilemma formulation and the dilemma matrix for one practice problem and for the subject's own problem were stored on PLATO DCS for each subject. The dilemma formulations were rated by a trained rater on six criteria of a correct dilemma formulation. If the formulation met a particular criterion, it was given a score of 1; if it did not meet the criterion, it was given a score of 0. Therefore, scores for each formulation could range from 0 to 6. The mean rating for the practice problem was 4.28, and the mean rating for the subject's own problem was 4.75, $t(39) = 1.29$, ns.

Each cell of both dilemma matrices was rated for correctness by the same rater. If the dilemma part, extrication route, or creative inquiry for a par-

Table 9.2 Performance Variables: PLATO Dilemma Counseling System (PLATO DCS).

Variable	N	M	SD
Number of keywords			
Dilemma phrasing practice	43	3.47	2.01
Dilemma matrix practice	42	3.21	2.65
Dilemma matrix own problem	43	1.77	1.85
Time			
3 dilemma phrasing practice			
problems	43	18.02	7.33
Finance	43	6.22	4.76
Obey	43	5.39	2.44
Drinking	43	6.40	3.65
Dilemma phrasing own			
problem	43	3.04	1.22
Dilemma matrix own problem	43	9.93	5.95
Solutions own problem	43	5.88	2.92
Entire dilemma counseling			
system	43	136.03	24.21

Note: Time is expressed in minutes.

ticular cell of the matrix was correct, it was given a score of 1; if it was incorrect, it was given a score of 0. Therefore, scores for each matrix could range from 0 to 15. The mean rating for the practice problem was 13.58, and the mean rating for the subject's own problem was 14.00, $t(30) = .82$, ns.

A correlational analysis indicated that the correctness of the dilemma formulation problems and the dilemma matrix problems was unrelated to the time to complete those problems.

Follow-Up Measures

The PLATO DCS group and the control group were assessed on two measures of problem improvement at the one-week follow-up session. For each subject, the measures of improvement were self-ratings of troublesomeness and degree of improvement. An ANCOVA was conducted on the troublesomeness rating for the one-week follow-up, with the rating of troublesomeness for the first session of the study as the covariable. Results indicated that the PLATO DCS group showed a greater reduction in problem troublesomeness as compared with the control group, $F(1, 74) = 5.87$, $p < .01$. Adjusted means for the two groups were 2.22 (PLATO DCS) and 4.97 (control).

A t test was conducted on the rating of degree of improvement for the one-week follow-up. Results indicated that the PLATO DCS group showed significantly greater improvement in their problems as compared with the control group, $t(75) = 4.40$, $p < .01$. Means for the two groups were 1.95 (PLATO DCS) and 4.12 (control).

Intercorrelation of Personality, Performance, Evaluation, and Follow-Up Measures

Correlations were computed among the Neuroticism and Extraversion scores from the Maudsley Personality Inventory, the performance variables, the evaluation component scores, and the measures taken during the one-week follow-up session.[2] Subjects with higher neuroticism scores (1) spent more time completing their own dilemma matrix, $r(38) = .34$, $p < .05$, (2) spent more time generating solutions to their own problems, $r(38) = .35$, $p < .05$, (3) spent more total time in PLATO DCS, $r(38) = .52$, $p < .05$, (4) gave more positive evaluations of PLATO DCS as a counselor, $r(38) = .33$, $p < .05$, and (5) indicated greater improvement in their problems at the one-week follow-up, $r(36) = .42$, $p < .05$.

Subjects who spent more time generating solutions to their problems gave more positive evaluations of PLATO DCS as a counselor, $r(39) = .36$, $p < .05$, and experienced greater satisfaction in their use of PLATO DCS, $r(39) = .33$, $p < .05$. Subjects who spent more time working on the dilemma phrasing for their own problems also gave more positive evaluations of PLATO DCS as a counselor, $r(39) = .41$, $p < .05$, as did those subjects who spent more total time in PLATO DCS, $r(39) = .34$, $p < .05$.

Subjects with more positive evaluations of PLATO DCS as a teacher rated their best solutions as more adequate to solve their problems, $r(39) = .32$, $p < .05$. Subjects with more positive evaluations of PLATO DCS as a counselor also rated their best solutions as more adequate, $r(39) = .31$, $p < .05$. Finally, subjects who experienced greater satisfaction in their use of PLATO DCS found the solutions that they applied to their problems more helpful at the one-week follow-up, $r(33) = .34$, $p < .05$.

DISCUSSION

The results of this exploratory research generally tend to be quite supportive of PLATO DCS and its various functions. Students find the experience of interacting with a sophisticated computer counseling system highly stimulating and interesting. Such user enthusiasm probably serves as a strong motivater for acceptance of PLATO DCS in both its teaching and counseling functions.

Critics of personal computer counseling (Weizenbaum 1976, 1977) present concerns about the supposedly impersonal nature of solving psychological dilemmas on a computer. However, a majority (56%) of the participants in the present study felt that PLATO DCS was not too impersonal. In addition, a substantial proportion of the participants felt more at ease (42%) and more independent (45%) on the computer than if they saw a counselor. It is evident, however, that for most subjects, the computer is a professional resource to be sought in addition to the professional skills of the counselor. Of the current sample, 64% felt that it would be helpful to use PLATO DCS and to see a counselor to solve a personal problem.

These positive findings need to be balanced by several observations pointing to the need for additional research beyond this exploratory investigation. First, it would be desirable to test for placebo effects by a group of subjects who interact with the PLATO computer system but who did not use the procedures of systematic dilemma counseling. Second, it would be useful to expand the types of follow-up measures to include behavioral observations and ratings and possibly standardized personality tests. However, one obstacle in the way of such expansion of follow-up measures is the great diversity in range, complexity, and malleability of psychological dilemmas. Third, a comparative study of PLATO DCS alone, personal counseling alone, and PLATO DCS plus personal counseling would be useful. Fourth, the comparative study might involve clients drawn randomly from the many university campuses where PLATO DCS is available.

Generating and Judging Self-Help Dilemma Solutions

It should be noted that experimental research with PLATO DCS made certain demands on the participants. Clients were asked to interact with an experimental procedure that was at once novel in using a computer for personal counseling and unusual in expecting clients to teach and counsel themselves to generate solutions to their psychological problems.

It is of interest, therefore, that approximately two-thirds of the clients succeeded in generating solutions to their troubling psychological dilemmas. Furthermore, the adequacy of these solutions as judged by the clients themselves was quite high (M = 5.76, SD = 1.85; 8.00 = perfectly adequate for solving this dilemma). Judgment of the adequacy of solutions to psychological problems suggests an interesting area for research (Wagman 1979), especially when the problems are cognitively complex (as is true of psychological dilemmas) and when the process of comparing, ranking, and judging quality of solutions involves idiosyncratic personal values.

Correlational Findings

The correlational findings involving evaluation of PLATO DCS functions, adequacy of subjects' best solutions, and helpfulness of these solutions when applied to the subjects' problems are provocative. Although correlation coefficients are generally not reliably interpreted in terms of direction of causation, they seem to be highly illuminating in this first exploratory investigation of the effects of PLATO DCS.

Among the various correlational findings, the following pattern seems quite significant. Subjects who gave more positive evaluations to PLATO DCS as a counselor also spent more time generating solutions to their problems and rated their best solutions as more adequate. In turn, subjects who rated their best solutions as more adequate to solve their problems also expressed more positive evaluations of PLATO DCS as a teacher of the dilemma problem-solving method. This pattern taken as a whole suggests that subjects who experienced greater satisfaction in their use of PLATO DCS found the solutions that they applied to their problems more helpful at the one-week follow-up.

The above analyses and interpretations were based on the entire research sample. It is of interest that the Neuroticism–Stability factor of Maudsley's inventory (Eysenck 1959) was related to some of these evaluation performance and outcome variables. Thus, persons with higher Neuroticism scores spent more time generating solutions to their problems, spent more total time in PLATO DCS, gave more positive evaluations of PLATO DCS as a counselor, and indicated greater improvement in their problems at the one-week follow-up. Taken together, these findings might suggest that persons in greater need of counseling (i.e., maladjusted persons) respond positively to a computer by staying involved. They spend more time interacting with the computer and working on solving their personal dilemmas, resulting in stronger evaluations of the computer as a counselor and, significantly, greater improvement in their problems at the one-week follow-up. These findings will require cross-validation in future research, but it is of interest that Greist, Gustafson, and Strauss (1973) found that suicidal patients preferred interacting with a computer to a counselor (psychiatrist) and that the computer was more accurate in predicting suicidal attempts.

Finally, it should be pointed out that PLATO DCS participants rated the adequacy of their solutions to their problems prior to their evaluation of PLATO DCS, which, in turn, preceded the ratings of problem improvement by a week. Thus, it may be that the quality of the solutions created by interaction with PLATO DCS influenced the evaluation and the perceived usefulness of the system. In the present study, the mean value for the adequacy ratings was 5.76 (SD = 1.85) on an 8-point scale, in which 8 meant perfectly adequate for solving this dilemma. Thus, solutions generated by PLATO DCS were generally of high quality as rated by the subjects.

Future Research in Computer-Based Counseling

Computerized self-help counseling offers advantages to both client and counselor that could be explored by the computerization of other counseling techniques. From the point of view of the client, computer counseling prevents the buildup of dependency on a counselor for solving moderately difficult psychological problems. In addition, the computer can teach a method for solving future problems; this will further increase the autonomy of the client. Research on the use of problem-solving techniques for teaching and maintaining self-help or self-control procedures is currently very active (Goldfried and Davidson 1976; Mahoney 1974; Richards and Perri 1978).

From the point of view of the counselor, computerization of counseling procedures could result in significant advances because techniques must be very clearly and concisely articulated to make computer applications feasible (Taylor 1970). The computer could be used to model various counseling techniques. Counselors could then use the techniques as clients to achieve new perspectives in their work. In addition, research on counseling could be improved as a result of the standardization of procedures (Lange 1969). The process of computerization could therefore result in significant theoretical and practical advances.

Problem-solving approaches to counseling (Cochran et al. 1977; Dilley 1967; Krumboltz 1965) have recently been reviewed by Heppner (1978). Research on the possible computerization of problem-solving techniques in the counseling process could benefit greatly from the work of Newell, Shaw, and Simon, who have developed a theory of the elements of general problem solving (Newell and Simon 1958) and a computer program called The General Problem Solver, which models human thought (Newell, Shaw, and Simon 1963).

CONCLUSION

As in the case of dilemma counseling, it would appear that cognitive counseling approaches (Mahoney 1977) are most appropriate for computer applications. The particular advantage of the dilemma counseling technique for computer presentation is that the logic of the method is the logic of the computer; that is, the logic of conditionals that forms the basis for dilemma counseling (Wagman 1979) is also the logic of the computer. Future attempts at computerized counseling should be preceded by serious consideration of the match between the technique and the medium of presentation.

The flexibility, objectivity, and speed of the computer present admirable qualifications for any counselor (Kleinmuntz 1975; Sagan 1977). These qualifications summarize the potential of a modern computer system to aid clients in the solution of psychological problems. However, the actualization of this potential for the purpose of computer-based counseling depends on the skills of the counselors who construct the materials (Holden 1977; Palman 1978) for use on the computer.

The facilities of PLATO DCS for assisting persons in the solution of psychological dilemmas are currently being expanded (Wagman and Kerber

1980). The logical structures and processes of PLATO DCS would permit applications to populations other than college students. The type of population would define the specific content of the system (e.g., the common dilemmas of managers, executives, and supervisors; the career dilemmas of women; the practical and existential dilemmas of retired persons; and dilemmas in medical practice and genetic counseling). PLATO DCS has recently been published by Control Data Corporation (Wagman and Kerber 1978). As a result, PLATO DCS is currently available at a large number of colleges and universities throughout the United States and Canada.

Finally, the counseling service provided by PLATO DCS to university students and to other types of populations implies the use of the system for research, whereby data are collected and program content is devised and enlarged as knowledge and experience accumulate.

NOTES

1. It seems plausible that the time to complete various parts of the PLATO DCS lesson would be related to typing ability. However, all correlations between each subject's estimate of his or her typing ability and the times to complete designated parts of the lesson were not significant. For example, the correlation between typing ability and the total time to complete the PLATO DCS lesson was $-.13$. These results indicate that typing speed was probably *not* an important factor influencing progress through the lesson.

2. Of the 148 possible correlations among these measures, approximately eight would be significant by chance at the .05 level. Results indicated that 19 of the correlations were significant at the .05 level.

10

PLATO DCS, AN INTERACTIVE COMPUTER SYSTEM FOR PERSONAL COUNSELING: FURTHER DEVELOPMENT AND EVALUATION

The PLATO DCS teaches a generic method for solving life-choice problems and counsels persons regarding their current psychological dilemmas. Two newly developed solution components are described as additional resources for users of PLATO DCS. The specific and structural dilemma solution components contain 69 representative life-choice problems and over 400 specific and general solutions that assist users in solving their psychological dilemmas. Computer-based dilemma counseling was examined empirically by assessing self-reported problem improvement in two groups of undergraduate students treated on PLATO DCS (n = 48) or in a no-contact control group (n = 62). Students who used PLATO DCS showed significantly greater improvement in their problems than the control group one week after treatment. This difference tended to persist one month after treatment. Favorable subjective reactions to the teaching and counseling functions of PLATO DCS suggested that a modern computer system can be helpful in solving psychological dilemmas. PLATO DCS is available for research and application at numerous universities and colleges.

People often face life-choice problems that involve two possible actions and two corresponding aversive consequences. In general, these avoidance problems can be phrased: If I make a decision for action p, then unhappy consequence r will occur. If I make a decision for action q, then unhappy consequence s will occur. But I must either do action p or action q. Therefore, unhappy consequence r or unhappy consequence s must occur.

The resolution of avoidance–avoidance problems involves reasoning with

---

AUTHOR'S NOTE: This research project was supported by a grant from the University of Illinois Research Board.

implication, that is, "if, then" sequences (Inhelder and Piaget 1958). Unfortunately, a number of studies have shown that people have difficulty with such reasoning (Johnson-Laird and Wason 1971; Leahey and Wagman 1974; Roberge 1971; Wagman 1978; Wason 1964; Wason and Johnson-Laird 1972). In addition, the logical structure of the avoidance–avoidance problem seems to impose the inescapable necessity of enduring aversive consequences. The person feels trapped in the dilemma and helpless in the face of the negative outcomes. These difficulties are often intensified by the confused emotional state of the person who experiences the conflict. The dilemma counseling method (Wagman 1979) represents a systematic approach to the formulation and solution of avoidance–avoidance problems.

Application of the dilemma counseling method to an avoidance–avoidance problem first involves the careful formulation of the problem as a psychological dilemma. The dilemma is then resolved by use of the generalized dilemma matrix as shown in Table 8.1. The first column of the matrix presents five components of the dilemma formulation, which restate the basic assumptions of the problem. The second column of the matrix presents five extrication routes corresponding to the five dilemma components. The extrication routes encourage the client to negate the various assumptions of the problem. The third column of the matrix presents five creative inquiries that challenge the client to develop alternatives or new perspectives that are more realistic and more optimistic with respect to the consequences of the problem. These alternatives represent solutions to the original dilemma by eliminating the necessity of enduring aversive consequences.

The dilemma counseling method was originally shown to be effective for use by clients with the help of a counselor (Wagman 1979) and was later shown to be effective for use in a self-help form (Wagman 1981). The availability of the PLATO computer system at the University of Illinois at Urbana-Champaign allowed computer presentation of self-help dilemma counseling.

The PLATO DCS computer system at the University of Illinois at Urbana-Champaign (Alpert and Bitzer 1970; Smith and Sherwood 1976) links hundreds of graphical display terminals to a central computer. Each terminal is composed of a keyset that transmits the user's input to the computer and then to a display screen that shows computer-generated information. In their simplest form, materials presented on PLATO DCS consist of a display on the user's screen followed by the user's response to that display. The user reacts to each display by pressing a single key to move on to new material or by typing a word, sentence, or expression. A user's response might also be a question or a command to PLATO DCS to respond with a particular type of display. Thus, the PLATO DCS system allows for individualized interaction sequences between the user and the computer.

A client learns the dilemma counseling method on PLATO DCS by constructing the dilemma formulation and the dilemma matrix for several sample problems. The client is also required to generate possible solutions for the sample problems. The computer provides feedback to the client regarding the appropriateness of his or her work. A client applies the dilemma counseling method to his or her own problem by using the techniques that were learned by working on the sample problems. A more complete description of PLATO DCS and the dilemma counseling system can be found in Wagman (1980a) and in Wagman and Kerber (1979).

In Wagman (1980a) the effectiveness of PLATO DCS was compared to a no-contact control condition. Improvement that resulted from the use of PLATO DCS exceeded that obtained in the no-contact control condition (i.e., spontaneous remission). In addition, favorable reactions to the teaching and counseling functions of PLATO DCS suggested that many clients found the computer to be helpful in solving psychological dilemmas.

In the present study, the effectiveness of computer-based dilemma counseling was examined by assessing self-reported problem improvement in a group of undergraduate students treated on PLATO DCS and in a no-contact control group. This study differed in three important respects from the previous assessment of PLATO DCS. First, to assist clients in finding solutions for their problems, two solution sources were created on PLATO DCS: the specific dilemma solutions component and the structural dilemma solutions component. Second, problem improvement was evaluated on five scales designed to reflect overall improvement in addition to cognitive and affective aspects of improvement. As in the preceding study (Wagman 1980a), the assessment of improvement was based on self-ratings by each client; however, multiple measures of improvement were used as a more adequate assessment procedure. Finally, the present study included a one-month follow-up session in addition to the one-week session in the preceding study.

METHOD

Students who were experiencing troublesome psychological dilemmas were randomly assigned to a PLATO DCS group or to a no-contact control group. After two sessions on the computer, subjects in the PLATO DCS group completed a questionnaire on which they evaluated PLATO DCS. Subjects in both groups responded to a series of self-report measures of problem improvement at a one-week and a one-month follow-up session.

Subjects

There were 110 male and female introductory psychology students at the University of Illinois at Urbana-Champaign who served as subjects in connection with course requirements. These subjects were selected from a larger group of 200 students on the basis of the criteria to be described.

Procedure

Subjects initially met in large group sessions during which they wrote descriptions of several personal problems that were currently troubling them. They also rated the problems on several scales designed to assess the severity of the problems. To participate in subsequent sessions of the study, one of each subject's problems had to meet the following criteria: First, the problem was rated by the subject at or above 6 on a scale in which 1 meant "not at all troublesome" and 8 meant "extremely troublesome, interfering with my life." Second, the problem could be formulated as a dilemma.

Due to limitations on the availability of computer terminals for research, only 48 subjects could be accommodated on PLATO DCS. These subjects were randomly selected from the 110 students who met the criteria for this study. The remaining 62 subjects were assigned to the control condition.

Subjects in the experimental condition interacted with PLATO DCS during two sessions. Subjects initially spent up to two hours learning the dilemma counseling method. Two days later, subjects spent up to one hour applying the method to their dilemmas. At the conclusion of the second session, subjects rated the adequacy of the best solution they generated for their problems (1 = completely inadequate for solving this dilemma; 8 = perfectly adequate for solving this dilemma) and responded to a questionnaire on which they evaluated PLATO DCS.

All subjects participated in two follow-up sessions during which problem improvement was assessed on several self-report scales. The amount of time from the group sessions to the follow-up sessions was matched for PLATO DCS subjects and for control subjects. The follow-up sessions occurred at one week and at one month after the final session of PLATO DCS.

Treatment

PLATO DCS consists of three separate components. The dilemma counseling component teaches students how to use the dilemma counseling method and how to apply the method to their own dilemmas. The specific dilemma solutions component provides suggested solutions to a wide variety of psychological dilemmas. These components contain 69 representative life-choice problems and over 400 specific and general solutions. The material in these two components was selected on the basis of a content analysis of over 800 psychological dilemmas collected from undergraduates in an earlier study (Wagman 1979). There are 17 categories of problems included in each of the two components: curriculum, dating, dropout, drugs and smoking, extracurricular activities, family relationships, financial, fraternity–sorority, interpersonal relationships, intimate relationships, living accommodations, marriage, miscellaneous, occupational choice, study habits, summer, and transfer. Students could access the specific and/or the structural dilemma solutions components each time a solution was required for their own dilemmas. Detailed descriptions of the specific and structural dilemma solutions components are presented in Wagman and Kerber (1979).

Evaluation Measures

Subjects in the PLATO DCS group responded to a questionnaire that was designed to evaluate PLATO DCS. There were 18 items that referred to the dilemma counseling component, 12 items that referred to the specific dilemma solutions component, and 12 items that referred to the structural dilemma solutions component. There were three types of items. First, the subject rated the helpfulness of each component in finding solutions to his or her problem (1 = not at all helpful; 5 = extremely helpful). Second, the subject rated the usefulness of specific features of each component when working on PLATO DCS (1 = not at all useful; 5 = extremely useful). Finally, the subject agreed or disagreed with each of a series of statements referring to the particular components (1 = disagree; 5 = agree). Items of each type are discussed in the Results section below.

Follow-Up Measures

The PLATO DCS group and the control group were assessed on five measures of problem improvement for both the one-week and the one-month follow-up. Subjects rated the overall degree of improvement in their problems (1 = extremely improved; 8 = extremely worse). Subjects also rated the troublesomeness of the problem (1 = not at all troublesome; 8 = extremely troublesome, interfering with my life) and the manageableness of the problem (1 = extremely manageable, I can fully deal with it myself; 8 = extremely unmanageable, I must have considerable help to deal with it). Finally, subjects rated their affective reactions to the problems in terms of pleasant versus unpleasant feelings (1 = extremely pleasant; 8 = extremely unpleasant) and good versus bad feelings (1 = extremely good; 8 = extremely bad).

Subjects in the PLATO DCS group also responded to four additional items at both follow-up sessions. Subjects were asked how much free time they spent actively trying to solve their problems (1 = no time at all; 8 = a great deal of time) and how much effort they expended actively applying some solution to their problems (1 = no effort at all; 8 = a great deal of effort). Subjects also rated the helpfulness of the solution that they applied to their problems (1 = extremely helpful; 8 = extremely harmful) and any change in the severity of their problems as a result of applying the solution (1 = extremely improved; 8 = extremely worse).

RESULTS

Evaluation Measures

Subjects evaluated each of the three PLATO DCS components with respect to their helpfulness in solving the subjects' dilemmas. Of the subjects, 25% stated that the dilemma counseling component was extremely or considerably helpful in solving their dilemmas. This component was judged as being helpful by 71% of the subjects, and only 4% of the subjects stated that the component was not at all helpful.

Of the 48 subjects in the PLATO DCS group, 22 used the specific dilemma solutions component, and 8 used the structural dilemma solutions components. Of those subjects who used the specific component, 27% felt that it was extremely or considerably helpful in solving their dilemmas. This component was judged to be helpful by 46% of the subjects, and 27% felt that it was not at all helpful. Of those subjects who used the structural component, responses were distributed as follows: extremely or considerably helpful, 26%; helpful, 74%; not at all helpful, 0%.

Subjects also responded in an agree/disagree format to a series of statements about each component. Table 10.1 summarizes responses to 12 items pertaining to the three components on PLATO DCS.

A principal-components analysis was performed on the responses to 18 items concerning the dilemma counseling component. On the basis of the eigenvalues and interpretability, three components were extracted that accounted for 49% of the variance. A varimax rotation yielded three orthogonal components. Each item was identified with the component on which it loaded most highly.

Component 1 (26% of the variance) dealt with the evaluation of PLATO DCS as a teacher. Items that loaded highly on this component included questions about specific parts of the dilemma counseling component (e.g., the dilemma phrasing problems and the dilemma matrix problems). Subjects with high scores on this component thought that the various parts of PLATO DCS were useful when learning the dilemma counseling method. They also favored using PLATO DCS as opposed to a printed booklet to learn the method, and they believed that they could independently apply the dilemma method on completion of PLATO DCS.

Component 2 (13% of the variance) dealt with the global evaluation of PLATO DCS. Subjects with high scores on this component thought that PLATO DCS was helpful in solving their problems, found PLATO DCS to be interesting to work on, desired to use PLATO DCS again to solve a problem and thought it would be useful to see a counselor and use the materials on PLATO DCS.

Finally, Component 3 (11% of the variance) dealt with the evaluation

Table 10.1 Evaluation of PLATO DCS.

Component	n	%Disagree	% Neutral	% Agree
Dilemma	48			
Interesting to work on		2	29	69
Rather use a printed booklet		73	10	17
Could independently apply the method		13	21	67
Would use lesson again		21	27	52
Too impersonal		54	25	21
Feel more at ease on PLATO DCS than if I saw a counselor		31	29	40
Useful to see counselor *and* use PLATO DCS		15	13	73
Feel more independent on PLATO DCS than if I saw a counselor		31	25	44
Specific	22			
Could find a similar problem		55	5	41
Solutions are helpful		41	18	41
Structural				
Could find a similar problem	8	38	38	25
Solutions were helpful	7	57	29	14

Note: PLATO DCS = PLATO Dilemma Counseling System. The disagree category consists of ratings of 1 or 2 and the agree category consists of ratings of 4 or 5 on a scale in which 1 means "disagree" and 5 means "agree." Values are rounded to the nearest whole percentage.

of PLATO DCS as a counselor. Subjects with high scores on this component felt that PLATO DCS was not too impersonal. They also felt that they were more at ease and more independent when they used PLATO DCS to solve a problem as opposed to when they saw counselors.

Follow-Up Measures

Table 10.2 shows the intercorrelations of the five follow-up measures at both the one-week and the one-month follow-up sessions. With respect to the overall improvement rating, the PLATO DCS group tended to report greater improvement than did the control group at the one-week follow-up session, $t(108) = 1.62$, $p < .11$, and at the one-month follow-up session, $t(107) = 1.71$, $p < .09$. Means and standard deviations for these analyses are shown in Table 10.3.

For the four self-ratings of improvement, multivariate analyses of covariance (MANCOVAs) were conducted for each follow-up session.[1] For these analyses, the covariates were the ratings on the four measures of improve-

Table 10.2   Intercorrelations of Measures of Improvement: One-Week and One-Month Follow-Up Sessions.

Variable	1	2	3	4	5
1. Improve	—	.72	.76	.69	.75
2. Trouble	.66	—	.79	.77	.81
3. Manage	.53	.70	—	.68	.72
4. Pleasant	.54	.68	.53	—	.92
5. Good	.51	.64	.52	.92	—

Note: Correlations for the one-week session are below the diagonal. All correlations are significant at the .01 level.

ment taken from the first session of the study. Unadjusted means and standard deviations for these analyses are shown in Table 10.3.

The PLATO DCS group showed significantly greater improvement in their problems than did the control group at the one-week follow-up, $F(4, 101) = 3.80$, $p < .01$. Univariate analyses on the *adjusted* group means indicated that the PLATO DCS group (4.64) felt more pleasant than the control group (5.68) at the one-week follow-up, $F(1, 104) = 13.69$, $p < .01$. Also, the PLATO DCS group ($M = 4.52$) experienced more good feelings than the control group ($M = 5.29$) at the one-week session, $F(1, 104) = 8.09$, $p < .01$.

At the one-month follow-up, the PLATO DCS group tended to show greater improvement than did the control group, $F(4, 101) = 2.23$, $p < .08$. Univariate analyses on the adjusted means indicated that the PLATO DCS group (3.62) felt significantly more pleasant than the control group (4.47) at the one-month follow-up, $F(1, 104) = 6.39$, $p < .05$.

Intercorrelation of Follow-Up and Evaluation Measures

Correlations were computed among the evaluation component scores and the follow-up measures taken during the one-week and the one-month follow-up sessions. The component that represented a global evaluation of PLATO DCS was related to several measures taken during the follow-up sessions. Subjects with more positive evaluations of the dilemma counseling component stated that during the first week they (1) spent more free time trying to solve their problems, $r(46) = .41$, $p < .01$, (2) exerted more effort trying to apply some solution to their problems, $r(46) = .44$, $p < .05$, (3) found the solution that they applied to their problems more helpful, $r(43) = .31$, $p < .05$, and (4) found the solution that they applied to their problems led to greater improvement, $r(43) = .36$, $p < .05$. Subjects with more positive evaluations also stated that during the first month they exerted more effort trying to apply some solution to their problems, $r(45) = .34$, $p < .05$.

Subjects who rated their best solutions as more adequate to solve their problems gave more positive global evaluations of the dilemma counseling component, $r(46) = .36$, $p < .05$, and gave more positive evaluations of PLATO DCS as a counselor, $r(46) = .47$, $p < .01$. Also, at the one-week follow-up session, subjects who rated their best solutions as more adequate to solve their problems found the solutions that they applied to their problems more helpful, $r(43) = .31$, $p < .05$, and found the solutions that they applied led to greater improvement in their problems, $r(43) = .37$, $p < .05$. In turn, subjects who found the solutions that they applied to be more helpful showed a greater reduction in (1) the troublesomeness of their problems at the one-week follow-up session, $r(43) = .42$, $p < .01$, (2) the unpleasant feelings generated by their problems at the one-week follow-up, $r(43) = .36$, $p < .05$, (3) the bad feelings generated by their problems at the one-week follow-up, $r(43) = .35$, $p < .05$, (4) the troublesomeness of their problems at the one-month follow-up, $r(42) = .36$, $p < .05$, and (5) the bad feelings generated by their problems at the one-month follow-up, $r(42) = .34$, $p < .05$. Subjects who

Table 10.3 Means and Standard Deviations for Measures of Improvement in the Control Group and the PLATO DCS Group: Pretest, One-Week, and One-Month Follow-Up Sessions.

Variable	Pretest		One-Week Follow-Up		One-Month Follow-Up	
	M	SD	M	SD	M	SD
Control Group (n = 62)						
Improve	—	—	3.65	1.42	3.27	1.44
Trouble	6.79	.81	4.58	1.85	3.98	1.91
Manage	5.50	1.30	3.90	1.82	3.44	1.83
Pleasant	6.71	.91	5.82	1.27	4.61	1.57
Good	6.37	.93	5.42	1.19	4.29	1.83
PLATO DCS Group (n = 48)						
Improve	—	—	3.25	1.04	2.83	1.20
Trouble	6.21	.99	3.69	1.78	3.30	1.80
Manage	4.81	1.66	3.15	1.56	2.96	1.55
Pleasant	6.17	1.14	4.46	1.69	3.51	1.84
Good	5.81	1.16	4.35	1.59	3.38	1.87

Note: PLATO DCS = PLATO Computer-Based Dilemma Counseling System.

found the solutions that they applied led to greater improvement showed a greater reduction in (1) the troublesomeness of their problems at the one-week follow-up, $r(43) = .44$, $p < .01$, (2) the unpleasant feelings generated by their problems at the one-week follow-up, $r(43) = .31$, $p < .05$, and (3) the troublesomeness of their problems at the one-month follow-up, $r(42) = .30$, $p < .05$.

Computer-Assisted Versus Self-Generated Solutions

Two supplementary components were available on PLATO DCS for those subjects in the PLATO DCS group who desired additional help in solving their problems. Of the 48 subjects in the PLATO DCS group, 26 made use of one or both of these lessons (computer-assisted solutions group), and the remainder did not access the supplementary material (self-generated solutions group). These two PLATO DCS groups did not differ in overall improvement at either the one-week follow-up sessions, $t(46) = .69$, or the one-month follow-up session, $t(45) = 1.33$. A MANCOVA on the four measures of improvement for the one-week follow-up, $F(4, 39) = 2.09$, and for the one-month follow-up, $F(4, 38) = .88$, indicated that the two PLATO DCS groups did not differ in problem improvement. Unadjusted means and standard deviations for these analyses are shown in Table 10.4.

A series of t tests indicated that the computer-assisted solutions group and the self-generated solutions group did not differ on the evaluation component scores, solutions adequacy, or the additional follow-up measures.

Finally, separate correlation matrices involving the evaluation component scores, solution adequacy, and the follow-up measures were computed for the two PLATO DCS groups. One interesting difference was that the adequacy of the best solution was related to the evaluation of PLATO DCS as a teacher in the self-generated solutions group, $r(20) = .69$, $p < .01$, whereas adequacy was related to the evaluation of PLATO DCS as a counselor in the computer-assisted solutions group, $r(24) = .54$, $p < .01$.

DISCUSSION

In support of previous research (Wagman 1980a), this study indicated that PLATO DCS is an effective counselor for psychological dilemmas and is an effective teacher of the dilemma counseling method. Students who used PLATO DCS showed significantly greater improvement in their problems than did students in a no-contact control group. Also, the majority of students who used PLATO DCS agreed that they learned the dilemma counseling method well enough to independently apply the technique to a personal problem.

Table 10.4 Means and Standard Deviations for Measures of Improvement in the Computer-Assisted Solutions Group and the Self-Generated Solutions Group: Pretest, One-Week, and One-Month Follow-Up Sessions.

Variable	Pretest		One-Week Follow-Up		One-Month Follow-Up	
	M	SD	M	SD	M	SD
Computer-assisted solutions group (n = 26)						
Improve	—	—	3.15	1.01	3.04	1.18
Trouble	6.04	.96	3.62	1.83	3.27	1.99
Manage	4.62	1.75	3.42	1.75	3.08	1.62
Pleasant	6.08	1.06	4.35	1.57	3.69	1.85
Good	5.73	1.12	4.31	1.57	3.54	1.98
Self-generated solutions group (n = 22)[a]						
Improve	—	—	3.36	1.09	2.56	1.21
Trouble	6.41	1.01	3.77	1.74	3.33	1.59
Manage	5.05	1.56	2.82	1.26	2.81	1.47
Pleasant	6.27	1.24	4.59	1.84	3.29	1.85
Good	5.91	1.23	4.41	1.65	3.19	1.75

[a]For the self-generated solutions group at the one-month follow-up session, n = 21.

The present study included several changes from the previous assessment of PLATO DCS. First, the specific and structural dilemma solutions components were programmed on PLATO DCS to assist clients in finding solutions to their problems. Over half of the students in the PLATO DCS group accessed one or both of these components. Subjects in the self-generated solutions group appeared to view PLATO DCS as a teacher who would instruct them in a problem-solving technique that the subjects could apply without additional help. For these students, the specific and structural components were not necessary. Subjects in the computer-assisted solutions group appeared to view PLATO DCS as a counselor who would make suggestions about how to solve their dilemmas. For these students, the specific and structural components were a valuable source of possible solutions. It would be of interest to investigate whether such personality factors as dependency-autonomy (Gough 1976) or such intellectual factors as cognitive complexity (Harvey, Hunt, and Schroeder 1961) can distinguish students who self-generate solutions from students who access computer-generated solutions. The major difficulty with the two components was the range of problems: 55%

of the students using the specific component and 38% of those using the structural component could not find sample problems that were similar to their own problems. These components should be expanded to cover additional problem categories.

A second change in the present study involved the use of five self-report measures of problem improvement. These measures were intended to assess overall improvement in addition to cognitive and affective aspects of improvement. As shown in Table 10.2, the various measures of improvement were highly intercorrelated, suggesting that an independent assessment of different components of improvement was not achieved. However, several analyses indicated that the ratings of pleasant versus unpleasant and good versus bad feelings were more sensitive to the effects of treatment than the troublesomeness or manageableness ratings. It is interesting that measures of affect are the most sensitive measures of the effects of such a highly cognitive and rational procedure as dilemma counseling.

A major problem with the current evaluation procedure was that all measures of improvement were self-report scales and, thus, were subject to problems of reactivity. In future research, it would be important to include additional measures of improvement (e.g., behavioral assessments of peer reports). In addition, it would be desirable to control for a possible placebo effect through the inclusion of an experimental group in which subjects interacted with PLATO DCS but did not use PLATO DCS. PLATO DCS (Wagman and Kerber 1978) is available on several university PLATO DCS systems in Minnesota, Florida, Delaware, and Illinois. The availability of computer-based dilemma counseling will allow for additional research, perhaps with actual clients rather than with introductory psychology students. The additional research could contain clients drawn randomly from campuses where PLATO DCS is available and could compare treatment by PLATO DCS only, PLATO DCS and counselor, and counselor only.

The third change in the present study was the addition of a one-month follow-up session. After one month, the effects of treatment by PLATO DCS were approximately equaled by the rate of spontaneous remission (except for the pleasant–unpleasant improvement measure). The high rate of spontaneous remission probably was due to the moderate severity of the problems reported by the students. With these types of problems the value of PLATO DCS is not that improvement remains higher across time for treatment as opposed to untreated problems, but rather that improvement occurs more rapidly for treated problems.

The correlational findings in this study highlight the importance of solution adequacy as it relates to the evaluation of PLATO DCS and to problem improvement. More adequate solutions (as rated by the subjects) were associated with more positive evaluations of PLATO DCS and with greater problem improvement at the one-week follow-up session. Ratings of solution adequacy preceded the evaluation of PLATO DCS and the ratings of problem improvement. Thus, it may be that the quality of the solutions generated on PLATO DCS influenced the evaluation and the perceived usefulness of the system. The mean value for the adequacy ratings in the present study was 6.04 (SD = 1.44) on an 8-point scale, where 8 meant "perfectly adequate for solving this dilemma." Thus, solutions generated on PLATO DCS were generally of high quality as rated by the subjects.

Some psychologists may be concerned about the supposedly impersonal nature of solving psychological problems on a computer (Weizenbaum 1976, 1977). However, a majority (54%) of the subjects in this study felt that PLATO DCS was not too impersonal. In addition, a substantial percentage of the subjects felt more at ease (40%) and more independent (44%) on the computer than if they saw a counselor. On the other hand, for most subjects the computer is a resource to be sought in addition to the skills of a counselor. Of the current sample, 73% felt that it would be helpful to use PLATO DCS and see a counselor to solve a personal problem.

Perhaps the most important finding in this study is that students reacted very favorably to the teaching and counseling functions of a modern computer system. In addition to the attractiveness of PLATO DCS as a medium of presentation, the particular advantage of the dilemma counseling method for computer presentation is that the logic of the method is the logic of the computer (Wagman 1980a). Future attempts at computerized counseling should be preceded by serious consideration of the match between the technique and the medium of presentation (Tombaugh 1983). It would appear that cognitive approaches (Mahoney 1977) and problem-solving approaches to counseling (Heppner 1978; Duckworth 1983) rather than affective approaches to counseling (Colby, Watt, and Gilbert 1966; Weizenbaum 1965) are most appropriate for computer application (Selmi et al. 1982).

NOTES

1. The MANCOVAs reported here were conducted with the multivariance statistical program (Finn 1972).

11

SOLVING DILEMMAS BY COMPUTER OR COUNSELOR

SUMMARY

Results of studies in which either a human counselor or a computer was used to solve personal dilemmas are compared. Subjects were 415 undergraduate students. To increase stability of comparisons, the counselor groups are aggregated as are the computer groups and the control groups. Comparison tests are then made among the aggregated groups. Two types of comparisons are made: significance tests and comparisons for size of effects. Computer counseling was significantly more effective than the control condition as was standard counseling. Comparisons of size of effect indicate that the average person in the computer groups was moved to the 51st percentile of the counselor groups and to the 78th percentile of the control groups. Size of effect for general psychotherapy and counseling indicate movement to the 75th percentile of the control groups. Thus, the effect of computer counseling resembles the over-all effect for general therapy. Future comparison of computer and counselor methods, effectiveness, and reactions is discussed.

Traditional counseling uses the mode of the human counselor. Contemporary counseling also uses the mode of self-counseling (Benson 1975; Goldstein 1975). Innovative counseling that uses the mode of a computer has recently been developed (Bonifacio and Nolan 1978; Bringmann, Balance, and Giesbrecht 1972; Colby, Watt, and Gilbert 1966; Farmer 1976; Greist, Gustaf-

AUTHOR'S NOTE: The research project was supported by a grant from the University of Illinois Research Board.

son, and Strauss 1973; Greist, Klein, and Erdman 1976; Harris 1974; Klein-muntz 1975; Maola and Kane 1976; Melhus, Hershenson, and Vermillion 1973; Price 1974; Pyle and Stripling 1976; Slack and Slack 1977; Super 1970; Wagman 1980a; Wagman and Kerber 1980).

The present study compared the results of several studies in which either a human counselor or a computer was used as the mode of psychological counseling. Two studies concern PLATO DCS (Dilemma Counseling System), an interactive computer system for personal counseling. Two studies concern treatment of psychological dilemmas by an eclectic counselor or a dilemma counselor. The four studies use the same experimental design and dependent measures. In each study, a pre–post and treatment–no-contact control design was used.

Each study is briefly summarized, and the method for comparing the findings of the computer-based and counselor-based procedures is described.

Counselor-Based Studies

Undergraduate students with highly troubling psychological dilemmas (aversive–aversive conflicts) were randomly assigned to treatment and no-contact control conditions. There were two treatment conditions. In the eclectic treatment condition, the counselor used whatever procedures seemed appropriate for the particular case. Techniques included reflection of the client's feelings of frustration about being in the dilemma, relaxation procedures, reassurance and persuasion procedures, and provision of relevant suggestions and information. In the dilemma-treatment condition, the counselor used the method of Systematic Dilemma Counseling (Wagman 1979, 1980b). This method involves five sequenced and interrelated processes. These processes may be listed as (1) formulating the original problem as a psychological dilemma, (2) formulating the extrication route for each component, (3) formulating the creative inquiry for each route of extrication, (4) generating solutions for each creative inquiry, and (5) ranking and evaluating solutions. The generalized dilemma formulation and dilemma matrix was shown in Table 8.1.

Following individual treatment, either by the eclectic counselor or the dilemma counselor, clients wrote out solutions to their psychological dilemmas, ranked them according to quality, and for the best solution indicated its adequacy on a rating scale (1 = completely inadequate for solving this dilemma, 8 = perfectly adequate for solving this dilemma). One week later, in a follow-up session, measures of troublesomeness of problem (1 = not at all troublesome, 8 = extremely troublesome, interfering with my life) and improvement in problem as a result of applying this solution (1 = extremely improved, 8 = no improvement at all) were administered. The time elapsed between the pretreatment session and the follow-up session was matched for treatment and control subjects.

Computer-Based Studies

In two studies (Wagman 1980a; Wagman and Kerber 1980), students with highly troubling psychological dilemmas were randomly assigned either to a treatment or a no-contact control condition. Treatment was given by PLATO DCS, an interactive computer system for personal counseling. The experimental design is essentially identical to the design of the counselor-based studies. In the first computer-based study (Wagman 1980a), PLATO DCS consisted of two components. The PLATO computer through the teaching component instructed the clients in a generic method of problem solving. PLATO DCS, through the counseling component, carefully guided the users in applying the method to their own problems. In the second computer-based study (Wagman and Kerber 1980), PLATO DCS was expanded by the addition of a solutions component. This component was created in response to the finding in the first computer-based study that one-third of the subjects could not self-generate solutions.

PLATO DCS has three components: Dilemma Counseling, Specific Dilemma Solutions, and Structural Dilemma Solutions. While working on one component, the user can access the other components. The Dilemma Counseling component has six parts. Part one introduces the dilemma counseling method. Parts two and three give the user practice in phrasing problems as dilemmas. Parts four and five give practice in generating solutions to these dilemmas, and Part six allows the user to apply the dilemma counseling method to a personal problem. From Part six, the user can access the Specific and Structural Dilemma Solutions components. These components contain 69 representative life-choice problems and over 400 specific and general solutions designed to assist the user in creatively solving his problems.

Each terminal on the PLATO system is composed of a keyset that transmits the user's input to the central computer and a display screen that shows computer-generated information. The keyset is composed of the standard typewriter characters plus special function keys that control the flow of a user through the PLATO materials. The display screen shows letters, figures, drawings, graphs, and other information typed by the user or produced by the computer. In their most simple form, materials presented on the PLATO display screen consist of a repeating sequence, that is, a display on the user's screen followed by the user's response to that display. The user reacts to each display by pressing a single key to move on to new material or by typing a word, sentence, or other expression. A user's response might also be a question or a command to PLATO to respond with a particular type of display. Thus, the PLATO system allows for individualized interaction sequences between the user and the computer.

METHOD

Groups Compared

Comparison of the counselor-based studies and the computer-based studies concerns eight treatment groups and four no-contact control groups. The treatment groups were the two eclectic counselor conditions, the two dilemma-counselor conditions, and the four PLATO DCS conditions of the computer-based studies. Each of the four studies contributes a no-contact control condition to the comparison.

To increase stability and reliability of comparsons (Epstein 1980), the four counselor groups are aggregated (Rosenthal 1978) as are the four computer groups and the four control groups. Comparison tests are then made among the aggregated counselor, computer, and control groups.

Computing and Interpreting Values in Size of Effect

To compute values in size of effect, the method used in a comparison of experimental and traditional teaching methods (Kulik, Kulik, and Cohen 1979) and in a comparison of therapy groups and control groups (Smith and Glass 1977) was used. The method was originally presented by Cohen (1969) in his book on statistical power analysis.

To compute values for size of effect for any measure, the following formula was used: (computer mean − counselor mean)/counselor standard deviation. Each treatment group was compared with the control group by means of the following formulas: (computer mean − control mean)/control standard deviation and (counselor mean − control mean)/control standard deviation.

Smith and Glass (1977) found an average effect of .68. They interpreted this size of effect as meaning that the average person in the therapy groups was moved to the 75th percentile of the control groups.

Kulik, Kulik, and Cohen (1979) found an average effect size of .49. They interpreted this size of effect to mean that the average student in the experimental teaching groups was moved to the 69th percentile of the traditional teaching groups.

Cohen (1969) interprets effect sizes centering around .50 as modest, those of .80 and higher as large, and those .20 and less as small. By these standards, effect sizes of .49 in the Kulik, Kulik, and Cohen (1979) study and .68 in the Smith and Glass (1977) study are in the moderate range. Cohen (1969) contrasts these medium effects with small effects that correspond to the order of magnitude of the difference in average IQ between twins and nontwins or in the difference in height between 15- and 16-year-old girls. Sizes of large effects are about the order of magnitude of the difference in IQ between a person with a Ph.D. degree and a typical first-year college student.

Measures

Measures include number of solutions, adequacy of best solution, reduction in troublesomeness of problem, and improvement in problem. In addition, the two computer-based studies contain measures of evaluation. These measures relate to subjects' reactions to being counseled by a computer and to preferences for computer-based or counselor-based counseling.

RESULTS

Computer versus Counselor

The mean number of solutions for the computer groups (4.64) did not differ significantly from the mean number of solutions for the counselor groups (4.50; $t_{255} = 1.39$, $p < .17$). The mean adequacy of solutions for the computer groups (6.07) did not differ significantly from that for the counselor groups (5.82; $t_{255} = 1.45$, $p < .15$).

The mean amount of improvement (1 = extremely improved; 8 = no improvement at all) for the computer groups (2.93) did not differ significantly from the mean amount of improvement for the counselor groups (2.80; $t_{255} = .78$, $p < .44$). The mean amount of troublesomeness (1 = not at all troublesome; 8 = extremely troublesome, interfering with my life) for the computer groups (3.33) did not differ significantly from that for the counselor groups (2.96; $t_{255} = 1.81$, $p < .07$). Table 11.1 shows means and standard deviations for this analysis.

Table 11.1 Means and Standard Deviations for Aggregated Computer, Counselor, and Control Groups.

	Computer Groups (n = 137)		Counselor Groups (n = 120)		Control Groups (n = 158)	
Measure	M	SD	M	SD	M	SD
No. of solutions	4.64	0.48	4.50	1.01	—	—
Adequacy of best solution	6.07	1.48	5.82	1.28	—	—
Improvement	2.93	1.05	2.80	1.54	3.89	1.42
Troublesomeness	3.33	1.78	2.96	1.50	4.89	1.85

Computer versus Control

The mean amount of improvement for the computer groups (2.93) was significantly greater than the mean amount of improvement for the control groups (3.89; $t_{293} = 6.66$, p < .001). The mean amount of troublesomeness for the computer groups (3.33) was significantly smaller than the mean amount of troublesomeness for the control groups (4.89; $t_{293} = 7.37$, p < .001). Table 11.1 shows means and standard deviations for the analysis.

Counselor versus Control

The mean improvement for the counselor groups (2.80) was significantly greater than the mean improvement for the control groups (3.89; $t_{276} = 6.04$, p < .001). The mean amount of troublesomeness for the counselor groups (2.96) was significantly smaller than that for the control groups (4.89; $t_{276} = 9.60$, p < .001). Table 11.1 shows means and standard deviations for the t-test analysis.

Size of Effect: Computer versus Counselor

Regarding number of solutions, the size of effect (.14) corresponds to moving the average person in the computer groups to the 56th percentile of the counselor groups. Regarding adequacy of best solution, the size of effect (.20) corresponds to moving the average person in the computer groups to the 58th percentile of the counselor groups. Regarding improvement, the size of effect (.08) corresponds to moving the average person in the computer groups to the 47th percentile (adjusted for directionality of scale) of the counselor groups. For troublesomeness, the size of effect (.25) corresponds to moving the average person in the computer groups to the 40th percentile (adjusted for directionality of scale) of the counselor groups. For all measures, the mean effect size was .17, this corresponds to moving the average person in the computer groups to the 51st percentile (adjusted for directionality of scale) of the counselor groups. Table 11.2 presents the values for this analysis.

Size of Effect: Computer versus Control

Regarding improvement, the size of effect (− .68) corresponds to moving the average person in the computer groups to the 75th percentile (adjusted for directionality of scale) of the control groups. For troublesomeness, the size of effect (− .84) corresponds to moving the average person in the computer groups to the 80th percentile (adjusted for directionality of scale) of the control groups. For all measures, the mean effect was − .76, this corresponds to moving the average person in the computer groups to the 78th per-

Table 11.2 Values for Size of Effect and Areas of Normal Curve Percentile for Comparison of Computer and Counselor Groups.

| Measure | Computer vs. Counselor | |
	Size of Effect	%
No. of solutions	0.14	56
Adequacy of best solutions	0.20	58
Improvement	0.08	47*
Troublesomeness	0.25	40*
Mean size of effect	0.17	51*

*Adjusted for directionality of scale.

centile (adjusted for directionality of scale) of the control groups. Table 11.3 presents values for this analysis.

Size of Effect: Counselor versus Control

Regarding improvement, the size of effect ($-.77$) corresponds to moving the average person in the counselor groups to the 78th percentile (adjusted for directionality of scale) of the control groups. For troublesomeness, the size of effect (-1.04) corresponds to moving the average person in the counselor groups to the 85th percentile (adjusted for directionality of scale) of the control groups. For all measures, the mean was $-.91$; this corresponds to moving the average person in the counselor groups to the 82nd percentile (adjusted for directionality of scale) of the control groups. Table 11.3 presents values for this analysis.

Table 11.3 Values for Size of Effect and Areas of Normal Curve Percentile for Comparison of Computer and Control Groups and of Counselor and Control Groups.

| Measure | Computer vs. Control | | Counselor vs. Control | |
	Size of Effect	%	Size of Effect	%
Improvement	-0.68	75	-0.77	78
Troublesomeness	-0.84	80	-1.04	85
Mean size of effect	-0.76	78	-0.91	82

Note: Percentiles are adjusted for directionality of scale.

Reactions to PLATO Dilemma Counseling System

Table 11.4 presents the reactions to the PLATO DCS in two studies (Wagman 1980a; Wagman and Kerber 1980). The data in Table 11.4 indicate that students in both studies reacted very favorably to PLATO DCS.

DISCUSSION

The data of the present study give some support for the usefulness of the computer-based counseling method. These findings indicate that the computer counseling was as effective as standard counseling for dilemma-type problems, producing as many good solutions to dilemmas and resulting in

Table 11.4 Percentages: Evaluation of PLATO DCS in Two Studies.

Item	Study 1 (n = 41)			Study 2 (n = 48)		
	Disagree	Neutral	Agree	Disagree	Neutral	Agree
Interesting to work on	10	29	62	2	29	69
Rather use a printed book- let	83	7	10	73	10	17
Could independently apply the method	2	12	86	13	21	67
Would use lesson again	40	21	38	21	27	52
Too impersonal	56	15	29	54	25	21
Feel more at ease on PLATO DCS than if I saw a counselor	34	24	42	31	29	40
Useful to see counselor and use PLATO DCS	14	21	64	15	13	73
Feel more independent on PLATO DCS than if I saw a counselor	21	33	45	31	25	44

Note: PLATO DCS = PLATO computer-based Dilemma Counseling System. The disagree category consists of ratings of 1 or 2 and the agree category consists of ratings of 4 or 5 on a scale in which 1 means "disagree" and 5 means "agree." Values are rounded to the nearest whole percentage.

as much improvement. In addition, computer counseling was significantly more effective than a control condition.

Reactions to the PLATO computer-based counseling system were generally very favorable. Students enjoyed the independence granted by solving problems with the aid of a computer. Many preferred the self-paced interaction with a computer to seeing a counselor. Many would prefer to see both a computer and a counselor so as to maximize the special benefits of each approach.

The comparative size of effects for computer, counselor, and control groups is interesting. These effects may be interpreted as meaning that the average person in the computer groups was moved to the 51st percentile of the counselor groups and the 78th percentile of the control groups. In comparison, the effects for all kinds of psychotherapy and counseling (Smith and Glass 1977) are interpreted as moving the average person in the therapy groups to the 75th percentile of the control groups. Thus, computer-counseling results in at least as much improvement as the overall effect for general therapy as reported by Smith and Glass.

Although computer-based counseling is a relatively new method, investigators have reported effective applications in a wide range from vocational counseling (Melhus, Hershenson, and Vermillion 1973) to psychotherapy (Slack and Slack 1977) and psychiatric interviewing (Greist, Klein, and Erdman 1976; Greist, Gustafson, and Strauss 1973). With further comparative research in these methods, effectiveness, and reactions, a better understanding of computers in mental health may be attained.

12

CONCLUSION

This book has presented an account of the fundamental nature of dilemmas. General and specific theories of the structure and content of dilemmas have been set forth.

Systematic accounts of the structure of dilemmas have included the very basic formulation as logical structures. These logical structures underlie specific psychological dilemmas. Logical operations on the basic structure such as those of identity, negation, correlation, and reciprocity are represented as specific and formal extrication routes from psychological dilemmas in general.

This structural theory of dilemmas was complemented by specific theories of the content of dilemmas. One such theory is represented by information theory. From the vantage point of information theory, dilemmas are deficient in information and operate under conditions of uncertainty. Information theory links uncertainty conditions of dilemmas to their resolution by the general logical routes of extrication that expand the information space of the dilemma.

Another specific theory concerned with the content of dilemmas is psychotherapy theory. From the standpoint of psychotherapy theory, the content of dilemmas was described in terms of the concept of anxiety that is the counterpart of the concept of uncertainty in information theory.

This book has presented research with the dilemma. Two research projects were laboratory studies of the dilemma. These laboratory studies focused on the fine detail of cognitive operations involved in reasoning with dilemmas. These studies revealed the ways in which the difficulty in reasoning with dilemmas can be surmounted.

The findings of these laboratory studies were then incorporated in an applied research study of the method and effects of systematic dilemma counseling. Encouraging results from this counselor-based method suggested the possibility of research with computer-based systematic dilemma counseling.

Theory also recommended the usefulness of a computer approach to dilemma counseling. The theoretical bridge was the equivalence of concepts in three domains: the logical structure of the psychological dilemma, the logical operations of the systematic dilemma counseling method, and the logic basis of the computer.

Two research studies concerned with the creation and effectiveness of the PLATO Computer-based Dilemma Counseling System, in use internationally for research, service, and teaching purposes, were presented.

In a final research study, a research method that permitted the integration of independent studies that compared computer-based and counselor-based solutions to dilemmas was given. It was tentatively concluded from these systematic comparisons that dilemma-type problems were treated about as effectively by the computer as by a counselor. An implication (Wagman 1983; Sampson and Pyle 1983) is that professional counselor time and experience might be conserved for other types of problems that were as yet (Erdman, Greist, Klein, and Jefferson 1981) beyond the scope of the computer acting as an intelligent assistant in the satisfactory resolution of dilemmas.

APPENDIX A

DILEMMA PROBLEMS AND CASE HISTORIES

Appendix A contains copies of booklets and instructions used in the experimental research that was presented in Chapter 6 (The Psychological Dilemma and Logical Extrication Routes). The following is a list of the sections of Appendix A.[1]

Section 1, booklet 1: Information sheet and Maudsley Personality Inventory (not reprinted).
Section 2, booklet 2: Case histories for experimental euphoric condition (Group A).
Section 3, booklet 2: Case histories for experimental dysphoric condition (Group B).
Section 4, booklet 3: Dilemma problems for experimental euphoric condition (Group A).
Section 5, booklet 3: Dilemma problems for experimental dysphoric condition (Group B).
Section 6, booklet 4: Dilemma problems for experimental euphoric condition (Group A).[2]
Section 7, booklet 4: Dilemma problems for experimental dysphoric condition (Group B).[3]

---

[1]For booklets 2, 3, 5, and 6 the control euphoric condition (Group C) is not reprinted since it is the same as the booklet for the experimental euphoric condition (Group A). Similarly, control dysphoric condition (Group D) is not reprinted since it is the same as the booklet for the experimental dysphoric condition (Group B).

[2]Booklet 4 is not reprinted for the control euphoric condition (Group C) since it is the same as booklet 4 for the experimental euphoric condition (Group A), except that the routes of extrication are not listed.

[3]Booklet 4 is not reprinted for the control dysphoric condition (Group D) since it is the same as booklet 4 for the experimental dysphoric condition (Group B), except that the routes of extrication are not listed.

Section 8, booklet 5: Dilemma problems for experimental euphoric condition (Group A).

Section 9, booklet 5: Dilemma problems for experimental dysphoric condition (Group B).

Section 10, booklet 6: Case histories for experimental euphoric condition (Group A).

Section 11, booklet 6: Case histories for experimental dysphoric condition (Group B).

Section 12, booklet 7: Experimental inquiry for experimental euphoric condition (Group A).[4]

Section 13, booklet 7: Experimental inquiry for control euphoric condition (Group C).[5]

SECTION 1, BOOKLET 1: INFORMATION SHEET

Identification Sheet

Please fill out the following information:
1. Name
2. ID Number
3. Sex: male _____ female _____
4. College _____
5. Expected major _____
6. Class: Fr. _____ So. _____ Jr. _____ Sr. _____
7. Current college grade point average if soph., jr., or sr. _____
8. If freshman, give approximate high school rank:

Top 10% _____
Top 25% _____
Top 50% _____
Top 75% _____
Bottom 25% _____

This information will be kept confidential.

SECTION 2, BOOKLET 2: CASE HISTORIES FOR EXPERIMENTAL EUPHORIC CONDITION (GROUP A)

Instructions

This booklet contains eight brief case histories. Imagine yourself in the role of trying to help this person with his/her problem. The first thing you

---

[4]Booklet 7 is not reprinted for the experimental dysphoric condition (Group B) since it is the same as booklet 7 for the experimental euphoric condition (Group A).

[5]Booklet 7 is not reprinted for the control dysphoric condition (Group D) since it is the same as booklet 7 for the control euphoric condition (Group C).

should do is to try to reformulate his/her problem into a dilemma of the form of:

If course of action A, then result B; and
if course of action C, then result D.
But either course of action A or course of action C.
Therefore, either result B or result D.

The general form of this dilemma is as follows:

If _____, then _____; and
if _____, then _____.
But either _____ or _____.
Therefore, either _____ or _____.

After you have completed this, we would like you to try to help this person find a *realistic* solution to his/her problem.

Space is provided after each item for your answer.

Please try to tackle each item as it comes. Do not omit any items, and do not turn back. When you are finished with the booklet, please raise your hand.

Code number:

_____

1. "For some time now—well—my future's been looking golden. I've always worked on ideas that—that were what I wanted to do. The question's been one of—well—I feel that my justification in life has been to create new and original architectural designs—sort of like what a great painter or writer feels—and—well—look at how we honor them and how they're considered builders of our culture—but even if I decide not to create new and original designs, it shouldn't matter—I can give people the unoriginal things they want and become rich at it. Money's just as good as originality, isn't it?"

PLEASE COMPLETE PARTS A AND B

A. If _____,
then _____ and
if _____,
then _____.
But either _____
or _____.
Therefore either _____
or _____.

B. What would be a realistic solution to this problem?

2. "The way I look at it — everything will be just terrific — just great — I've always wanted to be an engineer — electrical — get into research — that's my real interest — in high school I was very good in science and math — but I've spent my freshman and sophomore years as an education major, because I have a teacher's scholarship that requires that I be in education — and I have no other source of income when you come down to it — so, if I stay in education, then I'll be happy because I'll have financial security, and if I transfer into engineering in the beginning of my junior year — next semester — then I'll really be doing what I want to — it's going to work out — I'm sure I'm not overlooking anything."

PLEASE COMPLETE PARTS A AND B. (Not reprinted here since the format is the same as the format in item 1.)

3. "Well — as Billy's mother — I really don't think that there is any problem to be concerned about — of course, he's not like my other children who are very bright — Billy is mentally retarded — placing him in a special class for the educable mentally handicapped would be just fine — in that competition he'd succeed a lot and feel happier — and if he should be placed in a regular class of average students — he'd like that because he wouldn't be singled out as different, and kids then would never poke fun at him — I don't know what there is to be so worried about — I'm very sure that Billy will be quite happy and secure no matter how he's placed in school."

PLEASE COMPLETE PARTS A AND B. (Not reprinted here since the format is the same as the format in item 1.)

4. "J.B. — that's my boss — the company president — he expects me to take over responsibility for five additional big accounts — I'm pretty sure I can make it — you know how doctors exaggerate about things such as heart palpitations and fatigue — but even if I don't take over the additional responsibility — I'm sure J.B. had no one else in mind but me for vice president of the firm — there's really no other way to look at it."

PLEASE COMPLETE PARTS A AND B. (Not reprinted here since the format is the same as the format in item 1.)

5. "Yes — it's true that I've always hated big crowds — sort of feel like nervous or something — haven't cared for that reason to go to concerts and movies — but now it's going to be different — I just know it is — because I'll be going to college, and there you have to go to lectures — it won't be any different than being in a small classroom just because there are 400 students in the lecture room and all that crowd and noise — it won't bother me — I need those two courses that have lectures in them for my curriculum — they're required — and if sometimes I don't sort of just care to go to lecture — well then — I won't have

to worry about fainting or feeling nervous in the lecture hall — or — don't have to worry — worry about anything."
PLEASE COMPLETE PARTS A AND B. (Not reprinted here since the format is the same as the format in item 1.)

---

6. "Worry about people not liking me — about their belittling or rejecting me — never — not me — well — that's how it will be in the new dorm — I'll get in with a group of other kids — that'll prove that they really like me and respect me — and if I'm by myself and alone — well — that will just prove — that — not that they dislike me — that just couldn't be."
PLEASE COMPLETE PARTS A AND B. (Not reprinted here since the format is the same as the format in item 1.)

---

7. "For some weeks now I guess — I've been missing a lot of classes — just not going — I don't know what I did and where the time went — anyway — I missed a lot of work and papers and things — of course, I could go back and see all my instructors and find out what I missed and make it up, and if I did that I'd probably pass everything and — if I don't go back to classes for the rest of the semester — well, my instructors would understand — I'm sure they wouldn't give me E's — I don't suppose there's any hurry in making a decision — nothing realistically to worry about."
PLEASE COMPLETE PARTS A AND B. (Not reprinted here since the format is the same as the format in item 1.)

---

8. "You know how wives are — always concerned — these stomach or heart pains I have — I don't know why I told her — but I did — now — if I go to the doctors and take the tests — well — she won't nag me any more about my health. Of course — I'd really rather not know — if I don't go to the doctors — well, what you don't know can't hurt you — that's right, isn't it?"
PLEASE COMPLETE PARTS A AND B. (Not reprinted here since the format is the same as the format in item 1.)

SECTION 3, BOOKLET 2: CASE HISTORIES FOR EXPERIMENTAL DYSPHORIC CONDITION (GROUP B)

Instructions

This booklet contains eight brief case histories. Imagine yourself in the role of trying to help this person with his/her problem. The first thing you should do is to try to reformulate his/her problem into a dilemma of the form of:

If course of action A, then result B; and
if course of action C, then result D.
But either course of action A or course of action C.
Therefore, either result B or result D.

The general form of this dilemma is as follows:

If _____, then _____; and
if _____, then _____.
But either _____ or _____.
Therefore, either _____ or _____.

After you have completed this, we would like you to try to help this person find a *realistic* solution to his/her problem.

Space is provided after each item for your answer.

Please try to tackle each item as it comes. Do not omit any items, and do not turn back. When you are finished with the booklet, please raise your hand.

Code number:

_____

1. "For some time now — well — this has been hanging me up. I've always worked on ideas that — that were what I wanted to do. The question's been one of — well — I feel that my justification in life has been to create new and original architectural designs — sort of like what a great painter or writer feels — but — most of them starved to death or — died poor. Well, you can paint or write without too much money, but who'll pay for buildings? — I can make money — but that's just it — you'll only get it if you build what everyone wants — I just can't manage to see my way out of this one."

PLEASE COMPLETE PARTS A AND B

A. If _____.
   then _____; and
   if _____,
   then _____.
   But either _____
   or _____.
   Therefore, either _____
   or _____.
B. What would be a realistic solution to this problem?

_____

2. "Well — I really wanted to become an engineer — I was good in math and science and designing in high school — but it was a financial need — be-

cause I kind of thought I might like teaching, too — but now — after two years in education — I don't know — I have this teacher's scholarship that I can keep as long as I'm in the secondary education curriculum — but I don't want to be a teacher anymore — I really want to go into electrical engineering research — that's what really interests me — but I can't afford to drop the scholarship and I have to stay in secondary education in order to keep it — this thing has had me really frustrated for two years, and now that I'm ready to begin my junior year, I have just got to get this thing straightened out one way or another."

PLEASE COMPLETE PARTS A AND B. (Not reprinted here since the format is the same as the format in item 1.)

---

3. "Either way seems unhappy for my child. I have other very bright children, but Billy is mentally retarded. He comes home crying almost every day because the other boys call him names — they're so mean to him — just because he's in a special class for the educable mentally handicapped, but last spring Billy was in a regular class and he did so poorly against these average children that after a while he stubbornly refused to go back to school. We want him to have the best possible education and also to be personally happy and secure."

PLEASE COMPLETE PARTS A AND B. (Not reprinted here since the format is the same as the format in item 1.)

---

4. "J.B. — that's my boss — the company president — he expects me to take over the responsibility of five additional big accounts — I don't think I can make it — I already have fatigue and heart palpitations — but he says I'm vice president material and my wife expects it of me — or maybe I do of myself — should I accept the responsibility or turn it down?"

PLEASE COMPLETE PARTS A AND B. (Not reprinted here since the format is the same as the format in item 1.)

---

5. "I hate crowds — well, really — I'm afraid of crowds — it makes me feel just awful — I know I'm going to faint and sometimes I have — well, whenever I'm in a big crowd — I haven't gone to movies or concerts for a long time — now I'm starting college and I have to go to lectures — I tried to avoid scheduling classes with lectures, but two are required for my curriculum — a small classroom may be all right — but a big lecture hall with lots of students — I know either I'll run out or faint."

PLEASE COMPLETE PARTS A AND B. (Not reprinted here since the format is the same as the format in item 1.)

---

6. "I don't like being alone in the dorms when everyone else is out having a good time. But when I'm out with the group, they just chatter and they all seem so superficial. Then I wish I were by myself again. You know they

never talk about anything very serious or intellectual. But after a while I get kind of jittery by myself—I seem to feel tense all the time. I'm more and more discouraged—it's been this way for a long time—looks like there's no solution. It just seems hopeless."

PLEASE COMPLETE PARTS A AND B. (Not reprinted here since the format is the same as the format in item 1.)

---

7. "For some time now—a few weeks—maybe more—missing a lot of classes—lots of papers and exams and things—now—I don't know if I can go back and face my teachers and—well—maybe I should just continue this way the rest of the semester and take E's—I don't know how I can ever catch up with all of the work—even then I might not pass everything—well maybe some things—but if I go back I have to explain everything to all the instructors and all that—even trying to think about it—it's just terrible—it's got me down and—I just can't think straight anymore."

PLEASE COMPLETE PARTS A AND B. (Not reprinted here since the format is the same as the format in item 1.)

---

8. "My wife keeps nagging—nagging—nagging. She wants me to go in for a physical check-up—why did I tell her about the stomach or chest pains—well, they're not that bad—anyway—they come and go—but supposing the doctors and tests found something—very serious—maybe a heart condition—I wouldn't want to know about that—well, you know—but she never stops with nagging about my going to see the doctors—just thinking about that gives me a big pain."

PLEASE COMPLETE PARTS A AND B. (Not reprinted here since the format is the same as the format in item 1.)

SECTION 4, BOOKLET 3: DILEMMA PROBLEMS FOR EXPERIMENTAL EUPHORIC CONDITION (GROUP A)

Instructions

This booklet contains eight items posed in the form of personal dilemmas in which the individual involved is facing a significant problem.

How would you *help him/her* find a *realistic* solution to his/her problem?

Space is provided after each item for your answer.

Please try to tackle each item as it comes. Do not omit any items, and do not turn back. When you are finished with the booklet, please raise your hand.

Code Number:

1. It is easy to please women. If I take a second job, then she will not complain about not having nice things around the house, and if I do not take a second job, then she will not complain about being lonely. But either I must take a second job or not take a second job, and therefore either she will not complain about not having nice things around the house or she will not complain about being lonely.
WHAT WOULD BE A REALISTIC SOLUTION TO THIS PROBLEM? (Space was provided for response.)

2. If I make good grades, then I will not be defeating my own potentialities; and if I do not make good grades, then men will not be jealous or dislike me. But I must either make very good grades or not make very good grades, and therefore either I will not be defeating my own potentialities or men will not be jealous or dislike me.
WHAT WOULD BE A REALISTIC SOLUTION TO THIS PROBLEM? (Space was provided for response.)

3. If I am aggressive, then I will be successful in business; and if I am not aggressive, then I will be liked by many people. But I must either be aggressive or not aggressive, and therefore either I will be successful in business or I will be liked by many people. Either way there is no problem.
WHAT WOULD BE A REALISTIC SOLUTION TO THIS PROBLEM? (Space was provided for response.)

4. Like most housewives, I feel quite optimistic. If I don't take the job, then I am sure not to feel guilty; and if I do take the job, then I am sure not to wreck my marriage. But I must either take a job or not take a job, and therefore I am bound either not to feel guilty or not to wreck my marriage.
WHAT WOULD BE A REALISTIC SOLUTION TO THIS PROBLEM? (Space was provided for response.)

5. If you act as an individual, then you have integrity; and if you don't act as an individual, then you have friends. But you must either act as an individual or not act as an individual, and therefore either you have integrity or you have friends.
WHAT WOULD BE A REALISTIC SOLUTION TO THIS PROBLEM? (Space was provided for response.)

6. If I get divorced, it will not be a private admission of my personal failure; and if I do not get divorced, it will not be a public admission of my personal failure. But I must either get divorced or not get divorced, and therefore I must either not privately admit my personal failure or not publicly admit my personal failure.

WHAT WOULD BE A REALISTIC SOLUTION TO THIS PROBLEM? (Space was provided for response.)

_____

7. If I avoid the draft, then I will not be wounded; and if I don't avoid the draft, then I will not be judged a coward. But I must either avoid the draft or not avoid the draft, and therefore I will either not be wounded or not be judged a coward.
WHAT WOULD BE A REALISTIC SOLUTION TO THIS PROBLEM? (Space was provided for response.)

_____

8. If I cheat on my income tax, then I will be richer; and if I do not cheat on my income tax, then I will not be detected and punished. But I must either cheat on my income tax or not cheat on my income tax, and therefore I must either be rich or not be detected and punished.
WHAT WOULD BE A REALISTIC SOLUTION TO THIS PROBLEM? (Space was provided for response.)

_____

SECTION 5, BOOKLET 3: DILEMMA PROBLEMS FOR EXPERIMENTAL DYSPHORIC CONDITION (GROUP B)

Instructions

This booklet contains eight items posed in the form of personal dilemmas in which the individual involved is facing a significant problem.

How would you *help him/her* find a *realistic* solution to his/her problem?

Space is provided after each item for your answer.

Please try to tackle each item as it comes. Do not omit any items, and do not turn back. When you are finished with the booklet, please raise your hand.

Code Number:

_____

1. There is no pleasing women. If I take a second job, then she is sure to complain of loneliness; and if I don't take a second job, then she is sure to complain of not having nice things for the home. But I've just got to either take a second job or not take a second job, and therefore I must either hear complaints of loneliness or of not having nice home furnishings.
WHAT WOULD BE A REALISTIC SOLUTION TO THIS PROBLEM? (Space was provided for response.)

_____

2. If I make very good grades, then men will be jealous and dislike me;

and if I do not make very good grades, then I will be defeating my own potentialities. But I must either make very good grades or not make very good grades, and therefore either men will be jealous and dislike me or I will be defeating my own potentialities.

WHAT WOULD BE A REALISTIC SOLUTION TO THIS PROBLEM? (Space was provided for response.) _____

3. If I am aggressive, then I will be disliked by many people; and if I am not aggressive, then I will be unsuccessful in business. But I must either be aggressive or not be aggressive, and therefore I will be disliked by many people or I will be unsuccessful.

WHAT WOULD BE A REALISTIC SOLUTION TO THIS PROBLEM? (Space was provided for response.) _____

4. Like most housewives, I feel quite desperate. If I don't take a job, then I am sure to wreck my marriage; and if I do take a job, then I am sure to feel guilty. But I must either take a job, or not take a job, and therefore I am bound to wreck my marriage or to feel guilty.

WHAT WOULD BE A REALISTIC SOLUTION TO THIS PROBLEM? (Space was provided for response.) _____

5. If you act as an individual, then you have no friends; and if you don't act as an individual, then you have no integrity. But you must either act as an individual or not act as an individual, and therefore either you have no friends or you have no integrity.

WHAT WOULD BE A REALISTIC SOLUTION TO THIS PROBLEM? (Space was provided for response.) _____

6. If I get divorced, it will be a public admission of my personal failure; and if I do not get divorced, it will be a private admission of my personal failure. But I must either get divorced or not get divorced, and therefore I must publicly admit my personal failure or privately admit my personal failure.

WHAT WOULD BE A REALISTIC SOLUTION TO THIS PROBLEM? (Space was provided for response.) _____

7. If I avoid the draft, I will be judged a coward; and if I don't avoid the draft, I will be wounded. But I must either avoid the draft or not avoid the draft, and therefore I will either be judged a coward or I will be wounded.

WHAT WOULD BE A REALISTIC SOLUTION TO THIS PROBLEM? (Space was provided for response.) _____

8. If I cheat on my income tax, I will be detected and punished; and if

I do not cheat on my income tax, I will be poorer. But I must either cheat on my income tax or not cheat on my income tax, and therefore I must either be detected and punished or be poorer.
WHAT WOULD BE A REALISTIC SOLUTION TO THIS PROBLEM? (Space was provided for response.)

SECTION 6, BOOKLET 4: DILEMMA PROBLEMS FOR EXPERIMENTAL EUPHORIC CONDITION (GROUP A)

Instructions

This booklet contains eight items posed in the form of personal dilemmas in which the individual involved is facing a significant problem.

In your opinion, which of the alternatives following each problem would be most helpful to this person?

Please select the one alternative you feel would constitute the most *realistic* solution, and indicate your choice by placing an "X" at the left of the alternative you choose.

Please try to tackle each item as it comes. Do not omit any items, and do not turn back. When you are finished with the booklet, please raise your hand.

Code Number:
_____

1. If I become a scientist, then I will not have limited intellectual satisfaction; and if I go into business, then I will not have limited income. But I must either become a scientist or go into business, and therefore I will either not have limited intellectual satisfaction or not have a limited income.
WHICH ALTERNATIVE WOULD CONSTITUTE A REALISTIC SOLUTION TO THIS PROBLEM?

_____ 1. You are not restricted to either becoming a scientist or going into business.

_____ 2. Not having limited intellectual satisfaction is not necessarily good.

_____ 3. If you become a scientist, then you will have a limited income, and if you go into business, then you will have limited intellectual satisfaction.

_____ 4. Not having a limited income is not necessarily good.

_____ 5. Going into business will not necessarily lead to not having a limited income.

_____ 6. Becoming a scientist will not necessarily lead to not having limited intellectual satisfaction.

_____ 7. Other (including no solution). Specify.

_____

2. Do you think I have an inferiority complex? If people pay attention to me, it must be because they are not afraid to compete with me; and if people do not pay attention to me, it must be because they are not afraid to ignore me. But people must either pay attention to me or not pay attention to me, and therefore people are either not afraid to compete with me or people are not afraid to ignore me.

WHICH ALTERNATIVE WOULD CONSTITUTE A REALISTIC SOLUTION TO THIS PROBLEM?

_____ 1. From people not paying attention to you, it does not necessarily follow that they are not afraid to ignore you.

_____ 2. People not being afraid to ignore you is not necessarily good.

_____ 3. People not being afraid to compete with you is not necessarily good.

_____ 4. There are other alternatives besides people paying attention to you or people not paying attention to you.

_____ 5. If people pay attention to you, it must be because they are afraid to ignore you; and if people do not pay attention to you, it must be because they are afraid to compete with you.

_____ 6. Other (including no solution). Specify.

_____

3. I am really lovable. If I call for a date, then I will not be lonely; and if I do not call for a date, then I will not be turned down. But I must either call for a date or not call for a date, and therefore I must either not be lonely or not be turned down.

WHICH ALTERNATIVE WOULD CONSTITUTE A REALISTIC SOLUTION TO THIS PROBLEM?

_____ 1. Not being lonely is not necessarily good.

_____ 2. If you call for a date, then you will be turned down; and if you do not call for a date, then you will be lonely.

_____ 3. Calling for a date will not necessarily lead to not being lonely.

_____ 4. Not being turned down is not necessarily good.

_____ 5. Not calling for a date will not necessarily lead to not being turned down.

_____ 6. Other (including no solution). Specify.

_____

4. If I confess the infidelity to him, then he will not learn of it from someone else; and if I do not confess the infidelity to him, then he will not abandon me. But I must either tell him of the infidelity or not tell him, and therefore I must either not have him learn of it from someone else or not be abandoned.

WHICH ALTERNATIVE WOULD CONSTITUTE A REALISTIC SOLUTION TO THIS PROBLEM?

_____ 1. His not learning of it from someone else is not necessarily good.

_____ 2. Confessing the infidelity to him will not necessarily lead to his not learning of it from someone else.

_____ 3. Not being abandoned is not necessarily good.

_____ 4. Not confessing the infidelity to him will not necessarily lead to your not being abandoned.

_____ 5. You are not limited to either confessing the infidelity to him or not confessing the infidelity to him.

_____ 6. If you confess the infidelity to him, then he will abandon you; and if you do not confess the infidelity to him, then he will learn of it from someone else.

_____ 7. Other (including no solution). Specify.

_____

5. If I eat sweets, then I will not be nervous; and if I don't eat sweets, then I will not become overweight. But I must either eat sweets or not eat sweets, and therefore I must either not be nervous or not be overweight. WHICH ALTERNATIVE WOULD CONSTITUTE A REALISTIC SOLUTION TO THIS PROBLEM?

_____ 1. Not being nervous is not necessarily good.

_____ 2. If you eat sweets, then you will become overweight; and if you do not eat sweets, then you will be nervous.

_____ 3. Eating sweets will not necessarily lead to not being nervous.

_____ 4. Not eating sweets will not necessarily lead to not being overweight.

_____ 5. Not being overweight is not necessarily good.

_____ 6. You are not limited to eating sweets or not eating sweets.

_____ 7. Other (including no solution). Specify.

_____

6. I am happy and unbaffled. If I try to cook his mother's style, then he will not say that his mother's meals were always much better; and if I try to cook in my own style, then he will not say that my meals are second rate. But I must cook either in his mother's style or in my own style, and therefore I must either be told that his mother's meals were always much better or not be told that my meals are second rate. WHICH ALTERNATIVE WOULD CONSTITUTE A REALISTIC SOLUTION TO THIS PROBLEM?

_____ 1. Not saying that his mother's meals were always much better is not necessarily good.

_____ 2. Not saying that your meals are second rate is not necessarily good.

_____ 3. Cooking in your own style will not necessarily lead to his not saying that your meals are second rate.

_____ 4. If you cook in his mother's style, then he will say that your meals are second rate; and if you cook in your own style, then he will say that his mother's meals were always much better.

_____ 5. Cooking in his mother's style will not necessarily lead to his not saying that his mother's meals were always much better.

_____ 6. You do not have to restrict yourself to cooking in either his mother's style or in your own style.

_____ 7. Other (including no solution). Specify.

_____

7. If I clarify things for him, then he will not think that I am unable to help him, and if I don't clarify things for him, then he will not think I am degrading his intelligence. But I must either clarify things for him or not clarify things for him, and therefore either he will not think I am unable to help him or he will not think that I am degrading his intelligence.

WHICH ALTERNATIVE WOULD CONSTITUTE A REALISTIC SOLUTION TO THIS PROBLEM?

_____ 1. Not clarifying for him will not necessarily lead to his not thinking that you are degrading his intelligence.

_____ 2. Clarifying things for him will not necessarily lead to his not thinking that you are unable to help him.

_____ 3. His not thinking that you are not degrading his intelligence is not necessarily good.

_____ 4. His not thinking that you are not unable to help him is not necessarily good.

_____ 5. If you clarify things for him, then he will think you are degrading his intelligence, and if you do not clarify things for him, then he will think that you are unable to help him.

_____ 6. You are not restricted to either clarifying things for him or not clarifying things for him.

_____ 7. Other (including no solution). Specify.

_____

8. Dare I do it? If I do, then I will not be missing an opportunity; and if I don't, then I will not be taking advantage. But I must either do it or not do it, and therefore I must either not miss an opportunity or not take advantage.

WHICH ALTERNATIVE WOULD CONSTITUTE A REALISTIC SOLUTION TO THIS PROBLEM?

_____ 1. Not taking advantage is not necessarily good.

_____ 2. You are not restricted to either doing it or not doing it.

_____ 3. If you do it, then you will be taking advantage; and if you don't do it, then you will be missing an opportunity.

_____ 4. Doing it will not necessarily lead to not missing an opportunity.

_____ 5. Not missing an opportunity is not necessarily good.

_____ 6. Not doing it will not necessarily lead to not taking advantage.

_____ 7. Other (including no solution). Specify.

SECTION 7, BOOKLET 4: DILEMMA PROBLEMS FOR EXPERIMENTAL DYSPHORIC CONDITION (GROUP B)

Instructions

This booklet contains eight items posed in the form of personal dilemmas in which the individual involved is facing a significant problem.

In your opinion, which of the alternatives following each problem would be most helpful to this person?

Please select the one alternative which you feel would constitute the most *realistic* solution, and indicate your choice by placing an "X" at the left of the alternative you choose.

Please try to tackle each item as it comes. Do not omit any items, and do not turn back. When you are finished with the booklet, please raise your hand.

Code Number:

_____

1. If I become a scientist, then I will have a limited income; and if I go into business, then I will have limited intellectual satisfaction. But I must either become a scientist or go into business, and therefore I will either have a limited income or I will have limited intellectual satisfaction.

WHICH ALTERNATIVE WOULD CONSTITUTE A REALISTIC SOLUTION TO THIS PROBLEM?

_____ 1. You are not restricted to either becoming a scientist or going into business.

_____ 2. Having a limited income is not necessarily bad.

_____ 3. If you become a scientist, then you will not have limited intellectual satisfaction; and if you go into business, then you will not have a limited income.

_____ 4. Having limited intellectual satisfaction is not necessarily bad.

_____ 5. Going into business will not necessarily lead to having limited intellectual satisfaction.

_____ 6. Becoming a scientist will not necessarily lead to having a limited income.

_____ 7. Other (including no solution). Specify.

_____

2. Do you think I have a superiority complex? If people pay attention to me, it must be because they are afraid to ignore me; and if people do not pay attention to me, it must be because they are afraid to compete with me. But people must either pay attention to me or not pay attention to me, and therefore people are either afraid to ignore me or people are afraid to compete with me.

WHICH ALTERNATIVE WOULD CONSTITUTE A REALISTIC SOLUTION TO THIS PROBLEM?

_____ 1. From people not paying attention to you, it does not necessarily follow that they are afraid to compete with you.

_____ 2. People being afraid to compete with you is not necessarily bad.

_____ 3. People being afraid to ignore you is not necessarily bad.

_____ 4. There are other alternatives besides people paying attention to you or people not paying attention to you.

_____ 5. If people pay attention to you, then it is not because they are afraid to compete with you; and if people do not pay attention to you, it is not because they are afraid to ignore you.

_____ 6. From people paying attention to you, it does not necessarily follow that they are afraid to ignore you.

_____ 7. Other (including no solution). Specify.

_____

3. I am really unlovable. If I call for a date, then I will be turned down; and if I do not call for a date, then I will be lonely. But I must either call for a date or not call for a date, and therefore I must either be turned down or be lonely.

WHICH ALTERNATIVE WOULD CONSTITUTE A REALISTIC SOLUTION TO THIS PROBLEM?

_____ 1. Being turned down is not necessarily bad.

_____ 2. If you call for a date, then you will not be lonely; and if you do not call for a date, then you will not be turned down.

_____ 3. Calling for a date will not necessarily lead to your being turned down.

_____ 4. Being lonely is not necessarily bad.

_____ 5. Not calling for a date will not necessarily lead to your being lonely.

_____ 6. You need not restrict yourself to either calling for a date or not calling for a date.

_____ 7. Other (including no solution). Specify.

_____

4. If I confess the infidelity to him, then he will abandon me; and if I do not confess the infidelity to him, then he will learn of it from someone

else. But I must either tell him of the infidelity or not tell him, and therefore either he will abandon me or he will learn of it from someone else.

WHICH ALTERNATIVE WOULD CONSTITUTE A REALISTIC SOLUTION TO THIS PROBLEM?

_____ 1. Being abandoned is not necessarily bad.

_____ 2. Confessing the infidelity will not necessarily lead to his abandoning you.

_____ 3. His learning of it from someone else is not necessarily bad.

_____ 4. Not confessing the infidelity will not necessarily lead to his learning of it from someone else.

_____ 5. You are not limited to either confessing the infidelity to him or not confessing the infidelity to him.

_____ 6. If you confess the infidelity to him, then he will not learn of it from someone else, and if you do not confess the infidelity to him, then he will not abandon you.

_____ 7. Other (including no solution). Specify.

————————————

5. If I eat sweets, then I will become overweight; and if I don't eat sweets, then I will be nervous. But I must either eat sweets or not eat sweets, and therefore I must either be overweight or be nervous.

WHICH ALTERNATIVE WOULD CONSTITUTE A REALISTIC SOLUTION TO THIS PROBLEM?

_____ 1. Being overweight is not necessarily bad.

_____ 2. If you eat sweets, then you will not be nervous; and if you do not eat sweets, then you will not become overweight.

_____ 3. Eating sweets does not necessarily lead to being overweight.

_____ 4. Not eating sweets does not necessarily lead to being nervous.

_____ 5. Being nervous is not necessarily bad.

_____ 6. You are not limited to eating sweets or not eating sweets.

_____ 7. Other (including no solution). Specify.

————————————

6. I am baffled and unhappy. If I try to cook in his mother's style, then he will say that my meals are second rate; and if I try to cook in my own style, then he will say that his mother's meals were always much better. But I must cook either in his mother's style or in my own style, and therefore I must either be told that my meals are second rate or not as good as his mother used to make.

WHICH ALTERNATIVE WOULD CONSTITUTE A REALISTIC SOLUTION TO THIS PROBLEM?

_____ 1. Saying that your meals are second rate is not necessarily bad.

_____ 2. Saying that his mother's meals were always much better is not necessarily bad.

_____ 3. Cooking in your own style will not necessarily lead to his stating that his mother's meals were always much better.

_____ 4. If you cook in his mother's style, then he will not say that his mother's meals were always better; and if you cook in your own style, then he will not say that your meals are second rate.

_____ 5. Cooking in his mother's style will not necessarily lead to second-rate meals.

_____ 6. You do not have to restrict yourself to cooking either in his mother's style or in your own style.

_____ 7. Other (including no solution). Specify.

7. If I clarify things for him, then he will think I am degrading his intelligence; and if I don't clarify things for him, then he will think I am unable to help him. But I must either clarify things for him or not clarify things for him, and therefore either he will think that I am degrading his intelligence or he will think that I am unable to help him.

WHICH ALTERNATIVE WOULD CONSTITUTE A REALISTIC SOLUTION TO THIS PROBLEM?

_____ 1. Not clarifying things for him will not necessarily lead to his thinking that you are unable to help him.

_____ 2. Clarifying things for him will not necessarily lead to his thinking that you are degrading his intelligence.

_____ 3. His thinking that you are unable to help him is not necessarily bad.

_____ 4. His thinking that you are degrading his intelligence is not necessarily bad.

_____ 5. If you clarify things for him, then he will not think that you are unable to help him; and if you do not clarify things for him, then he will not think that you are degrading his intelligence.

_____ 6. You are not restricted to either clarifying things for him or not clarifying things for him.

_____ 7. Other (including no solution). Specify.

8. Dare I do it? If I do, then I will be taking advantage; and if I don't, then I will be missing an opportunity. But I must either do it or not do it, and therefore I must either take advantage or miss an opportunity.

WHICH ALTERNATIVE WOULD CONSTITUTE A REALISTIC SOLUTION TO THIS PROBLEM?

_____ 1. Missing an opportunity is not necessarily bad.

_____ 2. You are not restricted to either doing it or not doing it.

_____ 3. If you do it, then you will not miss an opportunity; and if you don't do it, then you will not take advantage.

_____ 4. Doing it will not necessarily lead to taking advantage.

_____ 5. Taking advantage is not necessarily bad.
_____ 6. Not doing it will not necessarily lead to missing an opportunity.
_____ 7. Other (including no solution). Specify.

SECTION 8, BOOKLET 5: DILEMMA PROBLEMS FOR EXPERIMENTAL EUPHORIC CONDITION (GROUP A)

Instructions

This booklet contains eight items posed in the form of personal dilemmas in which the individual involved is facing a significant problem.

In your opinion, which of the alternatives following each problem would be most helpful to this person?

Please select the one alternative which you feel would constitute the most *realistic* solution, and indicate your choice by placing an "X" at the left of the alternative you choose.

Please try to tackle each item as it comes. Do not omit any items, and do not turn back. When you are finished with the booklet, please raise your hand.

Code Number:

_____

1. There is a way out. If I mention that he was drunk last night, then he will not accuse me of being indifferent to him; and if I don't mention it, then he will not tell me to stop berating him. But I must either mention his drunkenness to him or not mention it to him, and therefore either he will not accuse me of being indifferent to him, or he will not tell me to stop berating him.
WHAT WOULD BE A REALISTIC SOLUTION TO THIS PROBLEM? (Space was provided for response.)

_____

2. If they laugh at my jokes, then it's only because they do not hate me; and if they don't laugh at my jokes, then it's only because they do not feel sorry for me. But they must either laugh at my jokes or not laugh at my jokes, and therefore they either do not hate me or they do not feel sorry for me.
WHAT WOULD BE A REALISTIC SOLUTION TO THIS PROBLEM? (Space was provided for response.)

_____

3. If I stop doing it, then I will not continue to feel humiliated; and if I do not stop doing it, then I will not miss the pleasure. But I must either stop doing it or not stop doing it, and therefore I must either not continue to feel humiliated or not miss the pleasure.
WHAT WOULD BE A REALISTIC SOLUTION TO THIS PROBLEM? (Space was provided for response.)

_____

4. If she thinks the same as I do, then she will not be insulting my judgment; and if she does not think the same as I do, then it will not be very boring. But she must either think as I do or not think as I do, and therefore either she will not be insulting my judgment or it will not be very boring.
WHAT WOULD BE A REALISTIC SOLUTION TO THIS PROBLEM? (Space was provided for response.)

5. Which shall it be—speed or accuracy? If I work fast, then I will get much done; and if I am careful, then I will not make many errors. But I must either work fast or I must be careful, and therefore I either will get much done or I will not make many errors.
WHAT WOULD BE A REALISTIC SOLUTION TO THIS PROBLEM? (Space was provided for response.)

6. Politics is not crooked. If you vote for the regular party candidate, then there will be an experienced administration; and if you vote for the new reform party candidate, then graft will not continue. But I must either vote for the regular party candidate or for the new reform party candidate, and therefore there will either be an experienced administration or there will not be continued graft.
WHAT WOULD BE A REALISTIC SOLUTION TO THIS PROBLEM? (Space was provided for response.)

7. If I marry early, then I will have much security; and if I don't marry early, then I will have much of a career. But I must either marry early or not marry early, and therefore I must either have much security or have much of a career.
WHAT WOULD BE A REALISTIC SOLUTION TO THIS PROBLEM? (Space was provided for response.)

8. If I become a social worker, then my mother will not be unhappy; and if I become a banker, then my father will not be unhappy. But I must either become a social worker or a banker, and therefore either my mother will not be unhappy or my father will not be unhappy.
WHAT WOULD BE A REALISTIC SOLUTION TO THIS PROBLEM? (Space was provided for response.)

SECTION 9, BOOKLET 5: DILEMMA PROBLEMS FOR EXPERIMENTAL DYSPHORIC CONDITION (GROUP B)

Instructions

This booklet contains eight items posed in the form of personal dilemmas in which the individual involved is facing a significant problem.

In your opinion, which of the alternatives following each problem would be most helpful to this person?

Please select the one alternative you feel would constitute the most *realistic* solution, and indicate your choice by placing an "X" at the left of the alternative you choose.

Please try to tackle each item as it comes. Do not omit any items, and do not turn back. When you are finished with the booklet, please raise you hand.

Code Number:

_____

1. There is no way out. If I mention that he was drunk last night, then he will tell me to stop berating him; and if I don't mention it, then he will accuse me of being indifferent to him. But I must either mention his drunkenness to him or not mention it to him, and therefore I must either be told that I am berating him or that I am indifferent to him.

WHAT WOULD BE A REALISTIC SOLUTION TO THIS PROBLEM? (Space was provided for response.)

_____

2. If they laugh at my jokes, then it's only because they feel sorry for me; and if they don't laugh at my jokes, then it's because they hate me. But they must either laugh at my jokes or not laugh at my jokes, and therefore they either feel sorry for me or hate me.

WHAT WOULD BE A REALISTIC SOLUTION TO THIS PROBLEM? (Space was provided for response.)

_____

3. If I stop doing it, then I will miss the pleasure; and if I don't stop doing it, then I will continue to feel humiliated. But I must either stop doing it or not stop doing it, and therefore I must either miss the pleasure or feel humiliated.

WHAT WOULD BE A REALISTIC SOLUTION TO THIS PROBLEM? (Space was provided for response.)

_____

4. If she thinks the same as I do, then it will be very boring; and if she does not think the same as I do, then she will be insulting my judgment. But she must either think as I do or not think as I do, and therefore it will either be very boring or she will be insulting my judgment.

WHAT WOULD BE A REALISTIC SOLUTION TO THIS PROBLEM? (Space was provided for response.)

_____

5. Which shall it be—speed or accuracy? If I work fast, then I will make many errors; and if I am careful, then I will get little done. But I must either work fast or I must be careful, and therefore I either will make many errors or I will get little done.

WHAT WOULD BE A REALISTIC SOLUTION TO THIS PROBLEM? (Space was provided for response.)

_____

6. Politics is crooked. If you vote for the regular party candidate, then graft will continue; and if you vote for the new reform party candidate, then there will be an inexperienced administration. But I must vote either for the regular party candidate or the new reform party candidate, and therefore there either will be continued graft or an inexperienced administration.
WHAT WOULD BE A REALISTIC SOLUTION TO THIS PROBLEM? (Space was provided for response.)

_____

7. If I marry early, then I won't have much of a career; and if I don't marry early, then I won't have much security. But I must either marry early or not marry early, and therefore I must either not have much of a career or not have much security.
WHAT WOULD BE A REALISTIC SOLUTION TO THIS PROBLEM? (Space was provided for response.)

_____

8. If I become a social worker, then my father will be unhappy; and if I become a banker, then my mother will be unhappy. But I must either become a social worker or a banker, and therefore either my father will be unhappy or my mother will be unhappy.
WHAT WOULD BE A REALISTIC SOLUTION TO THIS PROBLEM? (Space was provided for response.)

SECTION 10, BOOKLET 6: CASE HISTORIES FOR EXPERIMENTAL EUPHORIC CONDITION (GROUP A)

Instructions

This booklet contains eight brief case histories. Imagine yourself in the role of trying to help this person with his/her problem. The first thing you should do is try to reformulate his/her problem into a dilemma of the form of:

If course of action A, then result B; and
if course of action C, then result D.
But either course of action A or course of action C.
Therefore, either result B or result D.

The general form of this dilemma is as follows:

If _____, then _____; and
if _____, then _____.

But either _____ or _____.
Therefore, either _____ or _____.

After you have completed this, we would like you to try to help this person find a *realistic* solution to his/her problem.

Space is provided after each item for your answer.

Please try to tackle each item as it comes. Do not omit any items, and do not turn back. When you are finished with the booklet, please raise your hand.

Code number:
_____

1. "I think that now I've had enough with school for a while — I'd like to kind of roam around with a buddy — maybe go to California — not be saddled with a bunch of clothes and stuff — just go like we are — and make it on our own for — well, maybe even a whole year — uh — uh — my mom — she — she — wants me to stay in and continue in premed and become a doctor like my dad — well — if I don't make California, then my mom will be happy and proud of me — if I do go, I could really find out about myself and what I really want to do — but I guess it'll all work out all right, and I'll be happy making or not making the trip."

PLEASE COMPLETE PARTS A AND B

A. If _____
   then _____; and
   if _____
   then _____.
   But either _____
   or _____.
   Therefore either _____
   or _____.
B. What would be a realistic solution to this problem?

_____

2. "The way I look at it — it could work out very well either way — my father's in his 70s — a great guy — of course, his digestion isn't what it used to be; and my wife Helen has to spend a lot of extra time preparing his meals and caring in various ways for him, but she doesn't complain — if he went to an old folk's home, that would be a big load off her shoulders and — after all — it's not the worst thing — meanwhile, if he stays with us, then he will be with those who love him and want him around."

PLEASE COMPLETE PARTS A AND B. (Not reprinted here since the format is the same as the format in item 1.)

3. "But I really want to do something more—I've done my duty and had my three kids—done all the messy, grimy things with them—now I want a career—something to make me really important—I want to go to law school and become a lawyer—my little boy and girl—well—they can go to nursery school—I know my husband won't object to doing more around the house—if I go to law school for the next three years, I'm sure he'll be very thrilled and—well—I haven't discussed it with him yet—and if he doesn't agree—and I don't go to law school—then I'm sure I'll continue to be a very good mother and satisfied with being a mere housewife."
PLEASE COMPLETE PARTS A AND B. (Not reprinted here since the format is the same as the format in item 1.)

4. "Sure I'd like to get into better shape—lose all this flabbiness and get trim—exercise and dieting—that's the trick—of course—that's a lot of sweat—jogging and all that stuff—well—even for a middle-aged man like me—if I don't exercise and don't diet—I'll bet my doctor would still say that my chances of avoiding a cardiac are pretty fair."
PLEASE COMPLETE PARTS A AND B. (Not reprinted here since the format is the same as the format in item 1.)

5. "Everybody says I'm just an optimistic person—kind of a sunny disposition—I'm sure I won't have any regrets no matter how I decide—well, it's a little complicated—I'm from Canada—in a national competition, I won a $10,000 Science Foundation Fellowship, but I have to attend a Canadian university to use it—it's not good in the United States and—well—my boyfriend—he's going to be attending graduate school here in the States—and he wants me to be with him, and I guess I want to be also—well—if I go to school here in the States, then we'll both be quite happy—and if I go to a Canadian graduate school, the way I look at it is—is that then—I'd be able to continue my work in microbiology—as I said—I just always think about the brighter side of things—I guess I'm just that way."
PLEASE COMPLETE PARTS A AND B. (Not reprinted here since the format is the same as the format in item 1.)

6. "It never really occurred to me—that men could feel that way—I simply don't believe it—that they resent me because I'm the only woman in the freshman medical class—my grades and finishing at the head of my medical class can only result in their admiring me, and if I perform at an average level—then the men in the class will certainly have no basis to resent me—there's really no problem."
PLEASE COMPLETE PARTS A AND B. (Not reprinted here since the format is the same as the format in item 1.)

7. "But I know for sure—for sure, I tell you—that the medical chief made an incorrect diagnosis—I'm just a medical student—what do I know?—but I know that he made an error in that particular case—how can I tell him? Well—my concern is with the patient—it's very serious for the patient—I thought all day yesterday and all through last night about the other possibility—not telling him—that way—he couldn't get offended and ruin my career —it's no big problem—no big problem, I tell you."

PLEASE COMPLETE PARTS A AND B. (Not reprinted here since the format is the same as the format in item 1.)

8. "Some people have a phobia or something like that about flying— not me—even though we had a close call over San Francisco last year—everyone was pretty well scared to death—I got violently sick—but now it's somehow different—I'm sales manager of the company and my boss expects me to fly to New York—it's part of keeping my job and maybe even getting promoted—of course, there's really nothing to worry about—because even if I don't fly to New York on business—well, I admit it would be a relief, and I don't think my boss would like me or respect me any the less for it—so— do you—it's really no sweat."

PLEASE COMPLETE PARTS A AND B. (Not reprinted here since the format is the same as the format in item 1.)

SECTION 11, BOOKLET 6: CASE HISTORIES FOR EXPERIMENTAL DYSPHORIC CONDITION (GROUP B)

Instructions

This booklet contains eight brief case histories. Imagine yourself in the role of trying to help this person with his/her problem. The first thing you should do is to try to reformulate his/her problem into a dilemma of the form of:

If course of action A, then result B; and
if course of action C, then result D.
But either course of action A or course of action C.
Therefore, either result B or result D.

The general form of this dilemma is as follows:

If _____, then _____; and
if _____, then _____.
But either _____ or _____.
Therefore, either _____ or _____.

After you have completed this, we would like you to try to help this person find a *realistic* solution to his/her problem.

Space is provided after each item for your answer.

Please try to tackle each item as it comes. Do not omit any items, and do not turn back. When you are finished with the booklet, please raise your hand.

Code number:

_____

1. "I'm supposed to register tomorrow for next semester — but I'm rather sick of school — I did pretty well my first year as a freshman in premed — my dad's a doctor — I think he knows how I feel — but my mother is very upset — she thinks I'll turn into a criminal of some kind — and — I just want a chance to move around the country for a while — maybe go to California with a buddy — take no money, no clothes, nothing — work our way across the country and back somehow — maybe not back to school even — after that — maybe after a year out of school — I'd be ready to come back — I've always had everything that I've wanted, and now I think I'd like to find out how it is to live a while without anything really — my mother's crying and real upset — maybe during the year I could really find out about myself — a lot of thinking — maybe reading — after a year I could really know whether I wanted to go on with school and premed and all that — I have to either — hurt my mother — or hurt myself."

PLEASE COMPLETE PARTS A AND B

A. If _____
    then _____; and
    if _____
    then _____.
    But either _____
    or _____.
    Therefore either _____
    or _____.

B. What would be a realistic solution to this problem?

_____

2. "My wife is always nagging — continuing complaining — well mostly — maybe it's about my father who lives with us — he's close to 70 now — in pretty fair health — has slowed up quite a bit — his digestion isn't what it used to be — he complains about her cooking — says it tastes like poison — Helen — that's my wife — she's angry about all the work — cleaning his room — special cooking — helping him in this way and that way — sometimes he gets to feeling pretty lonely and unhappy — she doesn't want that burden any more, she

says. She won't come out and say it, but I know she wants him put into an old folk's home. But I feel — that's — just — like already putting him in a cemetery — he deserves better than that — I know my wife has some affection for him, too — but staying with us — things seem to be boiling all the time in the house — and going to an old folk's home — well — is always bad — it's got me down — I don't know really what to do."

PLEASE COMPLETE PARTS A AND B. (Not reprinted here since the format is the same as the format in item 1.)

---

3. "Men — and my husband especially — they think they're the dominant class. They set the rules and judge. They can follow any career they want and take a job any time. Now I've done my duty and had three children, and I want to return to school — go to law school and become a lawyer — but my husband blows up each time I mention it — he insists that I stay at home just because the kids are too young — well, there are nursery schools, aren't there? — I want to do right by my kids and not fight so much with my husband — but I want to please myself also — am I asking too much? It's all very confusing to me."

PLEASE COMPLETE PARTS A AND B. (Not reprinted here since the format is the same as the format in item 1.)

---

4. "Sure I'd like to keep in better shape — but what kind of exercise and what kind of dieting — it's not easy — I don't like to be flabby, but when I do jogging and other exercises, I get a big appetite and eat a lot — but my doctor says, for a middle-aged man like me, that lots of exercise is important for preventing cardiac attacks, and so is lowering my weight."

PLEASE COMPLETE PARTS A AND B. (Not reprinted here since the format is the same as the format in item 1.)

---

5. "It's kind of complicated — I'm from Canada and they have a $10,000 Science Foundation Fellowship for graduate school — it was a special competitive award — but it's good only at a Canadian university — and my boyfriend — well — he's here in the United States — he will be going to graduate school in the U.S. — he wants me to be here, and I guess I want to be here, too — but my parents and the professors are putting pressure on me to attend a Canadian university and keep the scholarship — I have to decide soon — a lot of pressure is building up — I have to make a decision very quickly, and it seems — either way I'm going to lose something."

PLEASE COMPLETE PARTS A AND B. (Not reprinted here since the format is the same as the format in item 1.)

---

6. "I feel quite rotten — my first semester in medical school I stood at the head of the class. Now I'm all tensed up. I'm the only woman in the class and

the men resent my performance — and resent me even more. I want to be a physician — but I don't know how I can go on."

PLEASE COMPLETE PARTS A AND B. (Not reprinted here since the format is the same as the format in item 1.)

---

7. "But I know for sure — for sure, I tell you — that the medical chief made an incorrect diagnosis — I'm just a medical student — what do I know? — but I know that he made an error in that particular case — how can I tell him — he could ruin my career — but it's serious for the patient — very serious — it's been with me — I don't know — all possibilities — everything I've thought of — everything looks disastrous."

PLEASE COMPLETE PARTS A AND B. (Not reprinted here since the format is the same as the format in item 1.)

---

8. "Do you think maybe it's a phobia? — I don't know when it started — maybe it was last year when we nearly crashed over San Francisco — the plane just made it down — everybody was scared to death — I got violently sick — now I have to make some more business trips — my boss expects me as sales manager to go to New York — even the secretaries tease me about being scared to fly — but it isn't really a joking matter — I could get fired — my boss expects me to fly on all business trips — I'm sweating here just talking about flying."

PLEASE COMPLETE PARTS A AND B. (Not reprinted here since the format is the same as the format in item 1.)

SECTION 12, BOOKLET 7: EXPERIMENTAL INQUIRY FOR EXPERIMENTAL EUPHORIC CONDITION (GROUP A)

Instructions

This booklet contains a questionnaire designed to let you tell us how you feel about the experiment you have just participated in. Please try to answer each question as honestly as possible. Your answers will help us to determine some of the strengths and weaknesses of the experiment and will let us better understand some of the processes operative in a counseling situation.

Thank you for your help. Your cooperation is greatly appreciated.

Code Number:

EXPERIMENTAL INQUIRY

I. Booklets 2 and 3
1. How easy was it for you to put the case histories (booklet 2) into dilemma form?

_____ very easy
_____ moderately easy
_____ about as easy as difficult
_____ moderately difficult
_____ very difficult

2. Did you feel for the people involved that the problems were serious
   a) in the case histories (booklet 2)?

   _____ yes, very
   _____ yes, moderately
   _____ yes, somewhat
   _____ about as serious as not
   _____ no, definitely not

   b) in the dilemmas (booklet 3)?

   _____ yes, very
   _____ yes, moderately
   _____ yes, somewhat
   _____ about as serious as not
   _____ no, definitely not

3. Would you say that some problems were more serious than others
   a) for the case histories (booklet 2)?

   _____ yes
   _____ no
   _____ don't know

   b) for the dilemmas (booklet 3)?

   _____ yes
   _____ no
   _____ don't know

4. Did you feel the solutions you proposed were by and large adequate
   a) for the case histories (booklet 2)?

   _____ yes
   _____ no
   _____ don't know

   b) for the dilemmas (booklet 3)?

   _____ yes
   _____ no
   _____ don't know

5. Did you feel there was one type of solution better than any of the
   others
   a) for the case histories (booklet 2)?

   _____ yes
   _____ no
   _____ don't know

b) for the dilemmas (booklet 3)?

_____ yes

_____ no

_____ don't know

6. If you answered yes to question 5, at about what point in the experiment did you hit on the solution?

_____ about the beginning of booklet 2

_____ about the middle of booklet 2

_____ toward the end of booklet 2

_____ about the beginning of booklet 3

_____ about the middle of booklet 3

_____ toward the end of booklet 3

_____ later on, during booklet 4

_____ later on, during booklet 5

_____ later on, during booklet 6

7. If you answered question 6, would you now say that the solution applies equally well to both case histories and dilemmas?

_____ yes

_____ no

_____ don't know

8. Have you ever been in situations like this, and if so, did you solve them in the same way you did here?

_____ yes, and in the same way

_____ yes, but not in the same way

_____ no

_____ don't know

9. Are there any answers you would want to change now on either the case histories or the dilemmas?

_____ yes

_____ no

_____ don't know

If so, which ones would you change, and how would you change them? At what point did you realize you wanted to change them?

II. Booklet 4

The six alternative solutions you were given are listed below in their general forms for a dilemma of the type:

If A, then B;
and if C, then D.
But either A or C.
Therefore, either B or D.

Solutions:

1. You are not necessarily restricted to A or C.
2. If A, then not necessarily B.
3. If C, then not necessarily D.
4. B is not necessarily good.
5. D is not necessarily good.
6. If A, then not D; and if C, then not B.

For many of the following questions you will be asked to refer to one or more of the solutions. Please do this by *referring to its number*.

1. Were you satisfied with the six alternatives given?

2. If not, did you feel that there were other alternatives not given? If so, how would you rate them in comparison to the alternatives given?

3. Which, if any, of the alternatives did you feel were not solutions?

4. Did you feel any of the alternatives were in fact equivalent to one another? Which ones?

5. If you felt that some of the alternatives were better solutions than some of the others, list them in the order to which they applied. For example, if you thought alternative 3 the best, please list it first.

6. Did you feel one alternative to be consistently better than the others? Which one?

7. The solutions differ in the degree to which they negate various parts of the dilemma. From the point of view of solving the dilemma, do you think it matters if a certain portion of the dilemma is negated, or if the dilemma as a whole is negated? If you feel that it does matter, which method is best, and which solution most typifies that method?

8. Did you feel that the solutions you gave in booklets 2 and 3 could be restated as one of these six alternatives?

9. Are there any answers you would want to change now? If so, which ones would you change, and how would you change them? At what point did you realize you wanted to change them?

III. Booklets 5 and 6

1. How easy was it for you to put the case histories (booklet 6) into dilemma form?

_____ very easy

_____ moderately easy
_____ about as easy as difficult
_____ moderately difficult
_____ very difficult

2. Did you feel for the people involved that the problems were serious
   a) in the case histories (booklet 6)?
   _____ yes, very
   _____ yes, moderately
   _____ yes, somewhat
   _____ about as serious as not
   _____ no, definitely not
   b) in the dilemmas (booklet 5)?
   _____ yes, very
   _____ yes, moderately
   _____ yes, somewhat
   _____ about as serious as not
   _____ no, definitely not

3. Would you say that some problems were more serious than others
   a) for the case histories (booklet 6)?
   _____ yes
   _____ no
   _____ don't know
   b) for the dilemmas (booklet 5)?
   _____ yes
   _____ no
   _____ don't know

4. Did you feel the solutions you proposed were by and large adequate
   a) for the case histories (booklet 6)?
   _____ yes
   _____ no
   _____ don't know
   b) for the dilemmas (booklet 5)?
   _____ yes
   _____ no
   _____ don't know

5. Did you feel there was one type of solution better than any of the
   others
   a) for the case histories (booklet 6)?
   _____ yes
   _____ no
   _____ don't know

b) for the dilemmas (booklet 5)?

_____ yes

_____ no

_____ don't know

6. Do you feel that you now better understand what would be a good solution to problems such as these?

_____ yes

_____ no

_____ don't know

7. Are there any answers you would want to change now?

_____ yes

_____ no

_____ don't know

If so, which ones would you change, and how would you change them? At what point did you realize you wanted to change them?

IV. General

1. Do you think it helpful for a client in a counseling or psychotherapeutic situation to formulate his problem in a logical form?

_____ yes

_____ no

_____ don't know

If so, who should formulate the problem, the client or the counselor?

_____ client

_____ counselor

_____ about both equally

_____ don't know

2. Whose responsibility is it to solve the problem?

_____ client

_____ counselor

_____ about both equally

_____ don't know

3. How should the problem be solved? Should the solution be one of a logical negation of the dilemma, or should the solution be guided by the client's emotions in the matter?

_____ logical solution

_____ emotional solution

_____ about both equally

_____ don't know

4. How satisfactory is a logical solution to the client? Does it relieve his

tensions and frustrations and allow him to continue with the normal process of day-to-day living?

_____ logical solution quite satisfactory

_____ logical solution fairly satisfactory

_____ logical solution not satisfactory

_____ don't know

5. Do you consider placing the dilemma in a logical form as artificial, or is it a valid way of characterizing the underlying personality dynamics in a dilemma situation? In other words, is the logical form a way of arbitrarily organizing your difficulties, or is it really an expression of those difficulties?

_____ logical form is arbitrary and artificial

_____ logical form is a realistic expression of problems

_____ don't know

6. The essence of a true logical dilemma is that there is no way out unless you change one or other of the conditions, that is, negate it. Otherwise, what must follow can only be the unfolding of the logical alternatives as stated in the conditions of the dilemma. Would you say that the problems encountered by the individuals were true logical dilemmas?

_____ yes

_____ no

_____ don't know

7. How would you characterize persons usually involved in dilemmas of the type that you were asked to solve?

_____ extroverted and outgoing

_____ introverted and shy and withdrawn

_____ about both equally

_____ don't know

8. What type of person do you think most adequately solves his problems by using logic?

_____ extroverted and outgoing

_____ introverted and shy and withdrawn

_____ about both equally

_____ don't know

9. What type person do you think could most easily learn to apply a logical solution to his problems?

_____ extroverted and outgoing

_____ introverted and shy and withdrawn

_____ about both equally

_____ don't know

10. What type of person do you think could most benefit from learning to apply this type of solution?
_____ extroverted and outgoing
_____ introverted and shy and withdrawn
_____ about both equally
_____ don't know

11. Did you try to solve these problems by placing yourself in the situation given and imagining yourself in the other person's shoes?
_____ yes
_____ no
_____ don't know

12. Did you feel that you knew what the other person was going through?
_____ yes
_____ no
_____ don't know

13. Would you say that practice with these dilemmas has increased your understanding of problems in general and of ways of solving those problems?
_____ yes
_____ no
_____ don't know
If so, do you think it likely that you will use this knowledge
a) in helping a friend with his problem?
_____ yes
_____ no
_____ don't know
b) in trying to solve your own problems?
_____ yes
_____ no
_____ don't know

14. How would you characterize yourself?
_____ mainly extroverted and outgoing
_____ mainly introverted and shy and withdrawn
_____ don't know

SECTION 13, BOOKLET 7: EXPERIMENTAL INQUIRY FOR CONTROL EUPHORIC CONDITION (GROUP C)

Instructions

This booklet contains a questionnaire designed to let you tell us how you feel about the experiment you have just participated in. Please try to answer each question as honestly as possible. Your answers will help us to determine some of the strengths and weaknesses of the experiment and will let us better understand some of the processes operative in a counseling situation.

Thank you for your help. Your cooperation is greatly appreciated.

Code Number:

I. Booklets 2 and 3

1. How easy was it for you to put the case histories (booklet 2) into dilemma form?

_____ very easy

_____ moderately easy

_____ about as easy as difficult

_____ moderately difficult

_____ very difficult

2. Did you feel for the people involved that the problems were serious

a) in the case histories (booklet 2)?

_____ yes, very

_____ yes, moderately

_____ yes, somewhat

_____ about as serious as not

_____ no, definitely not

b) in the dilemmas (booklet 3)?

_____ yes, very

_____ yes, moderately

_____ yes, somewhat

_____ about as serious as not

_____ no, definitely not

3. Would you say that some problems were more serious than others

a) for the case histories (booklet 2)?

_____ yes

_____ no

_____ don't know

b) for the dilemmas (booklet 3)?

_____ yes

_____ no

_____ don't know

4. Did you feel the solutions you proposed were by and large adequate

a) for the case histories (booklet 2)?

_____ yes

_____ no

_____ don't know

b) for the dilemmas (booklet 3)?

_____ yes

_____ no

_____ don't know

5. Did you feel there was one type of solution better than any of the others
   a) for the case histories (booklet 2)?

_____ yes

_____ no

_____ don't know

b) for the dilemmas (booklet 3)?

_____ yes

_____ no

_____ don't know

6. If you answered yes to question 5, at about what point in the experiment did you hit on the solution?

_____ about the beginning of booklet 2

_____ about the middle of booklet 2

_____ toward the end of booklet 2

_____ about the beginning of booklet 3

_____ about the middle of booklet 3

_____ toward the end of booklet 3

_____ later on, during booklet 4

_____ later on, during booklet 5

_____ later on, during booklet 6

7. If you answered question 6, would you now say that the solution applies equally well to both case histories and dilemmas?

_____ yes

_____ no

_____ don't know

8. Have you ever been in situations like this, and if so, did you solve them in the same way you did here?

_____ yes, and in the same way

_____ yes, but not in the same way

_____ no

_____ don't know

9. Are there any answers you would want to change now on either the case histories or the dilemmas?

    _____ yes

    _____ no

    _____ don't know

If so, which ones would you change, and how would you change them? At what point did you realize you wanted to change them?

II. Booklet 4

1. Did you feel that trying to solve another batch of dilemmas helped you to better understand what would be a good solution?

    _____ yes

    _____ no

    _____ don't know

2. Did you find that you could start to think of various solutions as formulas in which you could mechanically insert one or another aspect of each dilemma, or did you try to solve each problem on the basis of its own individual merits?

    _____ considered solutions as formulas

    _____ tried to solve each problem anew

    _____ don't know

3. Did you feel your solutions were by and large adequate?

    _____ yes

    _____ no

    _____ don't know

4. Are there any answers you would want to change now?

    _____ yes

    _____ no

    _____ don't know

If so, which ones would you change, and how would you change them? At what point did you realize you wanted to change them?

III. Booklets 5 and 6

1. How easy was it for you to put the case histories (booklet 6) into dilemma form?

    _____ very easy

    _____ moderately easy

    _____ about as easy as difficult

    _____ moderately difficult

    _____ very difficult

2. Did you feel for the people involved that the problems were serious
a) in the case histories (booklet 6)?

_____ yes, very

_____ yes, moderately

_____ yes, somewhat

_____ about as serious as not

_____ no, definitely not

b) in the dilemmas (booklet 5)?

_____ yes, very

_____ yes, moderately

_____ yes, somewhat

_____ about as serious as not

_____ no, definitely not

3. Would you say that some problems were more serious than others
a) for the case histories (booklet 6)?

_____ yes

_____ no

_____ don't know

b) for the dilemmas (booklet 5)?

_____ yes

_____ no

_____ don't know

4. Did you feel the solutions you proposed were by and large adequate
a) for the case histories (booklet 6)?

_____ yes

_____ no

_____ don't know

b) for the dilemmas (booklet 5)?

_____ yes

_____ no

_____ don't know

5. Did you feel there was one type of solution better than any of the
others
a) for the case histories (booklet 6)?

_____ yes

_____ no

_____ don't know

b) for the dilemmas (booklet 5)?

_____ yes

_____ no

_____ don't know

6. Do you feel that you now better understand what would be a good solution to problems such as these?

_____ yes

_____ no

_____ don't know

7. Are there any answers you would want to change now?

_____ yes

_____ no

_____ don't know

If so, which ones would you change, and how would you change them? At what point did you realize you wanted to change them?

IV. General

1. Do you think it helpful for a client in a counseling or psychotherapeutic situation to formulate his problem in a logical form?

_____ yes

_____ no

_____ don't know

If so, who should formulate the problem, the client or the counselor?

_____ client

_____ counselor

_____ about both equally

_____ don't know

2. Whose responsibility is it to solve the problem?

_____ client

_____ counselor

_____ about both equally

_____ don't know

3. How should the problem be solved? Should the solution be one of a logical negation of the dilemma, or should the solution be guided by the client's emotions in the matter?

_____ logical solution

_____ emotional solution

_____ about both equally

_____ don't know

4. How satisfactory is a logical solution to the client? Does it relieve his tensions and frustrations and allow him to continue with the normal process of day-to-day living?

_____ logical solution quite satisfactory

_____ logical solution fairly satisfactory

_____ logical solution not satisfactory

_____ don't know

5. Do you consider placing the dilemma in a logical form as artificial, or is it a valid way of characterizing the underlying personality dynamics in a dilemma situation? In other words, is the logical form a way of arbitrarily organizing your difficulties, or is it really an expression of those difficulties?

_____ logical form is arbitrary and artificial
_____ logical form is a realistic expression of problems
_____ don't know

6. The essence of a true logical dilemma is that there is no way out unless you change one or other of the conditions, that is, negate it. Otherwise, what must follow can only be the unfolding of the logical alternatives as stated in the conditions of the dilemma. Would you say that the problems encountered by the individuals were true logical dilemmas?

_____ yes
_____ no
_____ don't know

7. How would you characterize persons usually involved in dilemmas of the type that you were asked to solve?

_____ extroverted and outgoing
_____ introverted and shy and withdrawn
_____ about both equally
_____ don't know

8. What type of person do you think most adequately solves his problems by using logic?

_____ extroverted and outgoing
_____ introverted and shy and withdrawn
_____ about both equally
_____ don't know

9. What type person do you think could most easily learn to apply a logical solution to his problems?

_____ extroverted and outgoing
_____ introverted and shy and withdrawn
_____ about both equally
_____ don't know

10. What type of person do you think could most benefit from learning to apply this type of solution?

_____ extroverted and outgoing
_____ introverted and shy and withdrawn

_____ about both equally
_____ don't know

11. Did you try to solve these problems by placing yourself in the situation given and imagining yourself in the other person's shoes?

_____ yes
_____ no
_____ don't know

12. Did you feel that you knew what the other person was going through?

_____ yes
_____ no
_____ don't know

13. Would you say that practice with these dilemmas has increased your understanding of problems in general and of ways of solving those problems?

_____ yes
_____ no
_____ don't know

If so, do you think it likely that you will use this knowledge

a) in helping a friend with his problem?

_____ yes
_____ no
_____ don't know

b) in trying to solve your own problems?

_____ yes
_____ no
_____ don't know

14. How would you characterize yourself?

_____ mainly extroverted and outgoing
_____ mainly introverted and shy and withdrawn
_____ don't know

APPENDIX B

THE CODING MANUAL FOR DILEMMA SOLUTIONS

Appendix B contains the coding manual used in the experimental research in Chapter 6.

The coding manual is presented in two sections. The first section consists of a fundamental series of charts that present the complete coding of subjects' responses to the dilemma problems of booklets 2 to 6 (see Appendix A). The responses are scored according to type of solution. The second section of the coding manual consists of a selected commentary on the rationale for scoring solutions to dilemmas with special attention to the criteria used for difficult problems of scoring.

SECTION 1

Dysphoric

1   There are other alternatives besides p and q.
Do something else.
Someone else actively solves problems.
Some combination of p and q ("until" statements).
Some differentiation of p and q.
Try one course of action for a while and see.
Try one course; if not successful, try another.
Environmental change logically prior to p or q.
This drastically alters the nature of p.

2

3   Anything that negates the condition regardless of whether it is given as a historically presupposed condition, for example, historically presup-

posed: (1) p$\nrightarrow$r. Not historically presupposed: (2) p$\rightarrow$r, but p = (p₁, p₂, p₃, . . .) and some of these are such that they do not have r as a resultant. (3) p$\rightarrow$r, but some action t is such that it negates the bond (fly$\rightarrow$sick: take pills, see psychiatrist for fear, etc.). Note that this must be a negation of the action, and not of the quality of that action, unless that quality is specifically presupposed in p or q. A negation of the quality (don't worry about their resentment) is scored as 4 or 5. (4) p$\rightarrow$r now, but this is only a temporary state of affairs.

4

5 Anything implying the choice of one solution over another because of a qualitative determination relationship such as: is better than, is more important than, is easier than, gives greater happiness than, and so on. Also moral values: is the right thing, would cause guilt feelings, and so on. Here, note that the scoring is absolute rather than relativistic, in the sense that any one of the four terms, p, q, r, or s, along with a value judgment not part of the original term, will serve for the use of these categories. In addition, note that a response of the form "s is worse" will for dysphoric groups be coded as "r is not so bad." Also, responses of the form "Not s would be good" are taken as equivalent to the inverse "s would be bad," and hence again equivalent to "r is not so bad."

7 Problem reformulated in terms of another dilemma, that is, both alternatives given, or one alternative with criteria given where emphasis is fairly specifically on the criteria needing to be fulfilled, but there is no presupposition as to the direction of fulfillment. As paradigmatic here, see "unless" statements: p unless. . . . Also, this category embraces response items in which no real solution is given, including flip responses, "don't know" responses, cues for clarification (what is "it"?), and so on. Another paradigm is the "evaluate" statement: evaluate p in terms of x. . . .

8 One alternative arbitrarily picked, or one alternative with criteria given with explicit or implicit assumption that criteria will be fulfilled. Here, note that "if" statements taken as a presumption of fulfillment of criteria, that is, "take it if you really want to": inference that if clause modified action and/or describes conditions already existing, rather than sets forth hypothetical conditions for action.

6 as given

0 no response

10 no logical problem exists
    no problem so do whatever you wish
    no problem so do p (or q)

Euphoric

The guidelines here should follow the dysphoric criteria closely with the further observation that any solution of the dysphoric nature is scored according to the nondysphoric components or is scored according to the guidelines for solution 9, for example, (1) make the best grades possible and (2) find new friends who won't be jealous: (2) is ignored. Overcome fear of flying: part of solution 6 present and assumed here, but irrelevant to the euphoric dilemma and so scored as "fly": 9. One exception to especially be careful with in cross-referent scoring (cf. "differences" comments) is the case where the cross-referent is presented as a consequent rather than a presumed modifier of the action: Flying will only make you sick. Here, if consequent is emphasized as exclusive (e.g., "only"), score 2 or 3; if inclusive, score 4 or 5, the latter case being a qualitative judgment. Assume the inclusive sense where such is not explicitly exclusive or explicitly negative to the given consequent.

Booklet 2: Dysphoric

	Problem Number			
Solution	*1*	*2*	*3*	*4*
1	both other find out if it's only field could be happy in needs counseling small homes, where ideas more likely to be accepted alter ideas about work to make money	both other	both other quit professional help EMH until can handle regular	both other let doctor decide try, if too much, then pass on it accept on trial basis compromise take on as many as you can
2	original designs that people want either modify own tastes or make others agree with them make designs more feasible original with part-time other work environment where can be creative original not rich someone will accept them	get a loan (or scholarship or job) for engineering find some way to put self through E.E.	make other understand correction on discipline kids'll soon grow up won't necessarily call names compensate for teasing by special attention restructure situation around EMH avoid contact with other kids talk to parents	try to get assistant

(continued)

249

Booklet 2: Dysphoric (Continued)

	Problem Number			
Solution	1	2	3	4
3	unoriginal→no fame	stay↑not doing what want to do	tutor along with regular class brothers and sisters help	stress not bad physically, just mentally
4	not worth if makes unhappy happiness more fundamental to success poor not bad	worse to drop later E.E. regardless of money happiest in E.E. money not important	EMH best will adjust to name-calling needs better coped with in EMH learn to live with it ignore comments happier at EMH explain that names unimportant educ. more important, don't get discouraged with peers	bad health not bad
5	no fame not bad	better off in ed. not doing what want not bad	not holding own not bad	health more important than promotion may not be up to VP happier not taking not worth heart attack disappointing expectations not bad

7	decide depends on dedication depends on whether others like ideas take up a hobby	decide	decide don't know	decide consider health aspect first explain to boss/wife depends on strain find out about health work in factory and be content physical condition important talk to doctor needs more confidence refuse unless other duties lessened
9	original unoriginal try to sell own ideas if heavy for designs, original won't be happy original, conform original, world ready for a change maybe never truly wanted to be an architect	transfer stay transfer, worry about money later	EMH Regular tell him others don't understand EMH learning	take no what good is dead VP don't, not worth it shouldn't have to take it if he can't
Dilemma	if original, then not rich. If not original, then no fame.	If engineering, then no scholarship. If ed., not doing what want.	EMH, different. Reg., not up to rest of class.	Take, bad health. Don't, not fulfilling response expectation

Booklet 2: Dysphoric (Continued)

	Problem Number			
Solution	5	6	7	8
1	both other slowly get used to crowds counseling get assigned special lectures to small rooms see faculty member for help talk to lecturer	both other other group 1 or 2 friends dates go see doctor get good book get help	both other drop for semester and get problem cleared up see counselor drop hopeless courses, salvage others	other
2	overcome fear counseling for crowd fear adjust to lecture	alone+tense	go, but reveal as little as possible don't have to explain every detail	might be nothing might be curable overcome fear go to doctor and have him tell wife go to still own fears don't worry about being ill
3	get notes from someone	start intellectual conversation won't be so superficial when know you better adjust character to accept people	may not flunk	tell wife to shut up don't go, tell wife you went

#				
4	being not so bad	tense not so bad adjust/accept others learn to cope with world blend in better become interested in group	D's better than E's lecturers are there to help you some teachers are understanding effort would be well worthwhile do more harm if don't go not going is more embarrassing he'll feel better knowing he tried	best to know (about illness) accept fact that might be ill go, better than uncertainty life's worth worrying about better to catch it early make him accept, good or bad
5	missing lectures not so bad	bored not so bad	might be happier working than in school	being nagged not so bad
7	decide find out what causes fear don't know	decide depends on mood seems as if not interested tell group how you feel may solve problem if you can find background stop thinking of self find out why feel friends inferior	decide depends on how serious about school	decide realize your wife not the problem

(continued)

Booklet 2: Dysphoric (Continued)

		Problem Number		
Solution	*5*	*6*	*7*	*8*
9	go no lectures good to attend all of us have to learn to accept things	go out don't get involved in group	go back no find out why people so terrifying, then wouldn't miss class lose face rather than flunk get instructor's views go, even if flunk will salvage something	go no face it sooner he goes, easier to stop go, being ignorant won't make it go away important to know health go, wouldn't hurt anymore go, may die sooner if doesn't go
Dilemma	crowd, faint; not, miss lectures	alone, tense; not, bored	go, embarrassed; not, fail	go, worry about ill; not, wife nag

Booklet 2: Euphoric

		Problem Number		
Solution	1	2	3	4
1	both other try one, if doesn't work, try another	both other	both other let Billy decide let doctor decide	some other let boss/doctor decide take on as much as health permits
2	create→fame	may not like engineering	EMH→holding own	taking→fulfilling expectancy
3	not→fortune	ed→money	will be poked fun at	too sure of self, shouldn't expect so much might not get VP if don't
4	don't worry about fame or fortune	stay, since happiness for both but money for only one	will feel more successful in regular	dead VP no good money not worth health
5	original, since money→success but not happiness create, since rich either way don't worry about money no→ feeling of no accomplishment	transfer, not worth risking happiness would be unhappy as teacher happier in engineering staying in ed. for money is	only lose out in regular happier/better care in EMH EMH since both happy and successful more successful in EMH	good health not good

(continued)

255

Booklet 2: Euphoric (Continued)

Solution	Problem Number			
	1	2	3	4
	decide regardless of material wealth money not everything satisfaction more important than money doesn't really believe money as good	gyping self better to do what want won't like ed.		
7	decide create if possible, not if not do what comes naturally depends on age don't know get rid of self-centered views don't be so optimistic	decide	decide mother's attitude should be changed	decide talk with doctors/boss don't take more than can handle take unless doctor vetoes depends on how much want VP depends on health depends on age take unless too difficult
9	original no original for own satisfaction	transfer stay	regular EMH treat as normal, but give right type of care	take no don't this way won't ruin health

Problem Number

	5	6	7	8
10	no problem	no problem, transfer	what's the problem, Billy's happy	don't because of health take under doctor's care take care of health

Dilemma

	5	6	7	8
	create, fame; not, fortune	engineering, do what want; ed, money	EMH, hold his own; regular, not different	take, fulfill expectations; not, health not bad

Problem Number

Solution

	5	6	7	8
1	both other smaller school go, if can't take it, smaller classes counseling	both stop worrying go to group therapy and form relationship with someone there needs more confidence and psych. help	both find out why don't like classes, maybe drop out for a while	tell wife went, leave and return
2	may miss lectures	people may dislike person at end moving to dorm probably won't help	may fail	will still nag

257

(continued)

Booklet 2: Euphoric (Continued)

			Problem Number		
Solution	*5*	*6*	*7*	*8*
3	may feel faint	will not prove anything	instructors won't understand	what don't know can't hurt more to worry if leave ill, go should go because could get worse
4	will have trouble in large lectures, needs counseling may not get used to it school only makes it worse	get in with group, but don't worry about how they feel	passing not great	excuses could be bad mistakes
5	flunk if didn't go	proving nothing is not good	understanding not great	go, anyone would rather live longer better to go before too late not going could be fatal less to worry if knew what was wrong better safe than sorry
7	see doctor to get rid of problem salve fear of crowds try to cope with problem learn to live with it	be natural be yourself realize inferiority feelings take things as they come too worried about not mak-	find out why in slump, if doesn't care about school decide depends on importance of school	talk to wife

# / Situation			
no solution he should be nervous don't understand	ing friends keep it positive, hell with them learn to know self first be self, won't matter if alone what's the reasoning?	go back or quit go if passing important, not if not	
9 large lectures no get notes from someone adjust to others and stop worrying about crowds	go no seek out similar people find friends who like you for what you are act like you want to, friends will accept you enjoy company of others and gain self-confidence should move since not doing any good here	go no go if passing important	go no go before becomes more serious go to doctor without telling wife will have to go anyway since will have attack
10	wait til there's a problem		
Dilemma large crowd, lectures; no not sick	go, they like; not, proves nothing	go back, pass; not, teachers understand	go, no nag; not, no worry

Booklet 3: Dysphoric

Solution			Problem Number	
	1	*2*	*3*	*4*
1	both	both	both	both
	other	other	other	other
	find sitter first job		can't be one or other all the time	counseling
	wife work			job not giving guilt feelings
	let her decide		look for more subtle ways to get ahead	take actions not wrecking marriage or causing guilt
	take for a while		different business	try job for a while
	invest		be ambitious, not aggressive	
	save a little each month		aggressive with tact	
	if furnishings more important, relationship bad, leave		act neutral	
2	2nd job not interfering with life at home	true friends won't be jealous	aggressive ≠ pushy	sound marriage won't be wrecked
	if need money, complaints will stop	fight imposition on you	aggressive, but not imposing	not taking→wrecking marriage
	2nd job where could be with wife	high, but say low	aggressive→dislike	other factors will wreck marriage
	take and be comforting to wife	they really admire you	success→ like	
	have wife visit friends	reevaluate dislike because of grades	make people like you in other ways	
		dislike is really envy	success brings friends	
		associate with men encouraging scholarship	aggressive without hurting others	
		don't indicate competition	balance aggression with other more likable traits	
		those who dislike aren't friends		

	don't gloat, offer to help			
3	no, she'll learn to do with what she has persuade her to live on less work harder at first job build some of the things she wants talk, if she understood how you felt would be happy with present circumstances	if high grades interfere with more important matter, realize that grades do not equal potential	nonaggressive→failure	guilt offset by saving marriage if mate ok's job don't feel guilty guilt won't last long get over guilt feelings cope with the guilt ignore personal feelings mere guilt wrecking marriage
4	loneliness not bad	disregard emotional feelings self-respect more important if men jealous, they're immature best to fulfill potential don't worry about others better to get grades grades more important than men if these important then disregard others satisfy self first	people who don't like aren't friends anyway don't worry about others	guilt feelings → bad marriage, take if not taking wrecked marriage then marriage not worth it
5	old things not bad	disappointment not bad	more important to be liked	better to feel guilty money not as important as marriage guilt more easily coped with

(continued)

Booklet 3: Dysphoric (Continued)

	Problem Number			
Solution	1	2	3	4
7	decide talk with her both of you decide		decide depends on nature	decide don't understand seek understand of why the outcomes no solution talk to husband reach compromise with husband job iff* necessary
9	second job no	high grades average	aggressive no do what want, others dislike because jealous aggressive if $ the goal aggressive if like business	job no taking→harming spouse, don't job, how can you feel guilty if feel guilty, know it's wrong, don't do it why feel guilty? take it
Dilemma	second job, loneliness; not, no things	high, resentment; not, disappointment	aggression, dislike; not, no success	job, bad marriage; not, guilt

*iff = if and only if.

Problem Number

Solution	5	6	7	8
1	both other modify actions somewhat counseling	counseling separate	both other	both other see IRS about loopholes look harder for more budget money vote for lower taxes financial gain through legal channels increase deductions next time save money
2	dilemma is false won't lose friends develop less superficial friends don't go out of way to be different accept self and others will friends are individuals if don't, friends won't be close friends	strive for different environment cope with social problem divorce ≠ failure no reason to assign blame public will forget divorce, prove you're not a failure	won't be coward in everyone's eyes definition of coward relative and personal not a crowd	hire sharp lawyer and get away with it probably wouldn't be detected may not be caught

(continued)

263

Booklet 3: Dysphoric (Continued)

			Problem Number			
Solution	5	6	7	8		
3	won't lose integrity	will become public if don't admit it	may not be wounded may be in neutral zone noncombat job	will be poorer if get caught won't be poorer		
4	better to have no friends; these wishy-washy they're not worth it personal integrity more im-portant	don't worry about public will feel better if others know own peace of mind more im-portant better to admit failure pub-licly, so who cares if it's public divorce is no disgrace private admission is worse will be respected for ad-mission	learn to live with being a coward don't worry about public better take coward than dead do what you think is right, will have nothing bad to live with	being caught not so bad		
5	friends more important integrity not necessary for you	personal failure present in both, so don't because of public more comfortable to live with self better to admit to self	will lose fear of getting wounded through time facing fear not so bad	detected worse (than poorer) being poorer not as bad consequences greater for cheating better not to be published be content with being poor		

	Individual	Divorce	Avoid draft	Cheat
(cont.)			decide develop more logical thinking avoid if don't believe in serving decide on ethical basis why are these all the same don't know	personal integrity more important public disgrace worse don't cheat, will be happier money isn't everything not worth being put in jail for
7	decide try to answer question "why do you need integrity?" Solution depends on this.	decide divorce iff not possible to make marriage work		decide cheat iff need money if $ cheat, but not losing $ that much anyway
9	individual no don't if want to be liked	divorce no be true to self quit fooling self	avoid draft no avoid → saving life	cheat no no, won't accomplish anything no, can't spend money in jail punishment would be embarrassing everyone has to pay, why not you?
Dilemma	individual, no friends; not, no integrity	divorce, public failure; not, private failure	avoid, coward; not, wounded	cheat, caught; not, poor

Booklet 3: Euphoric

Solution	Problem Number			
	1	*2*	*3*	*4*
1	both wife work let wife decide other	both other	both be yourself	both other parttime take on trial basis try and see
2	will complain of nice things	won't fulfill potential	may be failure	will feel more guilty by wrecking marriage
3	will complain of loneliness	will be rejected	more liked and successful if aggressive few like person sitting back and letting others solve problem if not aggressive, will be stepped on	no, guilt can wreck marriage
4	not having nice things better 2nd job just→to fatigue and loneliness material things unimportant without health	fulfillment not great	being liked more important than business better to have friends than not	happier saving marriage better feeling guilty marriage too important to wreck job marriage more important than own feelings

#				
5	opportunity more important than wife's loneliness	high, otherwise only falling in hole better to please self than others grades more important better to fulfill potential friends like that you don't need	being success more important than having lot of friends	better not feeling guilty not worth it if marriage based on money
7	decide take iff necessary talk with wife depends on finances do what physically capable of depends on how materialistic wife is	get knowledge, if high grades equal this then get them depends on character decide	decide	if marriage saved only by money, look into it decide take job iff necessary realize no job→to guilt, and job→to wrecked marriage you and husband decide don't understand depends on financial needs if don't feel guilty about wrecked marriage, can't help
9	not, complain of loneliness take job no 2nd job with little outside time	high average perhaps high not give what you think, but could open more opportunities	aggressive no tact, but emphasize feelings of others if aggression harmful, then	no, guilt state of mind take no take if doesn't wreck marriage

(continued)

Booklet 3: Euphoric (Continued)

	Problem Number			
Solution	1	2	3	4
	get job and see what happens one job and budget more carefully	high, don't worry what others think poor if others' feelings more important defeating potentiality = defeating self	he doesn't care about others aggression, can be liked and successful	don't if wrecks marriage take, worry about guilt later save marriage take if can be wife and work take job rather than bad one paying a lot job would keep her interested in life while housewife would wane
10			no problem, so do either/both	
Dilemma	take, not complain of nice things; not, not complain of loneliness	high, fulfillment; average, no resentment	aggressive, successful; not, friends	take, no guilt; not, good marriage

Problem Number

Solution	5	6	7	8
1	both	both other counseling, most important to have inner peace	other	both other
2	individual→integrity	might privately admit failure	either way you're wounded can get hurt even if guard avoid→not wounded avoid→trouble avoid→guilty and self-conscious	if found, won't be richer will be caught and end up poor don't, would feel guilty will get caught cheat→rich cheating→bad name only get hurt if cheat lose personal and public integrity if cheat
3	if individual, friends; if not, pushover individual more like to have friends that statement not necessarily true people disrespect you—individual	personal failure can be detected anyway might publicly admit failure	if don't, public opinion might still be against	might still be caught

269

(continued)

Booklet 3: Euphoric *(Continued)*

			Problem Number		
Solution	5	6	7	8	
	individual, who wants stereotyped, idealized friend				
4	integrity not so hot	better to admit wrong than to suffer better to admit personally	better wounded than coward better not to be coward better soldier than coward be drafted, alternatives not worth it	more important not to cheat money not good in jail happier poorer with clean conscience richer not worth punishment rich not most important thing cheating not worth time or trouble bad things happen when cheat would only cheat self cheating→impossible to keep track of legitimate accomplishments	
5	better not to be a success than liked	more important don't consider self a failure	better live coward than dead hero	not detected not great	

7 individual, since friends both ways
more important to have respect for self
integrity better
not being individual = not friend of self, which is bad

happier divorced
divorce to live with feeling of guilt
personal happiness better than what society thinks
happy only by admitting can live only with public failure, lose at

decide
act how you think you should

decide
do what's best
don't worry about failure
forget what others think
depends on your sex

decide
don't know
depends on ethics
depends on whether worried about being judged coward
avoiding because of problem of being wounded is being coward

decide
depends on finances

9 individual
no

divorce
no
divorce, bad marriage = failure
divorce if marriage won't work
divorce, perhaps you have failed
divorce, don't worry about admitting failure

avoid
no
avoid if feel should
avoid, takes more courage
problem of wound doesn't justify avoiding
draft →being wounded

cheat
not
cheat if can get away with it
don't cheat because of punishment
if money means more than havoc, cheat

(continued)

Booklet 3: Euphoric (*Continued*)

Solution		Problem Number		
	5	6	7	8
10		divorce, happiness more important than failure private admission	no problem: indeed coward but not wounded, sign up if wants to look brave	
Dilemma	individual, integrity; not, friends	divorce, not private; not, not public	avoid, not wounded; no, not coward	cheat, richer; not, unde-tected

Booklet 4: Dysphoric

Solution	Problem Number			
	1	2	3	4
1	both other	both level self with others so won't be self-conscious counseling get involved in more group things	other blind date	other
2	won't have low income	pay attention because want to pay attention afraid to ig- nore reasoning faulty	somewhere there is some- one for you won't necessarily be turned down turned down because of de- featist attitude, have con- fidence make self more likable lower standards and you'll be happier	might not abandon you tell, he'll understand will still love you, abandon- ment not solely cause by infidelity will forgive you
3	won't have low intellect satisfaction	not paying attention, afraid to compete	won't necessarily be lonely	might not find out
4	why should $ be as impor- tant	afraid to ignore not bad	don't take being turned down personally, there are	better to tell than have it from someone else

(continued)

273

Booklet 4: Dysphoric (Continued)

Solution	Problem Number			
	1	2	3	4
	intellect more important than money; income can be compensated for so go for intellect		other reasons; being turned down keeps you humble; being turned down not bad; so what if turned down?	if not loyal, doesn't like him anyway so won't matter; worse to hear from other; easier on both to tell; be for own good if tell; if will find out, better chance with honesty
5	low intellectual satisfaction not bad	afraid to compete not bad	being lonely not bad	hearing it from other not bad
7	decide	decide; too simplified for answer; trying to too much; act natural; no superiority complex; superiority/inferiority complex; reevaluate relationships with others; help person understand why feels as does	decide; when knows why feels unloved will be no problem	decide

	5	6	7	8
9	scientist businessman	pay attention / not / don't expect people to be attracted by such a self-centered individual	call / don't / before calling weigh possibility of acceptance / call and hope you won't be turned down / try calling and see what happens	tell / no / tell, if doesn't abandon you, you're lucky / someone else, he'll stay longer / ask for forgiveness / hope he won't leave
Dilemma	scientist, poor; businessman, low intellectual satisfaction	pay attention, afraid to ignore; not, afraid to compete	call, turned down; not, lonely	confess, abandon; not, hear from someone else

		Problem Number		
Solution	5	6	7	8
1	both / other / consult doctor / exercise no overweight and no nervous	both / other / tell him to eat out / tell him to go to hell / let him decide / ask him if he would rather you stop cooking, can always hire a cook	both / other / do it so he thinks he did it / clarify subtly by asking questions / clarify when asked for approach problem as clarifying for self	both / other
2	exercise for weight problem	try to learn to cook better either way	tact, not seeing something† lower level IQ	do†taking advantage

(continued)

Booklet 4: Dysphoric (Continued)

Solution	Problem Number			
	5	6	7	8
		won't always be second rate talk to him, he may understand	clarify without degrading use tact will appreciate it in long run won't degrade if don't talk down	not→missing opportunity
3	something else to solve nervous overcome eating sweets to avoid nervous sweets not only thing to avoid nerves don't, you'll get over it doctor for nerves problem cope with nerves	he'll have to accept your cooking will get used to it maybe he'll forget about his mother's meals own, he can't compare the two develop and better own style own, there'll be something you can make better	won't think unable to help	
4	better not to be nervous being overweight not bad	being called 2nd rate not bad	worse to think can't help	taking advantage not so bad take advantage and see if like it: won't know before-hand

276

				don't be bothered by taking advantage / do it, it can't hurt
5	may be nervous and fat later on if eat sweets	own, don't worry about what he says / being first in own better than second in someone else's	unable to help not bad	take advantage if want to, but friendship more important than advantage / missing opportunity not so bad
7	decide / problem is that thinks will be nervous	decide / like it or lump it	decide / person too self-conscious	decide / what is "H"? / depends ....
9	sweets / no / how are sweets keeping him from getting so nervous	own / mother's / keep trying, sounds like he has the problem / own, ask for helpful criticism / do your best, if yells, tell him to do it himself (go eat out/go home)	clarify / no / tell him don't mean to put down but this is the way it is / clarify unless seems sure he knows H / clarify, worry about consequences later	do it / no / do if doesn't hurt anyway / do it, but don't misuse opportunity / don't, if means taking advantage of others / take advantage if worth the effort / if it feels good, do it
Dilemma	eat, overweight; not, nervous	mother's, second-rate; own, mother's better	clarify, degrade; not, unable to help	do it, take advantage; not, miss opportunity

Booklet 4: Euphoric

		Problem Number		
Solution	1	2	3	4
1	both other	both other be self and have them like you for that look within cultivate good points counseling try to get to know people so that they'll find out what you're really like	other	both other
2	won't have intellectual satisfaction	attention→wanting to compete people like happy people pay attention because like you don't worry so much; all these ideas only in your head he doesn't make such a large impression on everybody pay attention because of what you say	take chance on calling, will be lonely anyway if turned down	may still hear from others

278

3	won't be rich	not paying attention→not afraid to ignore	may be turned down anyway	if don't, may abandon later more likely to abandon if hear from someone else
4	intellectual satisfaction not great	forget them, concentrate on you work for self, don't worry about them quit worrying about people paying attention to you	you're better off lonely	not hearing from others not good
5	decide, but intellect satisfaction more reward than income scientist, since can have both mind more important than billfold decide, don't worry about the money	not afraid to ignore not so great	turned down not bad: 2nd call might be better turned down not as bad as being lonely	tell, better he doesn't hear from others probably kill you if heard elsewhere, so tell and leave worse to hear from others happier if confess tell him, maybe he should abandon you
7	decide depends on how important intellect satisfaction is	mingle, don't worry about competition he seems capable of mingling don't have inferiority complex worried about being ignored	decide	decide depends on whether he'll find out depends on whether married tell, unless he can't seem to grasp it

(continued)

Booklet 4: Euphoric (Continued)

	Problem Number			
Solution	1	2	3	4
		maybe say very little worthwhile which is why ignored / don't feel inferior / ignore those who ignore you / do something / don't know / decide		honesty always best
9	scientist / businessman / scientist is most rewarding / scientist→limited income	pay attention / no / don't worry about competition—you get to know self and others this way	call / no / calling→turned down	confess / no / might not abandon you / don't if will abandon you / if will abandon you, wait until someone else tells / if doesn't find out, won't be abandoned, but may understand
10			no problem, decide	
Dilemma	scientist, intellect; businessman, rich	attention, compete; not, ignore	call, not lonely; not, not turned down	confess, not hear elsewhere; not, not abandon

Problem Number

Solution	5	6	7	8
1	stop eating, smoke, then quit smoking other other way to calm down both	both other	both other clarify so he doesn't know let him decide clarify only when asked	both other
2	eating sweets→less nervous there's a better explanation for nervous than this	might say mom's meals better	might think can't help	might still miss opportunity
3	might still be fat	might be 2nd rate	might think you're degrading	might still take advantage
4	nervousness is good, it cleans your pores worse to be overweight, don't	own, since either way you lose	he's not worth helping if feels degraded may lose him if clarify	will lose integrity if taking advantage of others for own advancement
5	not fat not good	2nd rate not necessarily bad	not degrading not good	do or will regret it later
7	decide depends on whether over-weight	decide	decide his responses not restricted to being degraded or you unable to help	decide do if want to, but not if only taking advantage depends on whether anyone hurt

(continued)

Booklet 4: Euphoric (Continued)

		Problem Number		
Solution	5	6	7	8
9	sweets no eating→ overweight, stopping→ overcoming nerves sweets, if only way nerves can be overcome	own mother's cook 1st-rate meal own, important to be individual happier own may not cook as well in mom's style, but can't have her style compared to it	clarify no clarify ↑degrading maybe you're not capable of clarifying don't, making people feel inferior→ losing friends	depends on situations depends on end product do it don't do if end justifies risk do if safe do↑not taking advantage do if want to do if feel it important
Dilemma	sweets, no nerves; not, not fat	mom, won't say her meals better; not, won't say they're 2nd rate	clarify, help; not, not de-grade	do it, catch opportunity; not, not taking advantage

282

Booklet 5: Dysphoric

	Problem Number			
Solution	1	2	3	4
1	both other counseling ask feign amnesia tell him you love him and kiss him tell him he was life of the party tell it as a joke	other get better jokes quite telling jokes don't make lousy jokes	both other if dependency, try substitution many other ways to get pleasure counseling	both other let her be herself find someone else counseling find out how she thinks and if it's boring or insulting
2	tell, but don't scold tell in nonberating way tell→berate mention it casually	dilemma not true, causal link off laugh because jokes funny/like you if don't feel sorry for self, others won't reading attitudes wrong laughing→feeling sorry when tell joke don't expect reaction ideas about people warped tell them not to feel sorry	stop→missing pleasure missing pleasure overcome by getting rid of humiliation will feel rewarded if stop	same→boring may not be boring or insulting same can be enlightening

283

Booklet 5: Dysphoric (Continued)

	Problem Number			
Solution	1	2	3	4
3	not→indifference no, but pay attention to him	don't laugh because jokes not funny not laugh→hate	don't be humiliated not→humiliation social rules not enough to feel bad about humiliation = state of mind, do it cope with humiliation if right to you, don't worry about others, they cause the humiliation	different→insult different, opinions should be mutually respected she may not think of it at all accept that all people's in- telligence has not the same basis of fact wait until she says some- thing and don't take re- marks personally
4	berate not too bad if you have an understand- ing, neither outcome will be bad	feeling sorry not bad	humiliation worse pleasure not worth humili- ation pride more important than pleasure being humiliated not healthy, avoid it easier to miss pleasure can't feel pleasure if humil- iated missing pleasure not so bad	conformity wanted, so should like it he would rather be bored let her think as she wants, everything'll work out

5	being indifferent not too bad	let them hate you, best find out that they do better to be hated	humiliation not bad	your judgment could stand insulting, either way OK better to insult since→compromise speak own mind, good things could happen
7	decide talk with him about your relationship depends on whether you care	decide get over inferiority complex help person find out why feels this way everyone can't be funny	decide can't answer	decide if insulting judgment by being different, then this is not what she should insult if she agrees and it's boring, then you're boring; his judgment not the only right thing neither of you should think at all
9	tell no tell and accept consequences would be wise to be indifferent	laugh no	stop no if can't eliminate humiliation, eliminate action why feel humiliated, if enjoying it, do it do it continuously do it if gives pleasure	same different be open-minded, listen to constructive criticism you can learn from people who think differently
Dilemma	tell, berate; not, indifferent	laugh, feel sorry; not, hate	stop, miss pleasure; no, humiliation	same, boring; if not, insulting

Booklet 5: Dysphoric (Continued)

		Problem Number		
Solution	5	6	7	8
1	both other fastest with least number errors counseling	both other don't vote unless truly committed	both other try career first, if don't succeed marry if in love find security by living to-gether counseling career until ready for marriage	both other banker in the ghetto social worker in bank
2	fast†errors fast, then check work with remaining time	regular † graft neither statement true such claims not always true	marriage†no career marry into an occupation marry early and work hard start career and earn enough married without hurting career	decide, parents won't be un-happy long if they love you they'll be happy as long as you are
3	slow→ fewer errors→ faster speed	reform→inexperience reform, will have experi-enced advisors reform, can learn inexperience, can mature	career→security late†less security security can be overcome decide, both security and career are possible	mother won't be unhappy

4	errors not bad	experience is best accept the graft as part of it	no career not so bad security most important	decide, but don't worry about parents
5	better to do little right than lot wrong errors→lesser speed accuracy more important lose more time if work fast time gained in speed lost in corrections correct answers better than wrong ones	inexperience not always bad inexperience→incompetence will get more done because inexperienced inexperience better than graft, since can lessen new reform better than experienced graft graft worse remember that regular was once inexperienced don't worry about inexperience	better not to damage career since you'll resent decision security not that important best to find good career if looking for marriage for security, may be disastrous: marriage can wait career more important than security	don't worry about mom
7	decide depends on how important it is do whatever your boss wants	decide inexperience unless graft gives desired effects	decide	decide it's your life, you decide parents should be able to accept your decision; but if not, not your fault
9	fast slow speed kills, try for accuracy	regular reform fight regular reform, not experienced at graft	early marriage no if career valuable, marriage can wait	banker social worker
Dilemma	fast, errors; slow, little done	regular, graft; reform, inexperience	early, no career; not, no security	social worker, pop unhappy; banker, mom unhappy

Booklet 5: Euphoric

Solution		Problem Number		
	1	*2*	*3*	*4*
1	both other give him some attention tell if he brings it up ask him if he was drunk divorce him if he can't appreciate your concern	both other don't tell jokes tell and find out how really feel by asking tell better jokes	other both find another pleasure stop for a while and see what happens	both other let her be herself entitled to own opinions find out how she thinks, then see what reaction is find someone else if same boring don't analyze her
2	tell→not accuse of indifference	laughing doesn't determine hate laughing→not hating laugh because joke funny, like you, etc. don't base people's opinions on your jokes they may be expressing indifference	stopping→not humiliated	same→insulting same→boring
3	not→not berating	don't laugh because joke not funny not laughing→not feeling sorry	humiliation isn't pleasurable so it couldn't have been pleasurable	different can be boring

288

#				
4	worse to be berated	not hate not good	pleasure more important	same = mindless which he wouldn't like better not to be boring better to differ she will be bored if you think like this; maybe she should insult your judgment
5	told to stop berating not so bad	not pity not good	better to avoid humiliation missing pleasure better than feeling humiliated nothing worth feeling humiliated for	not boring, not good
7	decide don't know depends on how drunk he was	decide think positive problem is absurd/unrealistic tell jokes gain more self-confidence laughing→feeling sorry, not→hating so what watch your reactions to others' jokes and see if there really are only two alternatives	decide find out why humiliated for pleasure depends on how humiliated	decide same/different→insulting/ boring no solution either way OK
9	tell no	laugh not	do it don't	same not

(continued)

Booklet 5: Euphoric (Continued)

		Problem Number		
Solution	*1*	*2*	*3*	*4*
	tell in a nice way tell regardless of what he thinks tell→his telling you to stop berating don't tell if doesn't want you to not→berating better you berate than be indifferent best not to tell	let them laugh, don't care what they think don't laugh→not hate, keep telling don't laugh→hate	do it discreetly humiliation should be destroyed don't continue to feel humiliated humiliation wears off in time don't stop, no reason to be humiliated doing it→not feeling humiliated	same→not boring not→insult different, which naturally, so problem is ridiculous same boring resistance = spice always good and less boring to have different opinions
10		what problem?	no problem	no solution needed—no problem
Dilemma	tell, not indifferent; not, not berating	laugh, not hate; don't, not sorry	stop, not humiliated; not, not miss pleasure	same, not insult; not, not boring

290

Problem Number

Solution	5	6	7	8
1	both other medium slow, speed will come later	both other	both other medium wait a little and see how it works out marry when in love first try career and see	both other
2	fast→much done faster→more errors will be destroyed by carelessness haste makes waste accuracy saves more time in long run	regular→experienced	marrying→much security more security by marrying late	not being one or other→either parents being happy
3	not→no errors	graft and party not necessarily correlated, pick best candidate reform→cessation of graft	late→big career	banker→happy dad
4	accuracy more important/better speed not important if accuracy not there	better to stop graft inexperience better than graft method through which other	marrying only for security not good early may be mistake security not always good	happy mom not good

(continued)

291

Booklet 5: Euphoric (Continued)

	Problem Number			
Solution	5	6	7	8
5	quality before quantity a lot of wrong ≠ the careful correct answer	administration get experience not too good experience can→crookedness ethics more important than experience experience not always good	career more important	
6	no errors not so great	experience is better	late, since can have both career and security security better	happy dad not good
7	decide if correction needed for errors then slow depends on importance of errors	decide can't help reform iff graft exists vote for best party regardless of experience depends on which is better retain that which is acceptable don't know	decide don't if only for security marry when you want	if become either, either mom and pop unhappy decide banker/social worker→a parent being unhappy

292

9   fast
slow
fast→more errors
careful→not more done

makes little difference who wins, politics is crooked

regular
reform
reform→no experience
reform, graft only corrupts and makes government useless
experienced administration = graft, vote reform
vote for uncorruptible politician
get rid of graft
experience more reliable

early
late
career first
early→no career
don't if want big career

social worker
banker

Dilemma   fast, a lot done; not, no errors

regular, experience; reform, no graft

early, security; late, career

social worker, mom happy; banker, dad happy

Booklet 6: Dysphoric

	Problem Number			
Solution	*1*	*2*	*3*	*4*
1	both	both	both	both
	other	other	other	other
	travel during summer	pop decide	wait till kids older	get other doctor's opinion
	stay out for part of the year and decide whether to go back	visit often	go back for a while and see how it works	proper combination of diet and exercise
		try a home for a while		exercise moderately and curb appetite
	stay in school one more year	leave house for a while and decide when return		other diet
				don't exercise so much that you get hungry
2	mom would get over it	some homes are nice	make hubby see your point of view	medicine to subdue appetite
	comfort mom, write occasionally	more attention in OFH*	all men not like that	don't eat fattening foods
	explain, will lessen hurt	OFH not bad	husband may cool down	big appetite→eating a lot
		OFH→neglecting pop	she won't hurt anyone	develop will power
		better care at OFH	school, but don't tell	don't eat
		pop might be happy in OFH	going→neglect	must learn to eat properly
				exercise→eating too much
				will soon eat less

294

3	school→hurt self keep searching from where you are	you/dad/hire help pop stops complaining won't last forever Helen will understand	not getting job→being dominated	won't be bad for health
4	personal integrity most important	marriage more important good home best for all get rid of guilt about pop	neglecting kids not bad	health most important eating→being fat low calorie foods dieting easier than dying eating and exercising cancel, so that there should be no weight gain you'll be putting on weight so still be fit
5	California→hurt self (more)	being burden not bad	best to take care of kids	bad health not bad
7	decide	decide find some way to alleviate tension talk to wife wife should tolerate him unless becomes totally unbearable ask pop bury him	decide talk to husband depends on how old kids are	decide what does doctor say

(continued)

Booklet 6: Dysphoric (Continued)

	Problem Number			
Solution	*1*	*2*	*3*	*4*
9	school California try to get mom to realize circumstances try remotivation for school take a while off	stay OFH	school home don't you feel responsible for kids; why did you marry	exercise and diet no
10				no problem
Dilemma	California, mom unhappy; not, not find self	old folk's home, guilt; not, burden on wife	school, hurt kids; not, hurt self	exercise, eat alot; not, bad health

*OFH = old folk's home.

	Problem Number			
Solution	*5*	*6*	*7*	*8*
1	both other try a year in Canada	both other stay in medicine, but don't do things leading to re-sentment	both other ask tell patient to go to other doctor	both other see doctor give flying another chance, maybe you'll like it try flying again

#				
2	Canada→losing b.f.* b.f. goes to Canada visit can see b.f. later boyfriend may not be mad	ignore/overcome resentment doing well→resentment high, but offer aid to others resentment will turn into respect they'll learn to live with you you will respect you if you show strength of character	tell→ruined career would be glad to have diagnosis corrected you can't predict his reaction	realize flying not dangerous overcome fear counseling for fear
3	check into US scholarship USA→losing money USA, parents will get over it	average→failing potential	patient might not be endangered	talk to boss, will understand not flying→losing job
4	if loves you, will understand; if not, not worth it fellowship better losing b.f. not so bad b.f. and parents should understand either way	keep going, will eventually relax don't worry/bother about them high, will be worth it in long run get other feeling ridiculed, don't worry so what if resent, work to potential adjust to resentment can take it if want to what is their resentment resentment not worth giving up career	better to save life if help patient, won't have to worry about jeopardizing job he, not you, misses out if he fires you ruined career not important lifetime of guilt not worth it if doesn't understand then he's not worth it	getting sick not bad

(continued)

Booklet 6: Dysphoric (Continued)

		Problem Number		
Solution	5	6	7	8
5	happier in USA happiness more important than money	failing potential not bad	career more important	losing face/getting fired not bad
7	decide depends on finances/feelings depends on school quality	decide	decide	decide
9	Canada USA Canada, things'll work out if b.f. really loves you, won't want you to miss this opportunity	high average quitting school would be mistake drop if more important to have friends	tell no good doctor won't endanger life for personal reasons tell, if won't listen seek other doctor's support	fly no
10				
Dilemma	Canada, won't be with b.f.; not, won't have scholarship	high, resentment; average, fail potential	tell, ruin career; not, hurt patient	fly, sick; no, lose face

*b.f. = boyfriend

Booklet 6: Euphoric

Solution	_____ Problem Number _____			
	1	*2*	*3*	*4*
1	both other find self in school, if doesn't work go to Calif. try premed, and see	both other	both other night school part-time wait till kids older let husband decide	both other go to doctor and see what he says
2	California→finding self	will be burden	law school→career	I don't believe this, usually exercise helps cardiac arrest exercise→no heart trouble
3	California, being happy for self only way to make anyone else happy	won't be with loved ones loved ones love him more in house	no→good mother	exercise, only fooling self about cardiac lack of exercise→preventing cardiac, exercise→cardiac
4	happy both ways so don't go school, since would be sad if now sad better off staying put	happier/better staying OFH bad for mental health OFH terrible will feel guilty if don't keep him	kids need you more than you need career more important to be with kids extra work might not be as	good health not so good

(continued)

Booklet 6: Euphoric (Continued)

Solution			Problem Number	
	1	*2*	*3*	*4*
5	regret would make you hate her, go	need special attention in OFH	rewarding as you think	better to be healthy
	your happiness more important than hers, go	nice house preferable to burdening wife	too hard to go back after family	health more important than laziness
	will waste time and money in premed if not what wants	loved and wanted in OFH as well as here	children need attention they would otherwise miss	better to look trim than to chance a cardiac
	happier going to California	better care/treatment in OFH	law, since might regret it other wise	happier exercising
	could be cheating self, move, and patience if don't go	happier with people his own age	isn't satisfied as housewife	better chances for living longer with exercise
	may regret it later if don't go			having fair chances doesn't mean anything
				more gained by getting into shape
				exercise, better off in long run
				can't be in good health when fat, also would feel better

#			
7	decide depends on personality do what you want find self here and then de-cide depends on whether need to get away from it all is real or not	decide depends on how much bother he is don't know depends on wife stay unless causes problems depends on health	decide husband and wife decide go with husband's consent talk with husband what would happen to fam-ily, is marriage that stale sounds like didn't want to marry, you want some-thing important	decide depends on health
9	school California go if think it necessary do what you want to don't have to go away to find self go if you hate premed if don't go, may never know what you missed	OFH stay staying→not being with loved ones hire someone to help with work can't be good wife and mother if have to care for father	law school no nursery for kids not wise go if mate doesn't mind	exercise and diet no job, good health very im-portant work off fat, health and happiness strongly rela-ed save health lose weight diet if not doing so = not avoiding cardiac follow doctor's advice
10			no problem, talk to husband	
Dilemma	California, find self; not, mom happy	OFH, not burden; stays, loved	law school, fulfilled; not, good mother	exercise, good health, not, still avoid cardiac

(continued)

Booklet 6: Euphoric (Continued)

| | | | | *Problem Number* | | | |
Solution	5	6	7	8
1	both other try micro to find real love Canada until certain of re- lationship with b.f. try Canada and see	both other medium-high grades try high and wait and see	both other ask	both other quit if you hate your job
2	Canada→continue in micro- biology	high→resent, accept this high→admiration	may not benefit patient	won't meet expectations
3	USA→be with boyfriend	average→no resentment	not telling→ruined career	will be sick
4	happier in U.S. micro not good/important will only get horny if in Canada	admiration not so great good grades, don't worry about others impt. to get grades; satisfy self before other	benefiting patient not good	fear of airplanes more im- portant than job don't fly, since relief, and keep job either way

302

(continued)

would regret if passed up opportunity, fly
promotion more important than indifferent boss
fly, will be ahead in long run

decide
depends on whether phobia persists
fly unless you really can't
how much do you like getting sick
talk to boss

life more important than propriety/career
tell or would feel guilty
should be more interested in patient's health than career
will learn more if tell
patient more important
tell, don't be guilty about being responsible for loss of life
would be horrible if anything happened because didn't tell

decide
depends on how important patient is

better to worry about career than whether liked
do best since no problem either way
the lost resentment not worth the respect

decide
need more information

5
hell if went to U.S. and broke up
Canada and be satisfied since happy both ways
frustrated in U.S.
won't be happy with boyfriend
dissatisfied in U.S. in long run

7
decide
go to Canada or try for $ in U.S.
talk to boyfriend, probably want you to stay in Canada
Canada unless much $
depends on finances
depends on relationship with boyfriend

Booklet 6: Euphoric (Continued)

Solution	5	6	7	8
9	Canada USA USA if b.f. important Canada if can get along without b.f. Canada if need $ b.f. go to Canada USA and be happy if that's more important to her than continuing work	high average average→resentment	tell no no→hurt patient tell→ruined career tell because chief might harm patient tell, it's the right thing	fly no no→no promotion overcome fear of flying counseling to overcome fear flying→getting sick doesn't have to fly for promotion
10		no problem either way		
Dilemma	Canada, fellowship; not, boyfriend	high, admiration; average, no resentment	tell, benefit patient; not, benefit career	fly, meet expectations; don't not sick

SECTION 2. CODE: GROUP (DYSPHORIC VS EUPHORIC). BOOKLET DILEMMA SOLUTION

Selected Commentary

D

211 small homes where ideas more likely to be accepted; alter ideas about work to make money: both scored 1 because of implied differentiation of creative versus noncreative, the first dealing with *limited* creativity; the second with a differentiation not necessitated by the problem itself, since it is given that money can be had (implicitly).

212 either modify own tastes or make other's agree with them; environment where can be creative: the first is scored 2 because of reasons discussed in the priority conditions; the second is scored 2 because of the addition of a third condition between p and r that serves to negate r.

219 won't be happy original, conform; original, world ready for a change: the first scored 9 instead of 4 because of simple repetition of the "quality" associated with p, rather than an active relational comparison, or a moral absolute; the second scored 9 because of ambiguity.

229 transfer, worry about money later: not scored same as a "regardless" statement because of lack of negation of the quality or consequent: it merely delays the consequent action.

231 professional help: by itself this is always scored as 1, but if the aid offered is for the alleviation of some condition leading to one of the consequents, then it is accordingly scored as 4 or 5.

232 compensate for teasing by special attention: any "compensate" or "overcome" statement will be taken as negating the consequent action, rather than its quality. This is obvious for the "overcome" statement but is also justified for the "compensate" statement in that it does not readily suppose a separation of action and quality, but seems instead to offer a separate course of action.

234 will adjust to name-calling: in this case the "adjust" does not seem to deal with a course of action per se.

239 tell him others don't understand: here, it is not apparent that this will serve, or is intended, to negate the quality.

249 what good is dead VP?: this is partly cross-referential, and also not comparatively indicative.

263 adjust characters to accept people: here, the character is not explicitly presumed in p or q so that this can be taken as a differentiation of q.

267 may solve problem if can find background: however, it's not very clear what the nature of this solution is, or that it must logically follow from "finding background," hence, not scored as 1, but rather 7.

271   drop for a semester and get problem cleared up: category assignment based on "drop for a semester."

274   teachers will help: negation of negative quality.

279   (1) find out why people so terrifying, (2) then wouldn't miss class: (1) alone would be scored as in 267, but (2) qualified it by asserting a choice.

279   go, even if flunk, will salvage something: not scored as 5 because of cross-referential ties, that is, flunking is associated with p instead of q, and hence in this case is not a valid quality-bearing argument. Lose face rather than flunk: "rather" doesn't have the force of a relation between qualities strong enough to allow it scoring of 4 or 5.

282   don't worry about being ill: in this case not scored as 4 because of inclusion of "worry" in r, so that the response serves directly to contradict r.

289   the sooner he goes, the easier to stop; may die sooner if he doesn't go: neither of these deals with the problem per se. In the first, a condition is perhaps set up, but this is not made clear. However, the implication is that he will go sooner or later, and that given this, it *might* be better to go sooner. Hence, the 9 score. In the second, it effectively reasserts the negative quality of a cross-over, rather than of the dilemma itself.

311   wife work; invest; save a little each month; if furnishings more important, relationship bad, leave: the first three serve to negate the dependency between p and r and q and s, and this might seem to be solutions of the form 2 or 3. However, the implication here is that of a drastic restructuring of the environment which is logically prior to both p and q. Hence, the scoring is 1. The fourth solution obviously points out an alternative to p and q and is not scored as 4 or 5 because of the nature of the "if" statement.

331   look for more subtle ways to get ahead: again, in a number analogous to the first three responses of 311, the scoring is 1.

352   dilemma is false: according to the criteria any response of this nature is automatically scored as a negation of the first dependency given. Hence, score 2.

367   divorce if and only if it's not possible to make the marriage work: "if and only if" statements, as opposed to "if" statements, whether explicit or implicit, are statements of conditions to be fulfilled, but which are not assumed as fulfilled in one or another ways. They are therefore considered to be restatements of the dilemma, not transforms of it.

379   avoiding draft leads to saving life: this is presumed equivalent to the euphoric cross-over "avoid means not wounded" and thus irrelevant to the dysphoric dilemma, except where the cross-over is exclusive, that is, that "saving life" and "being coward" are mutually exclusive. Such cannot be assumed here, and the saving is based on the fact that one cause of action was repeated as the solution.

381 see IRS about loopholes; budget money; use legal channels for financial gain; increase deductions next time; save money: again these are exactly analogous to the first three examples given in 311, and to the example in 331.

387 if you need the money cheat, but you're not losing that much anyway: this is an example of the "whole-thought" condition; based on the "if" clause, scoring would be 9. However, the clause that follows implies a negation of the "if" clause, serving to transform it into an "iff" clause.

389 don't, can't spend money in jail; punishment would be embarrassing: both of these repeat the negative quality associated with one cause of action, but neither does it in an absolute sense, and neither does it in a relational sense, thus not meeting criteria for 4 or 5.

414 income can be compensated for, so go for intellect: unlike 232, the compensate statement is implicitly rather than strongly directed to the quality in the sense of the cultural "money-isn't-everything" value.

432 turned down because of defeatist attitude; have confidence: this is a case of a differentiation of the p–r bond such that an intermediary link, confidence or the lack of it, is response for the r. The "have confidence" thus serves to negate the cause of r, and scoring is accordingly 2.

439 call and hope you won't be turned down: the "hope" phrase does not serve as a negation of r, nor does it serve as a negation of the quality of r, since its implicit "better" quality is logically prior to and negated by the outcome of being turned down.

451 exercise leads to no overweight and no nervousness: here, the problem as a whole is being solved, rather than one or other of the bonds being negated. Hence, the solution is taken as logically prior to and different from p or q.

452 exercise for weight problem: now exercising is taken as a negation of one of the specific bonds and is no longer logically prior to p or q.

455 may be nervous and fat if eat sweets: this implies that the person will be nervous either way, and fat one way, and that hence being nervous is not so bad, but it's worse to be nervous and fat.

479 clarify unless he seems sure he knows it: this is not considered to be an "unless" statement, since the condition posed seems to be a trivial one. If there were the implication that the condition was responsible for the problem, scoring would be 7. As it is, it remains 9.

485 take advantage if want to, but friendship more important than advantage: the "whole-thought" criterion negates scoring based only on the "if" clause, since the focus is on "friendship more important." Scoring is thus 5, whether by this reasoning, or by the logical priority condition.

511 tell it as a joke: again, the p/q conditions seem sufficiently changed to warrant coding as 1.

532 missing pleasure overcome by getting rid of humiliation; will feel

rewarded if stop: the first is a standard "overcome" statement (cf. 232), while the second is scored as 2 because of inclusion of the quality as the resultant in the dilemma.

533   if it's right to you, don't worry about the others; they cause the humiliation: given the "whole-thought" criterion, this is not scored 4/5 because of the inclusion by the subject of the quality and result. Thus, the "don't worry" statement in this case serves to directly negate the q–s bond.

654   if he loves you, he'll understand; if not, he's not worth it: although two conditions are given here, they are of equal stature: hence, the "exclusive or" is assumed: either he understands, or he's not worth it. The first condition is taken, and thus serves as a negation of the quality: "not being with your boyfriend won't be so bad."

659   Canada, things'll work out; if he loves you, he won't want you to miss this opportunity: the first is too nebulous to classify as other than 9; the second is a standard "if" statement.

679   tell, if won't listen, see other doctor's support: normally the last clause would serve for a 1 classification. However, in this case it is quite obvious that the emphasis or point of the whole solution is directed toward telling, and not toward solving the problem of a ruined career.

E

215   create, since rich either way; decide regardless of material wealth: in a manner analogous to D455, the first is considered as equivalent to "being rich alone is not that great, since can be rich and famous." The second, although it does not give a cause of action, is similarly scored 5 because of its implication of a negative value on being rich.

224   stay, since happiness for both, but money for only one: again, scored in the same manner as the first solution in 215.

241   taken on as much as health permits: although this would normally be scored 7, the implication is that the restriction is not an all-or-none one.

244   dead VP no good: here, there is a definite negation of the quality attached to "taking the responsibility."

269   find friends who like you for what you are: unlike in the dysphoric dilemma, this solution is totally inappropriate, and thus scored as being on the basis of finding friends, that is, getting in with friends. Hence, solution 9.

281   tell your wife you went; leave and return: again, this is more appropriate to the dysphoric case. However, it can also be a solution of the euphoric dilemma as a whole, such a solution being a "have your cake and eat it, too" solution. The response permits both consequences and hence is scored as 1.

283   more to worry if become ill, go; go, because it could get worse: these fairly obviously negate the p–r bond. In this case, the quality is contained within the results, and hence the negation is coded as 3 rather than 5.

319   one job, and budget more carefully: the second portion of this response is inappropriate to the euphoric dilemma and is consequently ignored. Scoring is based on what's left.

329   perhaps high grades will not give you what you think but they could open more opportunities: based on the first phrase alone, scoring would have been 2. However, the second phrase makes it fairly obvious that the referent of the first phrase was the cross-over, the dysphoric condition. Scoring is then again based on only the fact that high grades as a case of action are desirable.

333   more liked and successful if aggressive: although they seem similar at first, there is an important difference both in coding and interpretation between solutions such as 224 and this. The difference is paradigmatically keyed by the word "more," which is interpreted here as a relational operator. Hence, "more liked if aggressive" relativistically entails "not liked if not aggressive," and thus serves as a direct negation of the q–s bond.

339   if aggressiveness is harmful, then he doesn't care about others: there are two aspects to be noted here: first, the solution seems to be a cross-over, and therefore inappropriate; second, the implied "don't worry about others" is asymmetric with regard to the dysphoric and euphoric conditions, such that it can't be scored as 4 or 5 in the euphoric case unless it also serves to express something of the nature of a cultural value, that is, money isn't everything.

349   no, guilt is a state of mind: again, this has meaning primarily in the "cross-over" sense.

353   individual, who wants stereotyped, idealized friends: classifying this as 3 rather than 5 was a difficult decision. It was partly based on the popular response that "friends like that aren't really friends," which could be one interpretation of the response. In support of this interpretation was the restriction of the consequent, "friends," to "stereotyped, idealized friends," in seeming opposition to plain, regular friends. Hence, though the response did contain the word "friends," this was taken as being somewhat in an ironic or sarcastic vein.

369   divorce, don't worry about admitting failure; divorce, happiness is more important than failure: the first is scored in like fashion to 339; and the second is scored 9 because the relational operator is made to refer to failure, inappropriately for the euphoric dilemma. If the response had simply been: "divorce, happiness more important," scoring would have been 5.

424   quit worrying about people paying attention to you: in this case, the nature of the dilemma was such that the "don't worry" was considered applicable, the dilemma not necessarily being as "euphoric" as the others.

427   mingle, don't worry about competition: this is analogous to 424, except that this is in part a strict "don't worry" statement. In 424 the quality of worrying is presupposed and has to be specifically negated, while such is not the case in a "don't worry" statement. However, because of the nebulous nature of the dilemma, it was felt best to score on anything else that might be part of the solution. Scoring of 7 was thus based on "mingle" with the possibility of the "don't worry" statement being a cross-over.

445   tell him, maybe he should abandon you: this is taken as "abandonment not necessarily bad" and therefore as "nonabandonment not necessarily good."

469   own, important to be individual: as with "regardless" statements and "don't worry" statements, one has to be careful with "important" statements. In the dysphoric conditions, such statements serve as a contrast to the negative qualities of the dysphoric dilemma, while they are not so uniformly contrasted in the euphoric conditions. Other factors must thus be considered in deciding whether such a contrast has been formed (cf. the second point mentioned in 339). It was decided in this case that the response only served to reiterate the positive quality. If the phrasing had been "more important," then scoring would have been 4 or 5.

479   don't, making people feel inferior leads to losing friends: here, the crossover has again been used. Scoring is thus based only on the "don't clarify."

519   tell regardless of what he thinks: as in 469, the decision made was that there was not enough of a contrast to warrant a 4 or 5.

529   let them laugh, don't care what they think: ditto

549   thinking the same doesn't mean it's boring: again, this solution is geared toward the dysphoric dilemma.

567   makes little difference who wins, politics is crooked: the first thing to notice about this response is that it is global — it deals with the dilemma as a whole. Its nature is such that it doesn't necessarily negate any consequent or quality in particular. However, a solution is not unambiguously proposed; hence, the 7 scoring.

577   don't marry early if it's only for security: the decision in this case, due in part to the content of the dilemma, was that this would be treated as an "iff" statement, rather than a simple "if." This was in part based on the presence of "only" in the response.

619   you don't have to go away to find yourself: scoring is based on "you don't have to go away" since there is no explicit statement to the effect

of staying because you can find yourself that way, too. If such were the case, scoring would be 4; as it is, it's 9.

629   hire someone to help with the work: this is irrelevant to the euphoric situation. However, the implication in any case is that the father will stay.

649   jog, good health is very important: again, the decision is that not enough of a contrast is present for a coding of 4 or 5.

654   will only get money if in Canada: scoring is based on negation of quality.

662   high grades lead to resentment, accept this: the nature of this response seems to imply an exclusive nature that admiration and resentment are mutually exclusive. In part, this is based on the fusion of the result and quality in this particular problem.

684   fear of airplanes more important than job: here, the question of fear is inappropriate, and scoring is based on the job not being that important.

NOTES

1. Assume an exclusive "or" in A or B statements: score as
   a) Unless repeats as p or q
   b) subject to priority condition of logical solutions.
2. Priority condition: logical solutions first where such are in the first "thoughts" given, this later usually coterminous with the unit of the sentence. Also, there is a further priority in strict logical versus nonstrict logical solutions, for example, architect example: either (1) modify own tastes or (2) make others agree with them. Since (2) is strict–logical whereas (1) is not, (i.e., 1 operates on conditions rather than on the consequents), score as 2 rather than 1.
3. "Reasoning false; both premises false; etc."; 2.
4. Also 9, before 7.
5. Regardless statements: p regardless of the money. In dysphoric this is scored 4/5 because of the negation of the quality, being equivalent to "don't worry about money." But, this has an asymmetry in euphoric statements, not having as much punch: here, score 9.

BIBLIOGRAPHY

Abelson, P., and Hammond, A. 1977. "The Electronics Revolution." *Science,* pp. 1087–92.

Adler, A. 1931. *What Life Should Mean to You.* Boston: Little, Brown.

―――― 1929. *The Practice and Theory of Individual Psychology.* New York: Humanities Press.

Alexander, I. E. 1982. "The Freud–Jung Relationship—The Other Side of Oedipus and Countertransference: Some Implications for Psychoanalytic Theory and Psychotherapy." *American Psychologist,* pp. 1009–18.

Alpert, D., and Bitzer, D. L. 1970. "Advances in Computer-Based Education." *Science,* pp. 1582–90.

Applebaum, S. A. 1982. "Challenges to Traditional Psychotherapy from the 'New Therapies.'" *American Psychologist,* pp. 1002–08.

Arieti, S. 1959. "Schizophrenia: The Manifest Symptomatology, the Psychodynamic and Formal Mechanisms." In *American Handbook of Psychiatry,* edited by S. Arieti, New York: Basic Books.

―――― 1955. *Interpretation of Schizophrenia.* New York: Brunner.

Bakan, D. 1967. *On Method.* San Francisco: Jossey-Bass.

Bartlett, F. C. 1958. *Thinking.* New York: Allen and Unwin.

Bear, G., and Hodun, A. 1975. "Implicational Principles and the Cognition of Confirmatory, Contradictory, Incomplete, and Irrelevant Information." *Journal of Personality and Social Psychology,* pp. 594–604.

Beck, A. T. 1976. *Cognitive Therapy and the Emotional Disorders.* New York: International Universities Press.

―――― 1970. "Cognitive Therapy: Nature and Relation to Behavior Therapy." *Behavior Therapy,* pp. 184–200.

Beech, J. 1980. "An Alternative Model to Account for the Clark and Chase Picture Verification Experiments." *Journal of Mental Imagery,* pp. 1–11.

Benjafield, J. 1983. "Some Psychological Hypotheses Concerning the Evolution of Constructs." *British Journal of Psychology,* pp. 47–60.

313

Benson, H. 1975. *The Relaxation Response.* New York: Avon.

Bertalanffy, L. von. 1968. *General Systems Theory: Foundations, Development, Applications.* New York: G. Braziller.

Bloom, B. F., and Broder, L. G. 1950. *Problem-Solving Processes of College Students.* Chicago: University of Chicago Press.

Bogartz, Richard S. 1967a. "Some Geometry of the Analysis of Variance." University of Illinois at Urbana-Champaign.

——— 1967b. "Algorithms for E(MS's), degrees of freedom, and sums of squares in fixed random, and mixed analysis of variance experimental design models with crossed and nested factors." University of Illinois at Urbana-Champaign.

Bonifacio, P., and Nolan, J. 1978. "Computer-Augmented counseling — Maintaining Student Services on a Limited Budget." *Journal of College Student Personnel,* pp. 398–401.

Boole, G. 1854. *An Investigation of the Laws of Thought.* New York: Macmillan.

Bourbaki, Nicolas, 1964. *Elements de Mathematique.* Paris: Hermann.

Bourne, L. E., and Guy, D. E. 1968. "Learning Conceptual Rules. II. The Role of Positive and Negative Instances." *Journal of Experimental Psychology,* pp. 488–94.

Breuer, J., and Freud, S., 1957. "Studies on Hysteria." In *Standard Edition of the Complete Psychological Works of Sigmund Freud, Volume II,* edited by James Strachey. New York: Basic Books.

Brichacek, V., Katetov, M., and Pultr, A. 1978. "A Model of Seemingly Irrational Solutions of a Task to Identify a Critical Set." *Journal of Mathematical Psychology,* pp. 220–48.

Bringmann, W. G., Balance, W. D., and Giesbrecht, C. L. 1972. "The Computer vs the Technologists." *Psychological Reports,* pp. 211–17.

Brinley, J. F., and Sardello, R. J. 1970. "Increasing the Utility of Negative Instances in Conjunctive Concept Identification." *Psychonomic Science,* pp. 101–02.

Brown, C., Keats, J., Keats, D., and Seggie, I. 1980. "Reasoning About Implication: A Comparison of Malysican and Australian Subjects." *Journal of Crosscultural Psychology,* pp. 394–410.

Bruner, J. S., Goodnow, J. J., and Austin, G. A. 1956. *A Study of Thinking.* New York: John Wiley.

Carroll, J. B. 1964. *Language and Thought.* Englewood Cliffs, NJ: Prentice Hall.

Catlin, J., and Jones, N. 1976. "Verifying Affirmative and Negative Sentences." *Psychological Review,* pp. 497–501.

Chapman, L. J., and Chapman, J. P. 1959. "Atmosphere Effect Reexamined." *Journal of Experimental Psychology,* pp. 220–26.

Chomsky, N. 1957. *Syntactic Structures.* The Hague: Mouton.

Clark, H. H. 1969. "Linguistic Processes in Deductive Reasoning." *Psychological Review,* pp. 387–404.

Cochran, D. J., Hoffman, S. C., Strand, K. H., and Warren, P. M. 1977. "Effects of Client/Computer Interaction on Career Decision-Making Processes." *Journal of Counseling Psychology,* pp. 308–12.

Cohen, J. 1969. *Statistical Power Analysis for the Behavioral Sciences.* New York: Academic Press.

Cohen, M. R. 1944. *A Preface to Logic.* New York: Holt.
_____ and Nagel, E. 1934. *An Introduction to Logic and Scientific Method.* New York: Harcourt and Brace.
Colby, K. M., Watt, J. B., and Gilbert, J. P. 1966. "A Computer Method of Psychotherapy: Preliminary Communication." *Journal of Nervous and Mental Disease,* pp. 148-52.
Cope, D. 1979. "Reasoning with Conditionals: The Effects of a Binary Restriction." *British Journal of Psychology,* pp. 121-26.
Copi, I. M. 1967. *Symbolic Logic.* New York: Macmillan.
Cotton, J. W. 1982. "Where is the Randomness for the Human Computer?" *Behavior Research Methods and Instrumentation,* pp. 59-70.
Darwin, C. 1871. *The Descent of Man.* London: Murray.
Davidson, M. 1969. "Positive Versus Negative Instances in Concept Identification Problems Matched for Logical Complexity of Solution Procedures." *Journal of Experimental Psychology,* pp. 369-73.
Demetriou, A., and Efklides, A. 1979. "Formal Operational Thinking in Young Adults as a Function of Education and Sex." *International Journal of Psychology,* pp. 241-53.
DeSoto, C., London, M., and Handel, S. 1965. "Social Reasoning and Spatial Paralogic." *Journal of Personality and Social Psychology,* pp. 513-21.
Dilley, J. S. 1967. "Decision-Making: A Dilemma and a Purpose for Counseling." *Personnel and Guidance Journal,* pp. 547-51.
DiLoreto, A. O. 1971. *Comparative Psychotherapy: An Experimental Analysis.* Chicago: Aldine-Atherton.
Dobson, D., and Dobson, K. 1981. "Problem-Solving Strategies in Depressed and Nondepressed College Students." *Cognitive Therapy and Research,* pp. 237-49.
Dollard, J., and Miller, N. E. 1950. *Personality and Psychotherapy.* New York: McGraw-Hill.
Dominowski, R. L. 1968. "Anagram Solving and Creativity: Effects of Letter Moves and Word Frequency." Presented at 9th Annual Meeting of Psychonomic Society, St. Louis.
Duckworth, D. H. 1983. "Evaluation of a Programme for Increasing Effectiveness of Personal Problem-Solving." *British Journal of Psychology,* pp. 119-28.
D'Zurilla, T. H., and Goldfried, M. R. 1971. "Problem-Solving and Behavior Modification." *Journal of Abnormal Psychology,* pp. 107-26.
Ellis, A. 1962. *Reason and Emotion in Psychotherapy.* New York: Lyle Stuart.
_____ 1958. "Rational Psychotherapy." *Journal of General Psychology,* pp. 35-49.
Epstein, S. 1980. "The Stability of Behavior: II. Implications for Psychological Research." *American Psychologist,* pp. 790-806.
Erdman, H. P., Greist, J. H., Klein, M. G., & Jefferson, J. W. 1981. "The Computer Psychiatrist: How Far Have We Come? Where Are We Heading? How Far Dare We Go?" *Behavior Research Methods and Instrumentation,* pp. 393-98.
Evans, J. 1980. "Current Issues in the Psychology of Reasoning." *British Journal of Psychology,* pp. 227-39.
Eysenck, H. J. 1963. *Eysenck Personality Inventory.* San Diego, CA: Educational & Industrial Testing Service.

———— 1959. *Maudsley Personality Inventory*. London: London University Press.

Farmer, H. 1976. "Inquiry Project—Computer-Assisted Counseling Centers for Adults." *Counseling Psychologist*, pp. 50–54.

Feather, N. T. 1967. "Evaluation of Religious and Neutral Arguments in Religious and Atheist Student Groups." *Australian Journal of Psychology*, pp. 3–12.

Fenichel, O. 1945. *The Psychoanalytic Theory of Neurosis*. New York: W. W. Norton.

Finn, F. D. 1972. *Multivariance: Univariate and multivariate analysis of variance, covariance, and regression*. Ann Arbor, Michigan: National Educational Resources, Inc.

Frankl, V. 1963. *Man's Search for Meaning*. Boston: Beacon Press.

———— 1962. "Psychiatry and Man's Quest for Meaning." *Journal of Religion and Health*, pp. 93–103.

———— 1959. "The Spiritual Dimension in Existential Analysis and Logotherapy." *Journal of Individual Psychology*, pp. 157–62.

Freud, S. 1966. *Psychopathology of Everyday Life*, edited by James Strachey. New York: W. W. Norton.

———— 1935. *A General Introduction to Psycho-Analysis*. New York: Liveright.

Furth, H. G., Youniss, J., and Ross, M. 1970. "Children's Utilization of Logical Symbols: An Interpretation of Conceptual Behavior Based on Piagetian Theory." *Developmental Psychology*, pp. 36–57.

Goldfried, M. R., and Davidson, G. C. 1976. *Clinical Behavior Therapy*. New York: Holt, Rinehart & Winston.

Goldfried, M. R., and Merbaum, M. (Eds.) 1973. *Behavior Change Through Self-Control*. New York: Holt, Rinehart & Winston.

Goldstein, A. 1975. "Relationship Enhancing Methods." In *Helping People Change*, edited by F. Kanfer and A. Goldstein, pp. 218–38. New York: Pergamon Press.

Gough, H. G. 1976. "Personality and Personality Assessment." *In Handbook of Industrial and Organizational Psychology*, edited by M. D. Dunnette. Chicago: Rand McNally.

Gough, P. B. 1966. "Verification of Sentences: The Effect of the Delay of Evidence and Sentence Length." *Journal of Verbal Learning and Verbal Behavior*, pp. 492–96.

———— 1965. "Grammatical Transformations and Speed of Understanding." *Journal of Verbal Learning and Verbal Behavior*, pp. 107–11.

Greist, J. H., Klein, M. H., and Erdman, H. P. 1976. "Routine On-Line Psychiatric Diagnosis by Computer." *American Journal of Psychiatry*, pp. 1405–08.

Griest, J. H., Gustafson, D. H., and Strauss, F. F. 1973. "A Computer Interview for Suicide Risk Prediction." *American Journal of Psychiatry*, pp. 1327–32.

Griggs, R. A., and Newstead, S. E. 1982. "The Role of Problem Structure in a Deductive Reasoning Task." *Journal of Experimental Psychology: Learning, Memory, and Cognition*, pp. 297–307.

Guilford, J. P. 1967. *The Structure of Intelligence*. New York: McGraw-Hill.

Harris, H. 1974. "The Computer: Guidance Tool of the Future." *Journal of Counseling Psychology*, pp. 331–39.

Harvey, O. J., Hunt, D. E., and Schroeder, H. N. 1961. *Conceptual Systems and Personality Organization*. New York: John Wiley.

Hays, William L. 1963. *Statistics*. New York: Holt, Rinehart & Winston.

Hebb, D. O. 1949. *The Organization of Behavior: A Neuropsychological Theory.* New York: John Wiley.

Henle, M. 1962. "On the Relation Between Logic and Thinking." *Psychological Review,* pp. 366–78.

———— and Michael, M. 1956. "The Influence of Attitudes on Syllogistic Reasoning." *Journal of Social Psychology,* pp. 115–27.

Heppner, P. P. 1978. "A Review of the Problem-Solving Literature and Its Relationship to the Counseling Process." *Journal of Counseling Psychology,* pp. 366–75.

Heron, W. T., and Hunter, W. S. 1922. *Studies of the Reliability of the Problem Box and the Maze with Human and Animal Subjects.* Baltimore: Williams and Wilkins.

Holden, C. 1977. "The Empathic Computer." *Science,* p. 32.

Holt, R. W. 1983. "An Introduction to the PLATO CAI System." *Behavior Research Methods and Instrumentation,* pp. 142–44.

Horney, K. 1939. *New Ways in Psychoanalysis.* New York: W. W. Norton.

Huttenlocker, J. 1968. "Constructing Spatial Images: A Strategy in Reasoning." *Psychological Review,* pp. 550–56.

Inhelder, B., and Piaget, J. 1958. *The Growth of Logical Thinking.* New York: Basic Books.

Janis, I. R., and Mann, L. 1976. "Coping with Decisional Conflict." *American Scientist,* pp. 657–67.

Janis, I. L., and Frick, F. 1943. "The Relationship Between Attitudes Toward Conclusions and Errors in Judging Logical Validity of Syllogisms." *Journal of Experimental Psychology,* pp. 73–77.

Johnson, A. M., Parrott, G. R., and Stratton, R. K. 1968. "Production and Judgment of Solutions to Five Problems." *Journal of Educational Psychology,* p. 59.

Johnson, D. M. 1972. *Systematic Introduction to the Psychology of Thinking.* New York: Harper and Row.

Johnson-Laird, P. N. 1969. "Reasoning with Ambiguous Sentences." *British Journal of Psychology,* pp. 17–23.

———— and Wason, P. C. 1971. "A Theoretical Analysis of Insight into a Logical Relation." *Cognitive Psychology,* pp. 134–38.

Jung, C. G. 1910. "Problems of Modern Psychotherapy." In *Collected Works,* edited by G. Adler, M. Frodham, & H. Read. Princeton, NJ: Princeton University Press.

Kant, I. 1885. *Introduction to Logic and Essay on the Mistaken Subtlety of the Four Figures.* New York: Longman's Green.

Kelly, G. A. 1955. *The Psychology of Personal Constructs.* New York: W. W. Norton.

Kendler, T. S. 1964. "Verbalization and Optional Reversal Shifts Among Kindergarten Children." *Journal of Verbal Learning and Verbal Behavior,* pp. 428–33.

Kleinmuntz, B. 1975. "The Computer as a Clinician." *American Psychologist,* pp. 379–87.

Koffka, K. 1935. *Principles of Gestalt Psychology.* New York: Harcourt and Brace.

Kohler, W. 1927. *The Mentality of Apes.* New York: Harcourt and Brace.

Krumboltz, J. D. 1965. "Behavioral Counseling: Rationale and Research." *Personnel and Guidance Journal,* pp. 383–87.

Kulik, J. A., Kulik, C. L., and Cohen, P. A. 1979. "A Meta-Analysis of Outcome

Studies of Keller's Personalized System of Instruction." *American Psychologist,* pp. 307–18.

Lange, P. J. 1969. "The On-Line Computer in Behavior Therapy Research." *American Psychologist,* pp. 236–39.

Lazarus, A. A. 1977. "Has Behavior Therapy Outlived Its Usefulness?" *American Psychologist,* pp. 550–54.

———— 1971. *Behavior Therapy and Beyond.* New York: McGraw-Hill.

Lazarus, R. S. 1982. "Thoughts on the Relations Between Emotion and Cognition." *American Psychologist,* pp. 1019–24.

———— 1966. *Psychological Stress and the Coping Process.* New York: McGraw-Hill.

Leahey, T. 1977. "Training reasoning with implication." *Journal of General Psychology,* pp. 63–73.

———— and Wagman, M. 1974. "The Modification of Fallacious Reasoning with Implication." *Journal of General Psychology,* pp. 277–85.

Lefford, A. 1946. "The Influence of Emotional Subject Matter on Logical Reasoning." *Journal of General Psychology,* pp. 127–51.

Lowry, J. 1966. "'AUTO-COUN,' a Computer-Based Automated Counseling Simulation System." *Personnel and Guidance Journal,* pp. 5–15.

Luchins, A. S., and Luchins, E. H. 1950. "New Experimental Attempts at Preventing Mechanization in Problem Solving." *Journal of General Psychology,* pp. 279–97.

Mahoney, M. J. 1977. "Reflections on the Cognitive Learning Trend in Psychotherapy." *American Psychologist,* pp. 5–13.

———— 1974. *Cognition and Behavior Modification.* Cambridge, MA: Ballinger.

Maier, N. R. F. 1933. "An Aspect of Human Reasoning." *British Journal of Psychology,* pp. 144–55.

Maola, J. F., and Kane, G. 1976. "Comparison of Computer Based Versus Counselor Based Occupational Information System with Disadvantaged Vocational Students." *Journal of Counseling Psychology,* pp. 163–65.

May, R. 1967. *Psychology and the Human Dilemma.* New York: Van Nostrand.

McDowell, J. J. 1982. "The Importance of Hemstein's Mathematical Statement of Law of Effect for Behavior Therapy." *American Psychologist,* pp. 771–79.

McFarland, S. G., and Thistlethwaite, D. L. 1970. "An Analysis of a Logical Consistency Model of Belief Change." *Journal of Personality and Social Psychology,* pp. 133–43.

McGuire, W. G. 1960. "A Syllogistic Analysis of Cognitive Relationships." *In Attitude Organization and Change,* edited by M. J. Rosenberg, pp. 65–111. New Haven, Ct: Yale University Press.

McMahon, L. 1963. "Grammatical Analysis as Part of Understanding a Sentence." Ph.D. dissertation, Harvard University.

Meichenbaum, D. 1977. *Cognitive-Behavior Modification: An Integrative Approach.* New York: Plenum.

Melhus, G. E., Hershenson, D. B., and Vermillion, M. E. 1973. "Computer-Assisted Versus Traditional Vocation Counseling with High and Low Readiness Clients." *Journal of Vocational Behavior,* pp. 137–44.

Mill, J. S. 1874. *A System of Logic.* New York: Harper.

Miller, J. G. 1965. "Living Systems: Basic Concepts." *Behavior Science,* pp. 193–237.

Miller, G. A., Galanter, A., and Pribram, T H. 1960. *Plans and the Structure of Behavior.* New York: Holt, Rinehart & Winston.

Mischel, W. 1977. "On the Future of Personality Measurement." *American Psychologist,* pp. 577–614.

―――― 1973. "Toward a Cognitive Social Learning Reconceptualization of Personality." *Psychological Review,* pp. 252–83.

Morgan, A. B. 1956. "Sex Differences in Adults on a Test of Logical Reasoning." *Psychological Reports,* pp. 227–30.

Morgan, J. J. B., and Morton, J. T. 1944. "The Distortion of Syllogistic Reasoning Produced by Personal Convictions." *Journal of Social Psychology,* pp. 39–59.

Mowrer, O. H. 1960. *Learning Theory and the Symbolic Processes.* New York: John Wiley.

Myers, J. L. 1972. *Fundamentals of Experimental Design.* Boston: Allyn and Bacon.

Mynatt, C. R., Doherty, M. E., and Tweney, R. D. 1978. "Consequences of Confirmation and Disconfirmation in a Simulated Research Environment." *Quarterly Journal of Experimental Psychology,* pp. 395–406.

―――― 1977. "Confirmation Bias in a Simulated Research Environment—Experimental Study of Scientific Inference." *Quarterly Journal of Experimental Psychology,* pp. 316–24.

Nagel, E. 1956. Logic Without Metaphysics. New York: Free Press.

Neeches, R. 1982. "Simulation Systems for Cognitive Psychology." *Behavior Research Methods and Instrumentation,* pp. 77–91.

Newell, A., Shaw, J. C., and Simon, H. A. 1963. "GPS, a Program that Simulates Human Thought." In *Computers and Thought,* edited by E. A. Feigenbaum and J. Feldman. New York: McGraw-Hill.

Newell, A., and Simon, H. A. 1958. "Heuristic Problem Solving: The Next Advance in Operations Research." *Operations Research,* p. 8.

Newman, P. 1974. "Effects of Directional and Neutral Category Labels in Bidimensional Rule-Learning Problems." *Memory and Cognition,* pp. 695–99.

Ormrod, J. 1979. "Cognitive Processes in the Solution of Three-Term Series Problems." *American Journal of Psychology,* pp. 235–55.

Osborn, A. F. 1963. *Applied Imagination.* New York: Scribners.

Palman, J. 1978. "Sympathetic Computers or Programmers." *Science,* p. 934.

Perls, F., Hefferline, R., and Goodman, P. 1965. *Gestalt Therapy.* New York: Dell.

Peterson, C. 1980. "Recognition of Noncontingency." *Journal of Personality and Social Psychology,* pp. 727–34.

Phillips, E. L., and Weiner, D. N. 1966. *Short-Term Psychotherapy and Structured Behavior Change.* New York: McGraw-Hill.

Phillips, W., and Epstein, M. 1979. "Word-Pair Encoding Using Similarity and Construct Processing." *Psychological Reports,* pp. 1267–75.

Piaget, J. 1970. "Piaget's Theory." In *Carmichael's Manual of Child Psychology,* edited by P. Mussen. New York: Wiley, pp. 703–32.

Piaget, J. 1949. *Traite du logique; essai du logistique operatoire [Treatise of logic; essay on operative logistic].* Paris: Librairie Armand Colin.

―――― and Inhelder, B. 1959. *La genese des structures logiques elementaires [The*

Genesis of the Elementary Logical Structure]. Neuchatel, Switzerland: Delachauz and Neistle.

Polya, G. 1945. *How to Solve It: A New Aspect of Mathematical Method*. Princeton, NJ: Princeton University Press.

Presson, C. C. 1982. "Strategies in Spatial Reasoning." *Journal of Experimental Psychology: Learning, Memory, and Cognition,* pp. 243–51.

Price, G. E. 1974. "Counselor and Computer Effectiveness in Helping Students Select Courses." *Journal of Counseling Psychology,* pp. 351–54.

Pyle, K. R., and Stripling, R. O. 1976. "The Counselor, the Computer and Career Development." *Vocational Guidance Quarterly,* pp. 71–75.

Quintanar, L. R., Crowell, C. R., Pryor, J. B., and Adamopoulos, J. 1982. "Human-Computer Interaction: A Preliminary Social Psychological Analysis. *Behavior Research Methods and Instrumentation,* pp. 210–20.

Raimy, V. 1975. *Misunderstanding of the Self*. San Francisco: Jossey-Bass.

Rank, O. 1945. *Will Therapy and Truth and Reality*. New York: Alfred A. Knopf.

Ratcliff, R., and McKoon, G. 1982. "Speed and Accuracy in the Processing of False Statements About Semantic Information." *Journal of Experimental Psychology: Learning, Memory, and Cognition,* pp. 16–36.

Revlin, R., and Mayer, R. E. 1978. *Human Reasoning*. New York: John Wiley.

Richards, S. C., and Perri, M. G. 1978. "Do Self-Control Treatments Last? An Evaluation of Behavioral Problem Solving and Faded Counselor Contact as Treatment Maintenance Strategies." *Journal of Counseling Psychology,* pp. 376–83.

Roberge, J. 1976a. "Effects of Negation on Adults' Disjunctive Reasoning Abilities." *Journal of General Psychology,* pp. 23–28.

_____ 1976b. "Reasoning with Exclusive Disjunction Arguments." *Quarterly Journal of Experimental Psychology,* pp. 419–27.

_____ 1974. "Effects of Negation on Adults' Comprehension of Fallacious Conditional and Disjunctive Arguments." *Journal of General Psychology,* pp. 287–94.

_____ 1971. "An Analysis of Response Patterns for Conditional Reasoning Schemes." *Psychonomic Science,* pp. 338–39.

_____ and Flexer, B. K. 1982. "The Formal Operational Reasoning Test." *Journal of General Psychology,* pp. 61–68.

Rogers, C. 1942. *Counseling and Psychotherapy*. Boston: Houghton-Mifflin.

Rosenthal, R. 1978. "Combining Results of Independent Studies." *Psychological Bulletin,* pp. 185–93.

Roth, E. 1979. "Facilitating Insight in a Reasoning Task." *British Journal of Psychology,* pp. 265–71.

Russell, B. 1904. "The Axiom of Infinity." *Hibbert Journal,* pp. 809–12.

Rychlack, J. 1968. *A Philosophy of Science for Personality Theory*. Boston: Houghton-Mifflin.

Sagan, C. 1977. *The Dragons of Eden*. New York: Random House.

Salatas, H., and Bourne, L. E. 1974. "Learning Conceptual Rules: III. Processes Contributing to Rule Difficulty." *Memory and Cognition,* pp. 549–53.

Sampson, J. P., Jr., and Pyle, K. R. 1983. "art de title" *Personnel and Guidance Journal,* pp. 283–87.

Sells, S. B. 1936. "The Atmosphere Effect, an Experimental Study of Reasoning." *Archives of Psychology.*

BIBLIOGRAPHY / 321

Selmi, P. M., Klein, M. H., Greist, J. H., Johnson, J. H., and Harris, W. G. 1982. "An Investigation of Computer-Assisted Cognitive-Behavior Therapy in the Treatment of Depression." *Behavior Research Methods and Instrumentation,* pp. 181–85.

Shannon, C. 1949. *Mathematical Theory of Communications.* Urbana: University of Illinois Press.

Sharma, K. N. 1960. "Analysis of a Test of Reasoning Ability." *Journal of Educational Psychology,* pp. 228–40.

Shaw, M. L. 1982. "Attending to Multiple Sources of Information. I. The Integration of Information in Decision Making." *Cognitive Psychology,* pp. 353–409.

Simon, A. J. 1957. *Administrative Behavior.* New York: Free Press.

Simpson, M. E., and Johnson, D. M. 1966. "Atmosphere and Conversion Errors in Syllogistic Reasoning." *Journal of Experimental Psychology,* pp. 197–200.

Slack, C. W., and Slack, W. V. 1974. "Good: We Are Listening to You Talk About Your Sadness." *Psychology Today,* pp. 62–65.

Slack, W. V., and Slack, C. W. 1977. "Talking to a Computer About Emotional Problems: A Comparative Study." *Psychotherapy: Theory, Research and Practice,* pp. 156–64.

Slobin, D. I. 1966. "Grammatical Transformation in Science Comprehension in Childhood and Adulthood." *Journal of Verbal Learning and Verbal Behavior,* pp. 219–27.

Smith, D. 1982. "Trends in Counseling and Psychotherapy." *American Psychologist,* pp. 802–09.

Smith, M. L., and Glass, G. B. 1977. "Meta-Analysis of Psychotherapy Outcome Studies." *American Psychologist,* pp. 735–60.

Smith, S. G., and Sherwood, B. A. 1976. "Educational Uses of the PLATO Computer System." *Science,* pp. 344–52.

Spencer, H. 1896. *The Principles of Sociology.* New York: D. Appleton and Co.

Spinoza, B. de. 1927. *The Philosophy of Spinoza,* edited by Joseph Ratner. New York: Modern Library.

Sullivan, H. S. 1964. *The Fusion of Psychiatry and Social Science.* New York: W. W. Norton.

———— 1954. *The Psychiatric Interview.* New York: W. W. Norton.

Super, D. E. (Ed.) 1970. *Computer Assisted Counseling.* New York: Teachers College Press.

Taplin, J., Staudenmayer, H., and Taddonio, J. 1974. "Developmental Changes in Conditional Reasoning: Linguistic or Logical?" *Journal of Experimental Child Psychology,* pp. 360–73.

Taylor, K. 1970. *Computer Applications in Psychotherapy: Bibliography and Abstracts.* PHS No. 1981. Washington, DC: U.S. Government Printing Office.

Terrell, D. B. 1967. *Logic: A Modern Introduction to Deductive Reasoning.* New York: Holt, Rinehart & Winston.

Thomas, E., and Hemenway, K. 1981. "Processing Instructions, Markedness, and Congruity Effects in a Sentence Verification Task." *Journal of Experimental Psychology: Human Perception and Performance,* pp. 701–18.

Tombaugh, J. W. 1983. "Research Methods for Computer Applications." *Behavior Research Methods and Instrumentation,* pp. 222–27.

Tweney, R., Doherty, M., Worner, W., Pliske, D., Mynatt, C., Gross, K., and Arkkelin, D. 1980. "Strategies of Rule Discovery in an Inference Task." *Quarterly Journal of Experimental Psychology,* pp. 109–23.

Tyler, L. 1969. *The Work of the Counselor,* 3rd Ed. New York: Appleton-Century-Crofts.

VanDuyne, P. C. 1976. "Necessity and Contingency in Reasoning." *Acta Psychologica,* pp. 85–101.

Von Domarus, E. 1944. "The Specific Laws of Logic in Schizophrenia." In *Language and Thought in Schizophrenia,* edited by J. S. Kasanin. Berkeley: University of California Press.

Wagman, M. 1983. "A Factor Analytic Study of the Psychological Implications of the Computer for the Individual and Society." *Behavior Research Methods and Instrumentation,* pp. 413–19.

_____ 1982. "Solving Dilemmas by Computer or Counselor." *Psychological Reports,* pp. 127–35.

_____ 1981. "Autonomous Mode of Systematic Dilemma Counseling." *Psychological Reports,* pp. 231–46.

_____ 1980a. "PLATO DCS, an Interactive Computer System for Personal Counseling." *Journal of Counseling Psychology,* pp. 16–30.

_____ 1980b. "Systematic Dilemma Counseling: Transition from Counselor Mode to Autonomous Mode." *Journal of Counseling Psychology,* pp. 171–78.

_____ 1979. "Systematic Dilemma Counseling: Theory, Method, Research." *Psychological Reports,* 55–72.

_____ 1978. "The Comparative Effects of Didactic-Correction and Self-Contradiction on Fallacious Scientific and Personal Reasoning." *Journal of General Psychology,* pp. 67–80.

_____ 1969. "Critique and Extension of Wason's Verification Bias Concept." Department of Psychology, University of Illinois.

_____ and Kerber, K. W. 1980. "PLATO DCS, an Interactive Computer System for Personal Counseling: Further Development and Evaluation." *Journal of Counseling Psychology,* pp. 31–39.

_____ 1979. "DCS, an Interactive Computer System for Personal Counseling: Technical Description and Performance Data." *JSAS Catalog of Selected Documents in Psychology,* p. 20.

_____ 1978. *Dilemma Counseling System.* Minneapolis, MN: Control Data Corporation.

Wason, P. C. 1968. "Reasoning About a Rule." *Quarterly Journal of Experimental Psychology,* pp. 273–81.

_____ 1964. "The Effect of Self-Contradiction on Fallacious Reasoning." *Quarterly Journal of Experimental Psychology,* pp. 30–34.

_____ 1960. "On the Failure to Eliminate Hypotheses in a Conceptual Task." *Quarterly Journal of Experimental Psychology,* pp. 129–240.

_____ and Johnson-Laird, P. N. 1972. *Psychology of Reasoning: Structure and Content.* London: Batsford.

Weizenbaum, J. 1977. "Computer as Therapist." *Science,* p. 354.

_____ 1976. *Computer Power and Human Reason: From Judgment to Calculation.* San Francisco: Freeman.

_____ 1965. "'ELIZA,' Computer Program for the Study of Natural Language Communication Between Man and Machine." *Communications of the Association for Computing Machinery,* pp. 36–45.

Wertheimer, M. 1959. *Productive Thinking.* New York: Harper.

Whitehead, A. N., and Russell, B. 1910–1913. *Principia Mathematica* (2nd ed.). Cambridge, England: Cambridge University Press.

Whitfield, J. W. 1947. "Rank Correlation Between Two Variables, One of Which is Ranked, the Other Dichotomous." *Biometrika,* pp. 292–96.

Williams, E. B. 1965. "Deductive Reasoning in Schizophrenia." *Journal of Abnormal and Social Psychology,* pp. 47–61.

Williams, R. L. 1979. "Imagery and Linguistic Factors Affecting the Solution of Linear Syllogism Problems." *Journal of Psycholinguistics,* pp. 123–240.

Wilkins, M. C. 1928. "The Effect of Changed Material on Ability to do Formal Syllogistic Reasoning." *Archives of Psychology.*

Wolpe, J. 1958. *Psychotherapy by Reciprocal Inhibition.* Stanford, CA: Stanford University Press.

Zagorski, H. J. 1974. "Automatic Data Processing System and Procedures: Computerized Academic Counseling System." *JSAS Catalog of Selected Documents in Psychology,* pp. 26–27.

INDEX

ABOUT THE AUTHOR

Morton Wagman is Professor of Psychology at the University of Illinois at Urbana-Champaign and is the originator of the PLATO Dilemma Counseling System. PLATO DCS is in use internationally for research, service, and instructional purposes at numerous colleges and universities, business, and government organizations. Dr. Wagman is a diplomate in Counseling Psychology, American Board of Professional Psychology.

Dr. Wagman has published widely in the area of psychology. His articles have appeared in *Psychological Reports, Journal of Counseling Psychology,* and *Journal of General Psychology*. He also has coauthored a book in general psychology.

Dr. Wagman holds a B.A. in mathematics from Columbia University and an M.A. and Ph.D. in psychology from the University of Michigan.

DATE DUE

GW SEP 09 1992			

GAYLORD | | | PRINTED IN U.S.A